Real Studies 11

REAL Studies Editors:
Josef Schmied
Christoph Haase
Matthias Hofmann

Series Advisors

Marina Bondi
Daniel Nkemleke
Gabriela Miššíková
Renata Povolná
Andrew Tollet
Andrew Wilson

**Previous Titles**

Vol. 1:   English for Central Europe – Interdisciplinary Saxon-Czech Perspectives
Vol. 2:   Stress Patterns of Nigerian English
Vol. 3:   Complexity and Coherence: Approaches to Linguistic Research and Language Teaching
Vol. 4:   English Projects in Teaching and Research in Central Europe
Vol. 5:   Academic Writing in Europe: Empirical Perspectives
Vol. 6:   Exploring Academic Writing in Cameroon English: A Corpus-Based Perspective
Vol. 7:   English for Academic Purposes: Practical and Theoretical Approaches
Vol. 8:   Academic Writing for South Eastern Europe: Practical and Theoretical Perspectives
Vol. 9:   Essays on Language in Societal Transformation: A Festschrift in Honour of Segun Awonusi
Vol. 10: Academic Writing Across Disciplines in Africa: From Students to Experts

**African Urban and Youth Languages:
The Rural-Urban Divide**

Edited by

Josef Schmied
Taiwo Oloruntoba-Oju

Cuvillier Verlag

**Bibliografische Information der Deutschen Nationalbibliothek**
Die Deutsche National bibliothek verzeichnet diese Publikation in der
Deutschen National bibliografie; detaillierte bibliografische Daten sind im
Internet über http://dnb.d-nb.de abrufbar.
1. Aufl. - Göttingen: Cuvillier, 2019

This book has been published with funding from the Alexander von Humboldt Foundation

© CUVILLIER VERLAG, Göttingen 2019
  Nonnenstieg 8, 37075 Göttingen
  Telefon: 0551-54724-0
  Telefax: 0551-54724-21
  www.cuvillier.de

Alle Rechte vorbehalten. Ohne ausdrückliche Genehmigung des Verlages ist es
nicht gestattet, das Buch oder Teile daraus auf fotomechanischem Weg
(Fotokopie, Mikrokopie) zu vervielfältigen.
1. Auflage, 2019
Gedruckt auf umweltfreundlichem, säurefreiem Papier aus nachhaltiger
Forstwirtschaft.

ISBN 978-3-7369-7081-6
eISBN 978-3-7369-6081-7

## Acknowledgements

We would like to acknowledge the support of several scholars and colleagues whose efforts have enhanced the quality of this publication. Members of the panel of reviewers are greatly appreciated for their time and efforts.

This publication and our collaboration at Chemnitz University of Technology, Germany, was made possible through the award of the Alexander von Humboldt Foundation's scholarship for a research stay at Chemnitz University of Technology, Germany, in 2017.

We are equally grateful to the Alexander von Humboldt Foundation for sponsoring this publication as one of the outcomes of the research stay in Germany.

The role played by the following editorial assistants is also acknowledged: Ajadi Razaq, Oluwasola Ojo and Chris Olawale at University of Ilorin as well as Marina Ivanova and Isabelle van der Bom at TU Chemnitz.

Taiwo Oloruntoba-Oju
Department of English, University of Ilorin
Research Fellow of the Alexander von Humboldt Foundation

Josef Schmied
Professor of English Language & Linguistics
Chemnitz University of Technology
D-09107 Chemnitz

# Contents

Imperative of Indigenous African Grammar and Rhetoric Perspectives in African Urban and Youth Scholarship
*Josef Schmied & Taiwo Oloruntoba-Oju*   1

"Hidden in Plain Sight": Indigenous African Languages as Urban and Youth Languages: Urban Hausa, Urban Igbo and Urban Yoruba in Nigeria   7
*Taiwo Oloruntoba-Oju*

Rural and urban metaphors in Sheng (Kenya) and Tsotsitaal (South Africa)
*Fridah Kanana Erastus & Ellen Hurst-Harosh*   35

The Grammar of Indigenous Languages in African Urban Youth Languages: Questioning in Camfranglais in Cameroon
*Comfort Beyang Oben Ojongnkpot*   53

Sheng as Fractal Language Practice
*Philip Rudd*   71

Is the term "Youth Language" not a Misnomer?
*Moufoutaou Adjeran & Gratien Atindogbe*   87

American English and Urban Nigerian Youth: Investigating the Influence on Tweets from Lagos and Kano
*Matthias Hofmann*   97

Makerere University English: Is there an emerging youth-urban variety?
*Sauda Namyalo*   117

Le Contact des Langues Chez les Jeunes Algériens Lecture d'un Corpus Sociolinguistique Hétérogène ("Language Contact among Young Algerians: Reading a Heterogeneous Sociolinguistic Corpus")
*Souheila Hedid*   135

Le Nouchi: une Menace ou un Tremplin pour la Promotion des Langues Ivoiriennes? ("Nouchi: A Threat or a Springboard for the Promotion of Ivorian Languages"?)
*Jean-Claude Dodo & Yves Youant*   147

The Urban Film Narrative as a Space of Linguistic Hybridity in Africa
*Shikuku Tsikhungu*   155

Urban-Rural and Modern-Traditional Identities through Popular Zambian Music
*Felix Banda*   163

# Imperative of Indigenous Grammar and Rhetoric Perspectives in African Urban and Youth Language Scholarship

*Josef Schmied &*
*Taiwo Oloruntoba-Oju*

Attempts to build a sociolinguistic profile for urban and youth languages have led to a multiplicity of perspectives, some of which would appear controversial. This is because ways of conceptualising urbanity and of characterising the associated forms of language vary according to scholar perspective. Scholar perspective may also sometimes conflict with the perceptions of speakers of these languages regarding the nature of these languages, or even their "languagehood" (Kerswill, 2013: 128), and with acceptability judgments within respective speech communities. While such issues are universal, African urban and youth language scholarship has had to grapple additionally with the problem of determining the true nature and sources of the so called urban and youth languages of Africa. This includes the problem of determining the base or constituent languages, as well as the applicability of extant western classifications to the languages (see, among others, Bosire, 2006; Hurst, 2017; Mazrui, 1995; Myers-Scotton, 1993; Oloruntoba-Oju, 2017).

A major difference between Western and African youth language practices is the widely acknowledged "mixilingualism" of the latter. The term "mixilingualism," employed by Brann (1989) in a different context, has since been adopted in the description of African urban and youth language practices, and particularly to describe "the unrelenting mixture of languages that is typical of Nigerian hip-hop," for example (Oloruntoba-Oju, 2018, p. 187; see also Odebunmi, 2010). Indeed, the adjective "extreme" has been used repeatedly to describe the extent of code-mixing and semantic manipulation in African youth languages compared with the situation in Western Europe (see for example, Kerswill, 2010, pp. 7, 9, 29). This difference has roots in the respective linguistic environments of the youth practices. There is, on the one hand, the superlative multilingualism of many African communities (with Nigeria alone hosting about 500 languages, for example, and all jostling for input into the urban and youth languages), and, on the other hand, the relatively homogenous linguistic circumstances of western countries. The difference poses a challenge for the characterization of African urban and youth languages and associated practices such as code alternation, language mixing and or "fused lects" (Auer, 1999).

Related to this challenge is the "urban-rural divide" in African youth languages. This divide manifests in the difficulty in determining the relative input of urbanity and rurality to the lexis and structure of African youth languages, and the disproportionate focus on urbanity and coloniality in the construction of African youth languages. The virtual absence of wholly indigenous, non-colonial or non-mixed languages of Africa in 'African' 'urban' and 'youth language' scholarship is a distinct manifestation of this disproportionate focus. This is the challenge that birthed this edition of *REAL*.

At the European Conference on African Studies (ECAS) that held in Basel, Switzerland, in 2017, a panel convened by one of the editors of this volume extensively discussed the rural-urban dimension in African youth languages, their classifications, and their predictive value for language change and social development. The panel's interest was in "theoretical reflections and empirical exposé on the urbanisation of indigenous (rural) languages, and the reciprocal ruralisation of 'urban,' especially colonial, languages" (Oloruntoba-Oju, 2017a). The panel also wanted to focus on those African urban and rural youth language varieties in which rurality or indigeneity was conspicuously expressed. This would signal, on the one hand, the fluid nature of youth language practices and, on the other hand, the resilience and transformative potential of indigenous language forms vis-à-vis modern language expressions. Another important dimension for the panel was the predictive value of youth languages and expressions for language development and language change in Africa. Finally, the panel sought to establish indigenous, non-colonial languages of Africa as a neglected but proper subject of study in youth languages. Some of the papers discussed at this panel were revised and peer reviewed for this special edition of REAL.

The validity of the urban-rural binary in the description of youth languages has no doubt been challenged in the research literature (e.g. Mufwene, 2010; Nassenstein, 2016). This is especially in view of the intertwining nature of urbanity and rurality in youth speech samples. A couple of studies of youth languages in rural locations have also been conducted, such as among the Tarok in Nigeria (see Blench and Longtau, 2016). Many of the so called 'urban' youth languages of Africa such as Sheng (Kenya), Tsotsitaal (South Africa), Nouchi (Abidjan), Ligali, Indoubil (DRC), Camfranglais (Cameroon), etc., have actually been shown to contain significant representations of rural-indigenous thought and linguistic systems, both in naturally occurring settings and in simulated forms such as music, theatre and the media (see Hurst and Erastus, 2018). This has suggested over time that the youth and so called urban languages invariably comprise a *glocal* fusion of the global and the local.

Still, more work needs to be done in order to isolate truly indigenous urban and youth languages of Africa – indigenous in the sense of having local or indigenous, rather than colonial languages, as base, or in the sense of being the dominant language in terms of lexical and structural input. While the hybridity of African urban and youth languages can almost be taken for granted, the constituent codes are not evenly distributed in output samples; the hierarchical distribution of lexical and structural elements in the languages therefore needs to be well investigated in order to establish the motivational and dominance patterns. Furthermore, given the fluidity of the age factor in the use of the referenced languages, the aptness of the term "youth language" needs to be further investigated within the context of Africa, and the distinguishing features relative to the general lingo of the respective speech communities established. Finally, there is a yawning need to investigate attitudinal perspectives to youth languages, in view of the connotation of "antilanguage" and "criminal milieu" that often trails the characterization of the languages.

Most of the contributions in this volume agree that, notwithstanding the multiplicity of the voices that characterize African Urban and Youth Languages and its scholarship, and notwithstanding the surface linguistic appearance of the languages and practices, the languages ultimately bear the mark and intensity of the rural and indigenous as a major, if not dominant, component. While some contributions acknowledge African urban and youth languages as "fractal practice," some others demonstrate how some of the languages bear the marks of a contest between different colonial language varieties, such as British vs. American English. Others, still, demonstrate that so called youth languages are invariably marked by domain characteristics that may not be valid in other domains. For example, in some university campuses, as a restricted domain, the general language of instruction (English in the cited cases) 'duels' with the indigenous language of the immediate environment for proprietary rights over youth expressions. Ultimately, the articles in this volume are united in the attempt to isolate *the mark of the indigenous* as a constant and indelible feature of all the varieties of African urban and youth languages. What follows below is a brief summary of the chapters of the volume.

In the opening chapter, Oloruntoba-Oju uses the phrase *hidden in plain sight* to refer to indigenous urban and youth languages or language practices that have been rendered "invisible" under the influence of the colonial factor in African urban and youth language scholarship. His examples are drawn from three Nigerian cities, Lagos, Kano and Onitsha. Lagos is the most populous city in Africa and is also home to youths from all rural regions in Nigeria. Oloruntoba-Oju's "preliminary survey" of indigenous language practices in this sprawling metropolis identifies a number of indigenous language based varieties, such as *Yoruba Eko* (Lagos Yoruba), and *Erea* ('Area'), spoken by "area boys" identified as class and occupational groups. There is also a brief discussion of *Otu Onitsha* and *Hausankano*, which are elaborated as the urban and youth languages of the Nigerian cities of Kano and Onitsha respectively. The varieties are generally marked by a high level of indigeneity right in the heart of the urban and modern centres.

Fridah Kanana Erastus and Ellen Hurst-Harosh examine the rural-urban dichotomy in African youth languages through comparative data from Kenya (Sheng) and South Africa (Tsotsitaal), with additional data from some rapidly urbanising rural towns of Kenya. The authors demonstrate that the so called 'urban' languages do not only draw from modern paradigms and languages in their linguistic performances, but also from archaic and rural forms, to create layers of meaning and indexicality. The authors emphasise the intermingling of these resources as material base for youth linguistic performances.

Comfort Ojongnkpot compares Camfranglais as an established youth variety with Ejagham (a Cameroonian language), with the purpose of establishing the rural roots of 'urban' Camfranglais. Her analysis derives from the perspective that the so called African Urban Youth Languages do not only communicate ideas, strengthen ties and create in-group identities, but also link the youth to their indigenous roots, and that youths appropriate rural roots elements to create an African identity. This presumption is borne out by comparing the question structure of Camfranglais with that of Ejagham (a South-Western Cameroon language). The findings reveal that the questioning pattern of Camfranglais is influenced by Ejagham, thus establishing a link to cultural roots which inevitably serve as markers of an African identity for Camfranglais users.

Philip Rudd's "Sheng as Fractal Language Practice" also proposes a reconceptualization of African Urban Youth Language as practice rather than as object. Reinforcing the analogy of fractals, the author argues that languages are not rigidly demarcated but composed of discrete fragments and amalgamated practices. Rudd traces the history of Sheng in order to demonstrate that its fragments comprise precolonial elements growing into a postcolonial context, hence its fractal nature. Though Sheng is fragmented and continually challenging, it has over time acquired standardizing features that confer legitimacy on it as an established lingual practice.

In examining the appropriateness of the term "youth language" to describe the language practices of youth, Moufoutaou Adjeran and Gratien Atindogbe argue that the term is a socio-demographic categorisation with socio-ethnic coloration, in addition to the implied meaning of age-grading. They underscore the inappropriateness of the term, arguing among other reasons that the youth language practices are hardly autonomous languages, contrary to the connotation conveyed by the nomenclature. Citing existing literature and drawing additional data from advertising billboards in the Republic of Benin, the authors observe that the 'youthness' of the so-called "youth language" is mainly noticeable at the level of lexis. The peculiarities of the sociolect are therefore examined through the sociolinguistic strategies of borrowing, truncating and what the authors refer to as 'inversion' or 'back slanging.'

For his part, Matthias Hofmann establishes Tweets as a youth language variety in Nigeria and as a promising source of corpus investigation into youth language varieties in general. Taking due cognizance of the peculiarities of the Nigerian sociolinguistic population, Hofmann examines the influence of American English on prepositional usage and orthography in the Tweets by young Nigerians. He concludes that Hausa English, which is spoken in the North of Nigeria, appears to be less impervious to American influence than Yoruba English spoken in the South of the country, judging from the evidence of the Tweets. Hofmann's work once again establishes the multiplicity of inputs into what is known as 'youth language' and also the fact that the youth varieties are determined by the sociolinguistic peculiarities or specific speech communities or specific domains of language use.

Saudah Namyalo investigates the variety of English spoken by Makerere University students' population, which she labels *Mak-Eng,* as a possible specimen of urban youth language. She examines the linguistic strategies of speakers as well as functions of the variety. Namyalo submits that *Mak-Eng* is an emerging urban youth language. She finds that the variety has the English language as its core but also employs metaphors and similar usages from the indigenous languages, especially Swahili. Similarities in the creative strategies of the variety (i.e. metaphor, semantic manipulation, borrowing, etc.), coupled with its function as a marker of identity, bring the variety in tandem with many other African Urban Youth languages.

Souheila Hedid examines the reality of the multilingualism of the Algerian linguistic terrain from attitudinal perspectives, focusing on the perception of young Algerians of this multilingualism. The author uses a triangulation methodology in an attempt to find answers to two interesting questions that are fundamental to the paper: how is the mixture of languages in the verbal interactions of young Algerians conceived? What representations do these speakers have of this phenomenon? The author concludes that the mixture of languages as confirmed by her study is not an aberration, and that if certain languages or language practices are preferred by young speakers, it is because they cater to very particular needs.

In their paper, Jean-Claude Dodo and Yves Youant acknowledge the increasing growth and popularity of Nouchi, focusing therefore on the predictive value of the phenomenon. The authors especially question whether the language constitutes a threat to the other Ivorian languages or not. They submit that Nouchi is not a threat to the other Ivorian languages, but rather an ally, a strategic partner for the promotion of the indigenous languages of Ivory Coast. This conclusion follows the authors' analysis of a corpus of Nouchi, which reveals massive borrowing of vocabulary items by Nouchi speakers from Ivorian languages, notwithstanding that its 'base' is considered to be French.

The separate contributions by Shikuku Tsikhungu and Felix Banda explore the deployment of urban linguistic dynamics in the domain of film and music. Tsikhungu's "The Urban Film Narrative as a Space of Linguistic Hybridity in Africa" locates Kenyan urban films as a prime site where many languages compete for space, resulting in linguistic hybridisation. The infusion of the dominant indigenous languages such as Lingala and Swahili in the mixed codes is noticeable. This hybridisation is readily accepted by film makers as a signpost marker for the average Nairobian to understand and relate to the films. The author argues that the hybridisation in the Kenyan urban film is a true reflection of the real world Kenyan urban city, where the urban dweller is surrounded by many languages. The city is therefore suffused with influences from the rural landscape, the urban landscape, and the linguascape between both.

Felix Banda also explores how musicians draw on diverse cultural materials (especially the linguistic and the musical) as semiotic fodder for their music. The deployment and fusion of elements from multiple languages is also a strategy to achieve multiple affiliations to different ethnolinguistic groups, regions and even nationalities. The idea that youth language is strategic, or motivated, is reinforced by this finding. The musical video of a popular Zambian musician JK (featuring Selma) and titled *Kapilipili* suggests, Banda notes, that heteroglossia and multiculturality are reflective of the transcultural and transmodal communication practices of youths.

In order to preserve the originality and creativity of individual authors, the editors refrained from standardising the original texts too much and only adapted passages where the intelligibility for an international readership may be restricted. The individual variation also shows the different conventions in academic writing in African institutions, where the fascinating topic of youth languages is persued. Thus this volume hopes to contribute to connecting individual authors and their styles to further promote original research in this area.

## References

Auer, P. (1999). From code-switching via language mixing to fused lects: Toward a dynamic typology of bilingual speech. *International Journal of Bilingualism, 3*(4): 309–332.

Blench, R. and Longtau, S. R. (2016). Tarok young people's speech. *Sociolinguistic Studies, 10*(1-2), 219-234. DOI: 10.1558/sols.v10i1-2.28316.

Bosire, M. (2006). Hybrid languages: The case of Sheng. In Arosanyin, O. F. & Pemberton, M. A. (Eds.). *Selected proceedings of the 36th annual conference on African linguistics*. Somerville, MA: Cascadilla Proceedings Project, 185-193.

Brann, C. M. (1989, November). The terminology of multilingualism. *Alsed-LSP Newsletter, 12*(2).

Hurst, E. (2017). African (Urban) Youth Languages. *Oxford Encyclopaedia Online*. DOI: 10.1093/acrefore/9780199384655.013.157.

Hurst, E., & Erastus, F. K. (Eds.). (2018). *African youth languages: New media, performing arts and sociolinguistic development*. Basingstoke: Palgrave Macmillan.

Kerswill, P. (2010). Youth Languages in Africa and Europe: Linguistic Subversion or Emerging Vernaculars? *Academic Presentation*. Accesssed 18 Aug. 2017 at http://www.lancaster.ac.uk/fass/doc_library/linguistics/kerswill/Kerswill-African-Studies-19-10-10.pdf.

Kerswill, P. (2013). Identity, ethnicity and place: The construction of youth language in London. In Auer, P., Hilpert, M., Stukenbrock, A. & Szmrecsanyi, B. (Eds.) *Space in Language and Linguistics*. Linguae and Litterae. Berlin/Boston: Walter de Gruyter, 128-164.

Mazrui, A. (1995). Slang and code-mixing: The case of Sheng in Kenya. *Arbeitspapiere*, 42, 168-179.

Mufwene, S. S. (2010). Globalization, Global English, and World English(es): Myths and Facts. In Coupland, N. (Ed.) *The Handbook of Language and Globalization*. Oxford: Wiley-Blackwell, 31-55.

Myers-Scotton, C. (1993). Common and uncommon ground: Social and structural factors in codeswitching. *Language in society, 22*(4), 475-503.

Nassenstein, N. (2016). Global repertoires and urban fluidity: Youth languages in Africa. *International Journal of the Sociology of Language*, 242, 171-193.

Odebunmi, A. (2010). Ideology and body part metaphors in Nigerian English. *Review of Cognitive Linguistics, 2*(8), 272-295.

Oloruntoba-Oju, T. (2017a). African indigenous languages as urban youth languages: The rural-urban exchange. *Panel presentation at the European Conference on African Studies conference*, University of Basel Basel, Switzerland, 29 June – 1 July, 2017.

Oloruntoba-Oju, T. (2018). Contestant hybridities: African urban youth language in Nigerian music and social media. In Hurst-Harosh, E., & Erastus, F. K. (Eds.). *African Youth Languages: New Media, Performing Arts and Sociolinguistic Development*. Palgrave Macmillan, 181-204.

# Hidden in Plain Sight: Indigenous African Languages as Urban and Youth Languages: Urban Hausa, Urban Igbo and Urban Yoruba in Nigeria

*Taiwo Oloruntoba-Oju* (University of Ilorin, Nigeria)

## 1. Introduction

An area of discursive conflict in the study of African urban and youth languages is the dominance of the colonial factor in the scholarly consideration of the character and sources of African urbanity and the associated languages. By this is meant the rather frequent assumption that African urbanity, and the associated languages, sprang almost invariably from colonial antecedents (see, for example, Mclaughlin, 2009: 2). As a result of this misconception, African urbanity and African urban languages have been studied more as colonial contact phenomena than as autonomous indigenous languages. Consequently, and incongruously, some of Africa's most populous cities, such as Lagos and Maiduguri in Nigeria, have been characterised as "cities that have not developed any urban language of their own" (Beck, 2010: 14).

While some work has recently focused on the versatility of African languages in urban and youth usage (see, especially, Nassenstein, 2015, 2017, in respect of rural-urban and youth languages in Congo and Rwanda), the exclusion of some of the densest metropolitan centres in Africa from the arc of mainstream "urban language" studies deserves to be addressed. One such city is Lagos, Nigeria. With World Atlas population estimates ranging between 18,000,000 and 21,000,000,[1] that is, five to six times the population of Berlin, Lagos is one of the most cited African cities in connection with the development of an urban youth culture (see Omoniyi, 2006). Therefore, a claim such as that African cities like Lagos "lack an urban language" (along with Addis Ababa, Monrovia, Gaborone, Windhoek, Bujumbura, Lilongwe, Kigali, Kampala, Maiduguri – cities specifically listed by Beck, 2010: 14), underscores, on the one hand, the relative paucity of information on the urban language phenomenon in these quite major and important African cities, and on the other hand the absence of scholarly consensus on what actually constitutes an "urban language" with particular reference to African situations. It is also due in part, as I would be suggesting in this chapter, to the presence of considerable if unwitting fixation with parameters linked to colonial antecedents.

In the sections that follow, I first demonstrate how some characterisations of African urban and or youth languages appear to follow the colonial trajectory almost to the point of fixation, resulting in analytical focus on features that render

---

[1] *Demographia* (2017, p. 41) cites a considerably lower figure of 13,910,000 for Lagos, which is however still four times the population of Berlin, and about 3 million more than in London.

the colonial factor rather prominent in the classification of the languages, while a number of indigenous urban languages are literally "hidden in plain sight" begging to be investigated and proclaimed. Next, I present an overview of Nigeria's sociolinguistic profile in relation to the country's urban and rural spaces. I also conduct a preliminary though fairly extensive survey in which I draw attention to three urban languages in three major Nigerian cities. These are: *Hausan Kano* (literally "the Hausa of Kano"), *Otu Onitsha*, the urban Igbo of Onitsha, and *Eko*, the urban Yoruba of Lagos, as major exemplars. In the final section, I project the Yoruba of the so called "Area Boys" of Lagos, which I term *Erea* in this chapter (for reasons that I will make clear), as a social dialect and an exemplar of an urban and youth language in Lagos.

My projections in this chapter derive from participant and non-participant observations, recording and analysis of sample conversations on the streets of Lagos, as well as an assessment of the relevant literature on the languages profiled in the chapter. My knowledge and intuition, as a native speaker of Yoruba with considerable familiarity with many Yoruba dialects including the Lagos dialect, and the associated "folk linguistics",[2] is also a useful tool in the consideration of the elements of urbanity in the languages. In addition, secondary sources of data are employed.

## 2. African urban and youth languages through the prism of the Colonial

Despite compelling evidence of old African urbanities relating to languages such as Wolof in Senegal, Swahili in Kenya, Ligali in the Congo, Akan in Ghana and Yoruba in Nigeria, African urban language scholarship has tended to either deny spatial and lingual urbanity to pre-colonial Africa, or downplay the influence of indigenous African languages in the growth and development of contemporary urban languages. This may well be a reflection of the perpetual politics of inequality that underlies north-south top-down theorising (cf. Rudd, 2017, and in this volume, on "monoglot ideologies"). As noted by Beck (2010: 18) referring to Coquery-Vidrovitch (1991), "the essentialist ascription of an intrinsic ethnification and rurality to Africa was not reconcilable with concepts of urbanity and Western modernity". Consequently, many characterizations of African urbanity and the associated languages automatically assume the predominant influence of western colonisation in the origination of both. "Urban speech" in Africa is generally dated to coincide with European entrance into the African polity; accordingly, "the urban vernaculars [that] have emerged to become the language(s) of the city [are] most often dominant African languages that show evidence of contact with a former colonial language" (McLaughlin, 2009: 2; also cited by Beck, 2010: 18, and Hurst, 2017, among others).

---

[2] I refer here to the common knowledge, intuitions and understanding of communities, and assumptions that they make, regarding the nature and structure of their languages and those of others. These are often expressed in the form of profiling statements or stories that can be depreciative or appreciative of the languages profiled.

African urban language scholarship does acknowledge gaps in the history of African urbanity. It, however, continues to "flirt" with the ramifications of these gaps. An example here is the idea that "a great many of African cities came into being during the colonial period, as a direct consequence of colonialism, and were originally planned and modelled on European cities" (McLaughlin, 2009: 7), which seems obviously exaggerated.[3] While some of the ancient African cities[4] have definitely expanded and modernised with the effluxion of time, and under catalytic interventions that have certainly included colonialism, it is also true that cities all over the world have always expanded and modernised under sundry internal and external influences.[5] More importantly, with the African pre-colonial urbanities came a corresponding linguistic complexity: "Nothing was more natural than for Africans to speak several languages and to learn the language of a neighbouring group when out-group interaction so demands" (Bamgbose, 1998; also cited in Oloruntoba-Oju, 2007).

My main argument here is that the characterisation of African urbanity as a creation of Europe seems to have also influenced the analytical orientation towards contemporary urban African languages, resulting perhaps unwittingly in the privileging of linguistic markers of coloniality, and in the frequent ignoring of clear signs of indigenous African influence in the classification of urban and youth languages. This would also have contributed to the apparent reluctance to characterise indigenous African languages as urban languages except in so far as they "show evidence of contact with a former colonial language" (Hurst 2017). As I elaborate below, a prominent example of the colonial orientation in African urban language scholarship is the characterisation of code-switching of indigenous with colonial languages as the main distinguishing feature of many African urban languages.

---

[3] On the contrary, in many African nations such as Nigeria, the colonialists largely exploited existing cities and their resources. "The British did not aspire to remake Nigeria in their own image, but concentrated their efforts in the field of economic exploitation" (Mann, 1990, p. 94, also citing Prator, 1968). Nor did the colonialists remodel most of the old African cities that they met on European cities. Rather, the colonial cities were constructed mostly according to the "cantonment" segregationist principle, often for the purpose of trade and for the comfort of colonial personnel, to protect them from what was sometimes called the "noxious odours of native habitation" (Curtin, 1985, p. 595, cited in Omolo-Okalebo, 2011: 34). Separate colonies or quarters were built for the European colonies; but no metros, no undergrounds, and no inland waterways for the subjugated cities. Education was mostly functional and to facilitate colonial rule. To offer a perspective, the first television station and first skyscraper in all of Africa were built in Ibadan, Nigeria, under African rule (albeit using World scientific and technological knowhow).

[4] The apparent insinuation that there would have been no urbanity in Africa but for western colonialisation ignores the pre-colonial African empires such as Ghana, Mali, Ọyọ (Yoruba) and Benin and the corresponding metropolises that were certainly large in terms of the spatial dynamics of the time – Mali in the 13$^{th}$/14$^{th}$ Century was reportedly surpassed in size only by the Mongol (China) empire (Levtzion, 1980; Shillington, 2005).

[5] Brown (1992) offered the perspective that deplorable conditions in some old African cities mimicked the state of development in the west a century or so earlier (see pp. 345-346; p. 360). The inference may be drawn that African cities would have developed on their own. The four centuries of slavery and deprivation of Africans are discounted from the narrative.

## 2.1. The problem of code-switching as a major classificatory parameter of African urban and youth languages

African urban and or youth languages such as Wolof and Sheng are predominantly described in terms of sundry mixtures with colonial languages. Thus, urban Wolof is unambiguously characterised as "a language that has arisen out of continuous sustained contact between Wolof and French" (McLaughlin, 2001: 159). Schindler, Legendre & Mbaye (2008) also state that "Urban Wolof is a mixture of Wolof, a West-Atlantic Niger-Congo language, and French that is spoken in the cities of Senegal" (even though the authors also elicited several features that have little if anything to do with code-switching). Similarly, the Kenyan Sheng is seen as largely characterised by Swahili and English code-mixing (Mazrui, 1995; Abdulaziz & Osinde, 1997), although this characterisation is also sometimes questioned (see the brief critique by Bosire, 2006). For Beck (2010: 18), the "particularities of the urban languages" include "code-switching, borrowing, structural reduction".

The point here is not to question the existence or prominence of code-switching or code-mixing in these languages, but to question the idea that code-mixing is a specific or defining attribute of urbanity, or that African urban languages, including urban Wolof, for example, must of necessity be characterised in relation to the colonial languages in their mix. The argument is that code-mixing or code-switching in itself is less a condition of coloniality or urbanity and more a condition of individual and societal bi- or multilingualism and of sundry conditioning contexts. Code-switching has after all been established as a language-alternation process available to and employed by bilingual or multilingual speakers, albeit at varying levels of competency/incompetency. Code-mixing combines this participant-specific orientation (also allowing for social variables such as education, age, gender and class) with a function specific orientation. The latter involves "message intrinsic" factors (code-mixing for specific topics, comments, messages), and "situational" factors such as addressee requirements, in- or out-group dynamics, inclusion or exclusion strategies – the so-called secrecy, endophora and exophora functions (Oloruntoba-Oju, 1999). Degree of formality/informality, domain dynamics and style are also part of the situational factors affecting code mixing (see Ritchie & Bhatia, 2004; Wardhaugh, 2006), and these considerations are accounted for by the "situational" and "metaphorical" types of code-mixing advanced by Blom and Gumperz (1972).

Code-mixing is therefore a discourse attribute that is not specific to any language or locale, since any language can incorporate as much or as little code-mixing as is contextually relevant or required (cf. Auer, 1998; Myers-Scotton, 1993; Poplack, 1980).[6]

---

[6] It is not questionable that code mixing can ultimately progress to a state of "language mixing" or "fused lects", in the manner of Auer (1999), where it becomes an "unspectacular affair" (Auer, 2000). Mix dynamics has been a huge area of linguistic and sociolinguistic research, from word internal mixing (Poplack 1980) to clause level hierarchical mixing (Myers-Scotton, 1993). When the lexicons of languages merge to the point that relevant lects and processes are not subject to discourse or participant variation, and the community of speakers are not even aware of any "mix" or "switch", then a new language emerges which will not be described in terms of two languages or in terms of code switching.

Bosire (2006) makes a similar point in rejecting the classification of Sheng as a code-mixed language. He observes, correctly in my view, that

> [...] there are all sorts of code switches that can and do go on in the Kenyan urban setting given the multiplicity of languages in the country especially in the urban areas where Sheng is most common [...] To restrict Sheng to any one of these switches would beg the question about what to call the other types of abundant code switching. (p. 187)

Although there is a tendency for code-mixing to occur more in urban spaces than in rural areas, as pointed out by Myers-Scotton (1993) among others, this is only a matter of intensity due to the increase in population flow. Even so, and even in comparable urban spaces, the major catalyst is not the population flow per se but the character of the population, in addition to other inherent dynamics (typically "adjustment in situational factors" – Myers-Scotton, 1993: 238), that activate code-switching or code-mixing. It is axiomatic that much less code-mixing would occur in urban areas with a huge but linguistically more homogenous population than in those with more heterogeneous ones (as the examples of Lagos and Kano in this chapter show). Conversely, much code-mixing would be attested in rural spaces with substantial bilingual or linguistically more heterogeneous populations. For example, in Nigeria, Ugot (2010) found substantial code-mixing in Biase, a (rural) local government area in Cross River State, which has "an estimated population of a little over one hundred thousand (100,000) scattered over sixty (60) villages" (p. 27); here, "the average Mbise indigene is a compound bilingual" (p. 29). Ayeomoni (2006) also investigated code-mixing amongst the Ikalẹ in Irele and Okitipupa Local Government Areas of Ondo State, also in Nigeria. Concentrating on the "education elite" (sic), he established that the code-switching and code-mixing phenomena "correlate positively with the educational attainment of individuals", noting that "the average child of the community starts to become bilingual from the primary school stage of his education. This, in effect, makes code-switching and code-mixing [to] manifest in the child's linguistic performance right from his early age" (p. 90). Code-switching and code-mixing are therefore indifferent to both rurality and urbanity.

My main argument here is that the incidence of code-mixing involving indigenous African languages and colonial languages (or with any other languages) should in any event not lead to a rejection of the classification of African urban languages as indigenous, especially when the languages have clear indigenous bases. For example, Bosire (2006) cited above also rejects the classification of Sheng (by Mazrui, 1995: 188) as "an urban variety of Swahili" albeit one that "has [also] been shaped by code switching ..." The basis for the rejection this time seems unclear, since the "differences" in the Swahili and Sheng utterances juxtaposed in the article consist in the morphological, syntactic and other grammatical manipulations of Swahili (for example, from Swahili *si-li* – "I am not eating" – to Sheng *si-ku-li* – "I am not eating"). As acknowledged by Bosire himself, the morphemic insert *ku* is "productive in some non-standard dialects of Swahili". It is therefore not clear why a language or language practice (Sheng) consisting structurally of many such examples cannot be termed a variety of the base, manipulated, language (Swahili). Bosire would eventually settle for the term "hybrid" as a description of Sheng. However, this only seems to return us to the start point of the argument, since the original attempt was to determine the linguistic components of Sheng and the dominance configuration of its "duelling" components. The conclusion that Sheng is a hybrid variety of Swahili mixed with other languages (Swahili being the host and base language), is thereby somehow avoided.

This seeming reticence about acknowledging the pre-eminence of indigenous African languages in the constitution of urban or youth languages contrasts significantly with the orientation in western urban and youth languages studies. Here, the languages continue to be regarded as varieties of the host languages, albeit with sundry foreign language influences in the form of insertions from migrant and other languages. For example, although London youth language is characterised as a "feature pool" (Chesire et al., 2011), still, Kerswill (2010) had noted, correctly in my view, that western "youth languages tend to be new *dialects of the host languages* (English, German, etc.)" (my emphasis).

To give some further perspective to this north-south contrast in ideological and analytical orientation, Beck (2010: 16) would also assert that "German as spoken and familiar today *has to be seen* as an urban language as well" (my emphasis). This peremptory assertion comes despite the fact that, as Beck herself continues, "we have neither an everyday nor a scientific recollection of that fact". Furthermore, notwithstanding the avalanche of loan words from English, French and other languages into German, and an abundance of code-mixing of the two languages to boot, it would appear enough in this instance to simply explain "urban German" in terms of "the relationship between urban and rural environments". It is therefore inexplicable that indigenous African languages spoken in African urban centres should be denied a similar classification. Equally inexplicable is why attempts to claim an African heritage for languages such as Sheng would now be considered a "disquieting (…) re-ethnification" (Beck, 2010: 27).

The foregoing critique has an obvious Africanist/postcolonialist ring to it; that is, it expresses an underlying concern with the promotion of African indigenous languages, many of which are already attrition prone, as even UNESCO would caution. However, this concern is not simply emotive or without objective basis, since alternative perspectives that locate African indigenous languages as agents of change do exist (see Ambrose, Read & Webb, 1998; Phaahla, 2014, among others).

Within the current context, the alternative classification of urban and youth languages such as Wolof and Sheng as variants of the (indigenous) host languages also exists. The example of Sheng being characterised as a variety of Swahili has been highlighted above. With regard to Wolof, Tamba (2014) notes, for example, that "a difference can be noticed between rural Wolof and urban Wolof, with the latter being a simplified version of the former" (p. 12). Tamba does acknowledge that "the Wolof spoken in urban areas is *often* characterized by the use of French-Wolof code-switching" (p. 4, my emphasis). However, she avoids earlier classifications of urban Wolof as an exclusively Wolof-French phenomenon. She insists that "the reader should not expect to find one characteristic of urban Wolof which consists of using French words from time to time in [the examples used in the dissertation]" (p. 5). Indeed, she had decided "not to add any French words throughout the examples used in this dissertation" (pp. 4-5), thereby treating code-switching properly as an incidental feature or at least as only one of the many features.

There are several other indigenous African languages with urban varieties for which code-mixing is an incidental rather than ultimately defining feature. These indigenous urban languages are literally hidden in plain sight. In the next section I conduct a brief survey of the Nigerian situation.

## 3. Nigeria's Sociolinguistic Profile and the Urban Languages

### 3.1. Nigeria's Multilingualism and the Major Indigenous Languages

The Nigerian linguistic landscape is marked generally by its extensive multilingualism and the hierarchical interaction of the indigenous languages with colonial languages. The country is credited with some 400-500 indigenous African languages, among which three – Hausa, Yoruba and Igbo, representing the major population centres (North, South West and South East) – are dominant. These indigenous languages are also the dominant languages of expression in the associated cities, as highlighted below:

| Dominant Indigenous Nigerian Languages | | Associated Nigerian Cities |
|---|---|---|
| Hausa | → | Kano, Kaduna, Sokoto |
| Igbo | → | Aba, Onitsha, Owerri |
| Yoruba | → | Abeokuta, Ibadan, Lagos |

Agheyisi (1984) classified Nigerian States into heterogeneous and homogenous states, based on their language use patterns, and she grouped Lagos and Kano States, as well as Anambra State (where Onitsha is) as "predominantly monolingual states". The major languages above also serve as the provincial languages of their respective regions. They are thus recognised in the country's constitution, where they are prescribed for use in the provincial legislatures, in addition to English. They also serve as the dominant languages of the major cities of the regions, and they are represented to varying degrees in the major cities outside their native regions.

The above background establishes a prima facie context for the employment of these indigenous languages as urban languages. However, Nigeria's dense multilingualism, and the complex interaction of indigenous languages both amongst themselves and with colonial languages, especially English, does complicate the nation's sociolinguistic profile. This relationship therefore requires a closer look within the context.

## 3.2. Diglossia: English, Pidgin English and Code-mixing in relation to Urban Nigerian Languages

The relationship between the indigenous languages and English in Nigeria is one of *diglossia* (whose terms have been repeatedly explicated since Ferguson, 1972). The advent of Western colonialism introduced English as a dominant language in Nigeria, becoming the language of bureaucracy, education, parliament, international relations, etc. In terms of spread, it is estimated that English (along with Nigerian Pidgin English) is spoken by 60% of Nigeria's population, thereby making the language one of the most commonly spoken languages in the country (*Ethnologue*, n.d.). English also became the language associated with prestige, leading to negative attitudes towards the various mother tongues (see Adegbija, 2004; Oloruntoba-Oju, 1994, among others). Within this diglossic or "multiglossic" context, English became the "high" language, while the other languages became the "low" languages in the country.

However, this global view of the English language in Nigeria tends to cloak its restrictive outlook with regard to wider communication within the polity. "Its penetration is not deep; few Nigerians, even among the well-educated, speak good Standard English. [...] English in Nigeria is best classified as a language of special information" (Mann, 1990: 93, also citing Ferguson, 1966). Scotton (1975) found that the use of English was also determined by participant-related functions, as "more frequent use of English seems to be by persons who (a) hold salaried jobs where there are likely to be co-workers and (b) have co-workers of another ethnic group" (p. 82). English also carries the negative connotations of officialdom and of braggadocio. Described as the language of alienation (Oloruntoba-Oju, 1994), English outside of officialdom is often resorted to when speakers want to be impersonal, show superiority, shun familiarity, or conceal ethnic identity.[7]

Pidgin English has also enjoyed a generous treatment in Nigerian sociolinguistic studies. The language is widely used as lingua franca in parts of the South-South region of Nigeria, especially in Benin City and the Niger Delta areas such as Warri and Ughelli. Pidgin is the native language of approximately 3 to 5 million people mainly concentrated in the Niger Delta region. Mann (1990: 99) conjectured that Pidgin is "probably the language of widest interethnic communication in Nigeria today. It has more speakers than English, is easier to acquire". Indeed, there have been calls to make Pidgin English an official language and lingua franca in Nigeria (Emenanjo 1985: 127, cited in Mous, 2003: 158), even if the prospects are quite daunting (Adegbija, 2004; Mann, 2009). A survey by Mann (2009) also indicated a progressively favourable attitude towards the use of "Anglophone Nigerian Pidgin" (ANP). Even members of the diplomatic corps have recently taken to the occasional expression in Pidgin English, and BBC now has a broadcast programme

---

[7] Mother tongue interference, however, gives away the speakers' ethnic identities and or their relative competence in spoken English.

in Nigerian Pidgin. Pidgin is also used extensively for national and electronic commercial and political advertisements, whereas, for this domain of advertorials, the indigenous languages thrive only in their provincial areas.

However, outside of the Benin and Delta areas referred to above, Pidgin English is not a language of spontaneous but of situational communication, deployed as the need may arise. The first choice of language even in urban areas is often the dominant language of the environment, or English. For example, Scotton (1975: 84) noted that "conversations at work with members of one's own ethnic group show less English and Pidgin used" in Lagos, albeit "a high percentage use English even in this intra-ethnic situation, perhaps because the domain, if not the situation, is public". In the study group, which comprised those who claim ability to use the respective languages, 96% said they had used Yoruba in the three days preceding the interview, as against 92% for English and 76% for Pidgin. Akere (1972) had similarly discovered a preference for the use of either the Ijẹbu-Ikorodu Yoruba dialect or Eko (Lagos urban dialect) amongst citizens of Ikorodu, a Lagos suburb. Also, attitudinal observations and surveys continue to indicate a lower preference for the use of Pidgin than other languages. Mann (2009) expressed the irony that attitudes among the "young generation (15-19 years) – currently considered ANP's main users and vectors – were the least favourable" due to its association with the uneducated. For many youthful users, Pidgin is a means of projecting a youth identity and culture, and is often reserved for "exotic" peer group or in-group expressions.

My own participant observation indicates that the use of Pidgin in an urban area like Lagos is both participant sensitive and class sensitive, and that the language is used more to bridge the class divide than the ethnic divide. In other words, the first choice of inter-ethnic communication is often English, even a smattering of English, rather than Pidgin, except where participant assessment indicates the need for a *linguistic climb down*, to Pidgin. In designated areas such as the popular markets, general participant assessment does indicate an automatic climb down to Pidgin where Yoruba is not possible; that is, it is generally assumed based on class sensitivity that Pidgin would be the next possible or appropriate level of language in such settings. Corroborating evidence for this attitude will be found in aesthetic expressions, including novels, plays and films, where, in the vast majority of cases, Pidgin English is still used to depict the uneducated, unsophisticated and or the poor.

A prominent linguistic fallout from Nigeria's sociolinguistic development as briefly sketched above is the extreme code-switching and code-mixing that characterises spoken languages in the country. This extreme code-mixing has been theorised as a result of the degraded importance of indigenous languages and the associated acquisition dynamics (Aladejana & Odejobi, 1999; Isola, 2010; Oloruntoba-Oju, 1994; Taiwo, 1976, among others). However, as noted earlier, code-mixing itself has been theorised generally as a bilingual/multilingual phenomenon. Therefore, classificatory accent has been on participant and functional factors, and not necessarily on spatial factors such as urbanity or rurality. The researches by Ugot and Ayeomoni in rural Ikalẹ cited above are instructive in this regard.

The point that code-mixing is not necessarily an attribute of locale therefore stands reiterated with regard to the Nigerian setting. The role of colonial languages especially English and French, and the actual extent of their use in specific cities can only be ascertained therefore with a close look at the patterns for each city. For example, the extent of use of English in the streets of Lagos is vastly different from its occurrence in the streets of Kano, as I will elaborate below. In the following section, I briefly survey the three predominant indigenous languages in the Nigerian cities and comment on their urbanity and their interface with colonial languages in these cities.

## 4. Urban and Youth Hausa, Urban and Youth Igbo and Urban and Youth Yoruba

### 4.1. Urban and Youth Hausa – *Hausan Kano* (Hausa in Kano)

Hausa enjoys a pre-eminence in northern Nigerian cities that is unparalleled by other languages in other regions. Paden (1968) noted that, prior to western colonisation, Hausa was spoken throughout southern Niger and northern Nigeria and had even developed into a lingua franca across much of Western Africa for purposes of trade (p. 200). *Ethnologue* (n.d.) also confirms that Hausa is the "de-facto provincial language in the north". Agheyisi (1984: 238), citing Adeniran (1979) and Post (1968) noted that Hausa had been established as the regional lingua franca since pre-colonial times.

British colonial policy of indirect rule further cemented this pre-eminence of Hausa in the north. The language was so entrenched that even after independence, Nigeria's post-independence Constitutions continued to recognize the disparity in attitudes towards and actual use of English between the south and the north. The Constitutions therefore prescribed the use of English for the regional assemblies of the West and South, while, as noted by Taiwo (2009: 5), they "recommended Hausa as the language of business in the northern house of assembly". Taiwo proceeded to observe that "in Southern Nigeria, English had pervaded the major public domains, [while] in the North, the language had limited functions in the public domain". To date, Hausa is the language of urbanity and of the streets in the northern cities of Kano, Kaduna, Sokoto, Bauchi and others.

Literature on the distinction between urban and rural Hausa is scanty, but there is sufficient indication that Urban Hausa as represented by the standard Hausa spoken in the city of Kano is perceived as different from rural Hausa. "Sometimes", notes Jones (2015: 41) "words that would be universally comprehensible in the cities may draw vacant stares in the village". The particulars of these differences are not always stated. However, dialectal strains seem to be an important factor in the distinction between urban and rural Hausa. Datumbishi (2013) observed that "people residing in cities (*birane; biran (sg)*) laughed when they heard rural pronunciations", although "no dialect was considered superior or inferior".

Musa and Altakhaineh (2015) also studied the Hausa spoken in Kano from the perspective of optimality theory and discovered that "syllable structure and weight are important in selecting the optimal reduplication candidate, where structures like CVCC or CCV are not permitted in the reduplicant since they are not permissible forms in Hausa's syllable structures" (p. 40).

Distinction between educated and non-educated Hausa speeches has also been considered, along with the implication of class as an important variable. This is the context within which colonial languages come into the description of the urban Hausa. Code-switching is, however, situational. For example, Jones (2015) notes that "Westernized urban Hausas will *sometimes* employ [English] words to show that they are of a more refined and educated urban class" (p. 41; my emphasis).

For its part, Hausa youth language is often an admixture of slangs and technological lexes. It is associated in the literature with two main features, namely technological register and in-group code usage, along with code-switching, semantic extension, neologisms, and the like (Bature 2002, cited by Chamo, 2011: 27). A good majority of the slangs elicited in these studies (up to 96% in Chamo, 2011) are Hausa based, that is, deriving from indigenous sources.[8] Hausa youth language also has a sizable representation in Hausa rap/hip-hop music which draws from both Hausa and English (Muhammad, 2015) with a predominance of Hausa usage.

Code-mixing involving Hausa and English, Arabic and English or Arabic-Hausa-English seems a common enough phenomenon in Hausa youth language, as well as what may be described as the "Hausafication" of Arabic and English words. Ahmed and Daura (1970) note a distinction between classical and modern Hausa, where the former is subject to Arabic influence, while the latter is subject to Western languages, especially French (Hausa in Niger) and English (Hausa in Nigeria). However, the scope and significance of the code mixing is also subject to the extent of a participant's immersion in Western education, a condition that excludes the vast majority of Hausa speakers. In view of this, the variety of Hausa code-mixed with English in urban Hausa cities is restricted to the elite and is largely excluded from the streets.

In summary, urban Hausa is marked at the phonological and lexical levels by a noticeably distinct "city pronunciation", and lexical usage that respectively amuses and bemuses rural Hausa speakers, whose pronunciation in turn also entertains urban residents. The city pronunciation is marked by the phonological and semantic Hausafication of Arabic, English and French words, while at the syntactic level, code-mixing with English or Pidgin English is noticeable among the westernized elite whereas code-mixing with Arabic is spread among the non-westernised majority. Since Hausa-Arabic code-mixing is also evident in rural communities, the real distinguishing mark of urban Hausa is the "city pronunciation" of Hausa

---

[8] Most slangs in this study are analysed as coinages (e.g. *babarkaharka* which literally means "big activity" in Hausa, but used as a slang in the data, is analysed as a coinage by the researcher).

words. Meanwhile, Hausa youth language is marked by the use of slangs, technological register and code-mixing with predominant Hausa usage.

## 4.2. Urban and Youth Igbo – Igbo in Onitsha

Onitsha in Anambra State, Nigeria, with a population of nearly eight million (*Demographia*, 2017: 22), is the principal city of the Igbo, an ethnic group in the South Eastern part of Nigeria. The status of Onitsha as a commercial city and gateway to the other parts of the country ensures some heterogeneous presence. However, a good majority of the inhabitants of Onitsha are also other Igbos who flock in from the hinterland. They speak Igbo language, albeit of several different dialects that are, mostly, mutually intelligible. As noted by Agheyisi (1984), cited earlier, the predominant language of the Igbo area is Igbo. It is also the language of the main cities of the Igbos.

Available literature on Igbo languages and dialects gives some insight into the nature of urban Igbo as spoken in Onitsha (see, for example, Ezuoke, 2018; Ikekeonwu, 1987; Nkamigbo & Eme, 2011; Obadan & Okolo-Obi, 2017; Onumajuru, 2017). Although the literature is not presented primarily as urban language or youth language research, the city setting of the researches and the thrust of their findings show an orientation towards urban-rural distinctions. Ikekeonwu (1987), cited by Obadan and Okolo Obi (2017: 347), identified two main dialects in Onitsha, the "Onitsha-Enu" and "Otu-Onitsha" dialects. The dialects belong to the "Inland West Igbo" dialect clusters. Nkamigbo and Eme (2011) also noted these dialects, which they explain as the standard dialect spoken by indigenes of Onitsha who live mostly in Enu-Onitsha ("interior Onitsha"), and Otu-Onitsha dialect spoken by the more heterogeneous community of traders and other visitors from various parts of Igbo land and beyond. "Otu", according to Nkamigbo and Eme (2011), "is the name of the main Onitsha market which accommodates people from other dialects and areas of Igbo" (p. 83). Also, according to Onumajuru (2017), citing Williamson (1972) and Emenanjo (1976), the two main varieties of Igbo in Onitsha, are the "highly specialized" "Onicha" dialect spoken by indigenes, and the "generalized form" dialect "spoken by traders and non-indigenes of Onitsha" (p. 773).

In all cited cases, the distinguishing features of the urban Igbo are represented in terms of dialectal or morphological distinctions vis-à-vis other dialects of (rural) Igbo (Onumajuru, 2017), or in terms of the preponderance of slang usages (Nkamigbo and Eme, 2011). The slangs are also Igbo based, albeit from several different dialects of Igbo. What this means, for Nkamigbo and Eme (2011), is that the slangs could ultimately enrich the Igbo language as a whole, that is, "permeate the different Igbo dialects and, with time, lose their status as slang expressions" (p. 92). This is a predictable trajectory.

It is noteworthy that the slangy variety, Otu-Onitsha, is found in the area inhabited by more heterogeneous speech communities, therefore resulting in a linguistic mix. It is also conceivable that the population comprises a significant if not predominant number of youths. Otu-Onitsha may therefore be termed a youth language as well, although the literature so far does not assess the language from this perspective. However, youth language in Igbo is generally analysed in the literature as comprising slang usage by young folks (see Eze & Odo, 2017; Nkamigbo, 2015) and seems mostly concerned with what has been described as "youth topoi, especially the mix of sex, money and sometimes crime" (Oloruntoba-Oju, 2017: 187).

The urban language scenario in Onitsha can therefore be seen as two different varieties, the Onicha dialect that is spoken largely by Onitsha indigenes, which could be distinguished dialectically from other Igbo forms and is representative of Standard Igbo, and the Otu-Onitsha dialect which, apart from being urban and considerably heteregenous, is also heavily characterized by forms of youth usage. Indeed, in the Otu-Onitsha dialect we find a strong example of indigenous African Urban and Youth (combined) language in Nigeria. It is also an example of the predictable trajectory in which youth expressions become absorbed into the mainstream when they are "adopted by the general urban population and [perhaps] subsequently become urban vernaculars themselves" (Mclaughlin, 2009: 8-9; also cited by Hurst, 2017).

### 4.3. Urban and Youth Yoruba – Yoruba in Lagos

Lagos is the commercial hub of Nigeria. It is also the country's international seaport and was, until December 1991, the capital city of the Nigerian government. Originally settled by the Aworis (a Yoruba ethnic group), the Lagos coastal area naturally drew diverse populations to the area and shaped the multilingual character of Lagos long before the first white man set foot on the coastal region (Losi, 1967; Brown, 1964; Eades, 1980). Eades observed that "the population of Lagos State in general is "often extremely mixed", due to its coastal network of lagoons and creeks, and that "this was true of Lagos itself, even before its growth as a trading port in the 18$^{th}$ century" (pp. 14-15). The invasion of the Lagos by the Edo speaking Benin Empire (c. 1550), and the return of freed slaves from Sierra Leone threw more language into the mix. Indeed, some areas of Lagos (such as Popo Aguda/Great Campos) were populated by Brazilian returnees, while returnee figures such as Herbert Macaulay were to become important in Nigerian political history. They were also responsible for the Brazilian and Caribbean architecture that dotted the Lagos skyline at the period (see Brook, 1987). It was the slave trade that brought the British to Lagos; the English language, though now a dominant player, was a late entrant into the early linguistic mix that characterised Lagos.

Despite this early heterogeneity, three factors were to strengthen the hold of the Yoruba language on the Lagos metropolis. The first was that Lagos was (and still is) largely surrounded by the ethnic Yoruba in hundreds of towns, villages and some cities in the South Western part of the country, who had continually been flocking in large numbers to the new metropolis. The migration of several other Nigerian ethnicities especially from the South Eastern part of the country but also from the north would further activate hetero-linguistic input to the sociolinguistic profile of Lagos, but the reality of monolingual Yoruba presence all around did lead to the predominance of Yoruba language in the city. Eades (1980: 15) was to note that "the indigenous Lagosians form an increasingly small proportion of the population [but] some parts of the city still resemble Yoruba towns elsewhere".

The second factor, ironically, was the effort of the missionaries who arrived earlier with Western trading vessels. Unlike the colonialists, their interest was more in hoisting the flag of religion rather than of the colonial language. It was this period that saw the translation of the English Bible into Yoruba by the returned slave Samuel Ajayi Crowther. This singular effort was to lead to the standardization of Yoruba, beyond the classical standard associated with the old *Ọyọ* (Yoruba) Empire.

The third factor, the establishment of schools and the beginning of literacy, was also ironically connected to missionary activity. The irony is that the said missionary activity and the beginning of westernised literacy initially strengthened Yoruba language rather than the colonial language – at least until the first "grammar" schools, colleges and universities took root amongst the populace. Music and theatre entertainment, with the famed itinerant Yoruba Travelling Theatre, was largely in Yoruba, and so were the important newspapers. Films were also largely in Yoruba, so much that one of the early film makers, Eddie Ugbomah, a non-Yoruba, would abandon film making in English after an initial bad run and the realization that "acceptance and production of Yoruba language films was the beginning of the commercial wisdom" (Adesanya, 1997: 14).

In 1975, the sociolinguist Scotton (now better known as Myers-Scotton), found that "the indigenous Yoruba probably comprise at least 75% of the population" of Lagos, and that "Yoruba [was] most widely known and also seem[ed] to be most heavily used in general, with 96% of those claiming an ability to speak Yoruba reporting they used it in the two or three days preceding the interview". Akere (1972) also studied the neighbouring Ikorodu Yoruba, most of whose citizens claimed a high level competence in standard Yoruba and full competence in Eko, the Yoruba spoken in the city of Lagos. The majority indicated that they used the indigenous Yoruba dialect most often, while the smallest number, "made up of young secondary school leavers in the sample", picked English (p. 348).

Scotton would also discover indices of linguistic heterogeneity in Lagos, for example, the presence of English as official language, and Pidgin English as a widely used means of interlingual communication. Subjects in her study also observed that inhabitants of Lagos tended to need more than one language to get by. However, the languages are functionally and domain oriented. English and Pidgin are more used in public domains; "in non-public situations, the [predominant] Yoruba assert themselves as Yoruba much more freely". Neither Scotton nor Akere's study cited above mentioned code-mixing, which may have been present but which was probably not so significant as to merit their observation at that point in time.

Decades later, the demography of Lagos has altered significantly. However, the Yoruba remain the dominant ethnic group (World Population Review, *n.d*). Adedun and Shodipe (2010: 121) also note that the central Lagos speech community "is a largely indigenous Yoruba community situated in the heart of Lagos city". Yoruba remains the predominant language of the region and of the metropolis. Significantly, Yoruba is the language of the markets and of the streets, the motor parks, of political campaign speeches addressed to indigenes, etc.[9]

### 4.3.1. *Yoruba Eko: Urban Yoruba of Lagos*

Of particular interest here is the urban dimension of Yoruba language. Urban Yoruba had long existed in Lagos and had been appreciated as different from the Yoruba of other Nigerian cities such as Ibadan and Osogbo, and of the hinterland. Referred to as "Yoruba Eko", or "Eko", the Yoruba spoken in Lagos in the early period had been noticeably urbanized. Eko is actually the indigenous name for the area. Although the area was named Lagos by the Portuguese in 1652, Eko remains the preferred name by the indigenes. It is the name given to a number of prominent locations and establishments, e.g. Eko Bridge, Eko Atlantic (planned new city within Lagos), Eko Hotels and Resorts, Eko FM (Radio), Eko Meridien, Eko Hospital, Eko College of Management and Technology, Eko Challenge Cup, etc. Indeed, the indigenous name, Eko, reverberates daily as all traffic headed for central Lagos is heralded by shouts of "Ekoo!" from innumerable commuter parks, moving buses and from bus stops.

The colonial influence on Lagos had always been acknowledged; however, there is considerable consensus amongst researchers and commentators that Eko consists largely of dialectal infusions from other Yoruba or neighbouring dialects. Ajetumobi (2003) describes the urbanization of Yoruba in Lagos as comprising loan words from neighbours, especially the Ijẹbus (Yoruba ethnic group) and from the conquering Bini (with close historical links to the Yoruba), leading to a clear distinction between the urban (Lagos) dialect and prototype Awori, spoken by "hinterland Aworis". Akere (1978) also referred to Eko as "Common Yoruba", which is close to Standard Yoruba, but includes sundry dialectal variations relating to the rural environment. Fosudo and Ademeso (2001) describe the creation of urban Yoruba in terms of "the contact between Eko [...] and other dialects such as Ẹgba, Ijẹbu, Ọyọ, Ibadan, Ijẹsha, Ilajẹ, etc" (p. 428). Similarly, Adedun and Shodipe (2010: 126), even as they discuss Yoruba-English bilingualism, acknowledge that Eko (Lagos Yoruba) is "deeply eclectic in terms of the various dialectal infusions" and that the dialectal influence comes mainly from conglom-

---

[9] Former Nigerian Federal Commissioner for Works, Femi Okunnu, recently argued fiercely that "the common language spoken in Lagos had always been Yoruba", notwithstanding the longstanding heterogeneity of the city's population (PMnews, 2017).

eration of different Yoruba-speaking people of Western Nigeria in Lagos, thus creating a Yoruba dialect diversity involving the infusion of phonological or lexical components of Yoruba dialects like Ijẹbu, Ẹgba, Ekiti, Ọyọ, etc".

Vestiges of early colonial contact are no doubt found in certain borrowed lexical items that have been Yorubanised or indigenized over time (e.g. "copper" – *kọbọ*; "crowbar"–*koroba*; "half-penny" – *eekpini*, "bread"– *buredi*, etc.). While some researchers have referred to these items specifically in relation to Lagos (see Akere, 1978; Fosudo and Ademeso, 2001), they are in reality globally present in Yoruba language and have no other equivalents in the language. In other words, it is not the case that the items under reference are only specific to Lagos or to urbanity. Furthermore, vestiges of early contact with other languages, especially Hausa and Arabic, are similarly present in Yoruba, e.g. (*al-basa – alubosa* ("onion"); *al-barka – alubarika* ("blessing"); *du"a – adura* ("prayer")). Since related processes such as borrowing, code-mixing and code-switching occur globally within the language, they would not qualify as specific urban features.

### 4.3.2. *Some Distinguishing Features of Yoruba Eko*

Eko is clearly not identified by the volume of code-mixing or other global features but by Lagos specific features of the speech. A general survey reveals that these can be appraised at two broad levels: that of dialectal variation (and de-dialectalisation) appraised in relation to the rural environment or to rural dialects, and that of sundry discourse forms and domain specific usages.

(a) Dialectal variation and de-dialectalisation

In "folk linguistics", non-Lagosian Yorubas anecdotally profile Eko as different in some ways from standard Yoruba or other dialects of Yoruba. For example, kids from Lagos are often playfully referred to as *ọmọ midẹ*, or *ọmọ mi kẹdẹ* ("children of *mi dẹ*"/"children of *mi kẹdẹ*"), where *mi-dẹ* or *mi kẹdẹ* is the phonosyntactic and morphophonemic variation of the standard Yoruba *mo-si* ("And I ..."), where *mo* (1sg – "I") is substituted with *mi* (1sg –"I") and *si* (conj- "and") is substituted with *dẹ*.

In Table 1, below, the subject pronoun (*mo*) in standard Yoruba is generally varied in the Eko variety with regard to the vowel /o/, which changes to /i/ in *mi*. In 1b and 1c, the conjunction "*si*" ("and"), and intensifier "*kan*" in standard Yoruba are substituted with *dẹ* and *kẹ dẹ* in Eko. *Kẹ dẹ* appears to be an influence from neighbouring Ijẹbu Yoruba dialect. However, this usage as a feature of Eko is so distinctive that it singularly identifies the variety wherever it is heard in all of Yoruba land.[10] In 1d and 1e below, the repetitive /i/ sound is often a source of mirth and is often attested in pejorative mimicking of Eko. It is also frequently associated with youthful or childish Eko.

---

[10] In the 2017 Yoruba film, *Sisi Eko* ("Lagos Girl") directed by Wale Rasak, the Eko language of the protagonist is depicted almost solely by the exaggerated employment of the usage (*mi dẹ, mi kẹdẹ, mi kẹdẹkẹ*).

|  | Standard Yoruba | Eko (Lagos Yoruba) |
|---|---|---|
| 1a. | **Mo** lọ<br>1sg PAST go<br>("I went") | **Mi** lọ<br>1sg PAST go<br>("I went") |
| b. | **Mo si** lọ<br>1sg PAST conj. go<br>(I and went – "I went")<br><br>/1sg PAST PRE-VERB go<br>"I did go" | **Mi dẹ** lọ<br>1sg PAST conj. go<br>(I and went – "I went") |
| c. | **Mo kan** lọ<br>1sg INT go<br>("I just went") | **Mikẹdẹ** lọ<br>1sg INT Conj go<br>I just and wentx<br>("I just went") |
| d. | **Mo** mi pin<br>1sgPASTswallow pin<br>("I swallowed a pin") | **Mi** mi pin<br>1sgPASTswallow pin<br>("I swallowed a pin") |
| e. | **Mo ni mo** mi pin<br>1sg say 1sg swallow pin<br>("I said I swallowed a pin") | **Mi ni mi** mi pin<br>1sg say 1sg swallow pin<br>("I said I swallowed a pin") |

**Table 1**: Dialectal variation in Eko, Urban Yoruba of Lagos, Nigeria

In addition to the examples above, several other forms of variation are evident in Eko compared with standard Yoruba and other Yoruba dialects. Observation shows variations by way of vowel deletion, substitution or lengthening (or a combination of those), or deletion or substitution of nasal consonants as in the following examples:

|  | Some variation patterns | Standard Yoruba and other Yoruba dialects (indicated in brackets) | Variation/Preference in Eko |
|---|---|---|---|
| 1. | Vowel deletion and vowel lengthening in negative constructions | a. **Emi o mọ̀**<br>1sg NEG know<br>("I don't know")<br>or<br>b. **Mi o mọ̀**<br>1sg NEG know<br>"I don't know"<br><br>c. **Mẹ mọ̀** (Ekiti dialect)<br>1sg NEG know<br>"I don't know"<br><br>d. **Me mọ̀** (Yagba dialect)<br>1sg NEG know<br>"I don't know" | **Mo-o mọ̀**<br>1sg NEG know<br>"I don't know" |

| | Some variation patterns | Standard Yoruba and other Yoruba dialects (indicated in brackets) | Variation/Preference in Eko |
|---|---|---|---|
| 2. | Deletion or substitution of nasal consonant | a. *In mò* (Ọyọ dialect)<br>1sg NEG know<br>"I don't know"<br>or<br>b. *Ng-o mò* (Ọyọ)<br>1sg NEG know<br>("I don't know")<br>c. *Ng-o de lọla* (Ọyọ)<br>1sgPROG arrive tomorrow<br>("I will arrive tomorrow") | *Mo-o mò*<br>1sg NEG know<br>"I don't know" |
| | | d. *Ola-ni-ng-o-de* (Ọyọ)<br>TomorrrowFOC.-is-1sg-PROG- arrive<br>("Tomorrow is when I will arrive") | *Mi ma-a de lọla*<br>1sg PROG arrive tomorrow<br>("I will arrive tomorrow")<br>or<br>*Ma-a de lola*<br>1sgPROG arrive tomorrow<br>("I will arrive tomorrow")<br><br>*Ola-ni-ma-a-de* (Ọyọ)<br>TomorrrowFOC.-is-1sg-PROG-arrive<br>("Tomorrow is when I will arrive") |
| 3. | Vowel substitution | a. *Won o lọ/ Won yoo lọ*<br>3pl FUT go<br>("They will go")<br><br>b. *Mọ lọ* (Ọyọ)<br>2sg-IMP-NEG<br>("Don't go") | *Won a lo /Won maa lọ*<br>3pl FUT go<br>("They will go")<br><br>*Ma lọ*<br>2sg-IMP-NEG<br>("Don't go") |
| 4. | Clause particle variation (determiners/ demonstratives) | a. *Omo naa*<br>Child that<br>("That child")<br><br>b. *Omo un* (Ọyọ)<br>Child that<br>("That child") | *Omo yen*<br>Child that<br>("That child") |
| 5. | Lexical variation | a. *Ng ma lu e*<br>1sg PROG beat 2sg<br>("I will beat you") | *Mi ma na e*<br>1sg PROG beat 2sg<br>("I will beat you") |

**Table 2** Further dialectal variation patterns in Eko, Urban Yoruba of Lagos, Nigeria

The above represents a preliminary survey. A full inventory of such dialectal variations must await substantive research focused on the relevant elements.

De-dialectisation: A general process of *de-dialectalisation*[11] seems evident even from the examples above. That is, urban Yoruba, especially Eko is de-dialectalised in relation to rural or other dialects of Yoruba (especially 2 – 4 in the table above). Yoruba immigrants from the hinterland tend to quickly learn to "step up" to Standard Yoruba or Eko in order not to be "branded" as *ara oke* (upland folks).

(b) Discourse forms and domain-specific usages

Many domain specific usages can be observed on the streets of Lagos. They include toponyms and terms that are contextually linked to the city. These usages are hardly attested in similar domains in Yoruba speaking areas outside of the Lagos metropolis. A specific domain is that of commuter traffic where quite a lot of Lagos specific commuter codes and slangs occur. Usages are also internally marked by various forms of semantic manipulation, idiomatisation and pidginisation. Notable discourse forms include, but are not limited to, the following:

(i) Commuter codes and slangs (and their pidginised and code-mixed variants)
(ii) Ethnic vocatives
(iii) Toponymic vocatives
(iv) Toponymic panegyrics
(v) Lagos slangs

**i-** Commuter codes and slangs: These are names and terms related to commuter traffic and they are quite peculiar to the Lagos environment. These occur in indigenous language, pidginised and code-mixed forms. Examples include:

*Indigenous language forms*: *danfo*; *molue* (names for commuter buses); *agbero* (motor park "tout" who hustles passengers); *o nwole o* ("he/she is alighting (the bus)"); *o nbole o* ("he/she is disembarking"), *durogbe* ("stop to carry him/her"), *w'egbee* ("check your side" [for oncoming traffic] usually said by bus driver to his *"conductor"* (motor boy/driver's assistant)), *o wa o* ("there is" – i.e. passenger has reached point of disembarkation); "I/he/she want(s) to alight"); *owo da nbi?* ("Where is the money here?" i.e. calling on passengers to pay – this contrasts with *esanwo* – "please pay" in most other Yoruba towns), *owo da nwaju*? ("Where is money at the front?" i.e. calling on passengers on the front seats beside the driver to pay up); *o loyun o ponmo o* ("he/she is pregnant and is carrying a baby too" – usually a warning by the conductor to the driver to be slow/cautious in reference to elderly or delicate passengers alighting/disembarking).

*Pidginised forms*: Some examples are shown in the table below.

---

[11] See Thelander (1980) for comparative notes on the process of de-dialectalisation.

| Yoruba | Pidgin | Gloss |
| --- | --- | --- |
| W'egbe e<br>2sg look side POSS<br>You look side yours | Your side | "Look out for oncoming traffic on your side"<br>(from bus driver to the "conductor") |
| Owo da nwaju?<br>Money INT front<br>Money where front | Money for front | "Passengers on front seat pay up" (from conductor to passengers) |
| O nbolẹ o<br>3sg PROG alight PARTI-CLE/ EXCL<br>He/she alighting | E dey come down o | "He/she [passenger] is alighting [from the bus]" (conductor alerting driver) |

**Table 3:** Pidginised forms of commuter codes and slangs

*Code-mixed forms*: The main type of code-switching in popular (street) usage in Lagos is Yoruba-Pidgin English code-mixing. The best examples will be found in the markets or in commuter traffic codes in the course of exchanges such as "conductor" regulations or announcements. The latter produces popular examples such as the following:

- Ikẹja *straight* (i.e. bus is commuting non-stop to Ikẹja)
- Maryland *ma wọle o* ("Maryland do not enter" i.e. passengers heading for Maryland should not get in [because the bus is not stopping there])
- Yaba *Under Bridge* ni o (i.e. bus is stopping at the bus stop near the bridge underpass at Yaba)
- *Wọle pẹlu changeẹ; enter with your change o* (i.e. only passengers who do not require change should alight)
- *Mi o ni change o – I no get change o* (I don't have small bills/coins for change – i.e. do not come in with big bills)
- *Hol your 100 naira o* ("Hold 100 naira note" – i.e. only those with a 100 naira note not requiring change are allowed in the bus)

**ii-** Ethnic vocatives: These are names by which other ethnicities are called. Again, the vocatives are hardly heard of outside of Lagos. They include: *ara oke* ("upland folks") *ọmọyibo / ọmọnna* ("child of Igbo/child of Nna" – Igbo citizen, *nna* being an Igbo referencing phrase), *aboki* (means "friend" in Hausa but is used generically to refer to Hausa immigrants in Lagos), *Ete* (reference to Cross-River State, especially Calabar, immigrants);

**iii-** Toponymic vocatives: This refers to naming relating to parts of Lagos: *Ọmọge Cele* ("Girls from Celestial area"); *Ọmọge Akoka* ("Campus Girl"; also *Akoka Boys* – Akoka is the location of the University of Lagos); *Alajọ Shomolu* (fabled thrift collector from Shomolu[12] – intelligent person); *Yaba left* ("Psychiatric person/patient"; "go check your head"); *Ero Gbobi* ("Gbobi passengers/commuters" – orthopaedic patients, Gbobi being the site of Lagos' foremost orthopaedic hospital; the term is also a slang reference to motorcyclists especially when they are driving dangerously).

**iv-** Toponymic panegyrics: This refers to Lagos specific praise sayings and self-praise: *Eko o gbagbęrę* ("Lagos does not accommodate slothfulness"); *Eko aromisalęgbęlęgbę* ("Lagos has waters enough to take care of the dry lands"); *Eko gbole o gbọle* ("Lagos accommodates the thief and the lazy"); *Eko wenjele* ("Lagos – the city where it happens"); *Owo Eko, Eko l'ongbe* ("Money made in Lagos stays in Lagos" – caution to the spendthrift); *Eko for show* (Lagos, a city given to flamboyance and braggadocio); *Eko l'àwa* ("We are Lagos folks"); *Eko lawà ta ti n jaye* ("We are in Lagos and we enjoy!"); *Eko o ni baję* ("Lagos will never be spoiled").

**v-** Lagos Slangs: These involve various forms of semantic manipulations, especially semantic and pragmatic extensions. Examples include the following:

*Won n ko mi ję* ("folks are eating me up" – admire/love me); *Bobo yen dun* ("the fellow is sweet" – gullible, easy to dupe); *ọmọyen dun* ("the babe is sweet" – sexual connotation); *Oloso* ("prostitute" – etymology unclear); *Ọsọmọ* ("who does girls" – randy fellow); *Orobolepa* ("abundance/congregation of ample (*orobo*), and slim (lepa), girls"); *O ta lęnu* (spicy – nice/delicious/beautiful); *Kondo alata* ("spicy baton" – "penis"); *eja* ("fish" – marijuana); *ejanla* ("big fish" – rich, influential); *Alaye* ("owner of the world" – person to be reckoned with or feared; influential; but sometimes used as peer reference); *Wagbọ węn* ("You will hear węn" – You will face serious anguish – *węn* is a snapping sound, onomatopoeic for neck breaking/death).

The coverage of the sociolinguistic profile of Lagos in the foregoing has privileged usages comprising solely of Yoruba Eko, the indigenous urban language of Lagos, Nigeria. The objective has been to give some indication of the vast range of this indigenous usage by several millions in the city. However, it is important to restate that other languages are in use in many different contexts, as already explained in the foregoing. These include Pidgin English, English, Outland or Upland Yoruba, Hausa, Igbo, other minority languages and several different combinations.

## 4.4. Erea: Language of the Area Boys of Lagos

The conflation of urban and youth language noted earlier can be observed in some of the samples already given above. Examples include the repeated /m/ and /i/

---

[12] Incidentally, Shomolu suburb in Lagos was the site of Scotton's (1975) research referred to earlier.

sounds in (*mi ni mi mi ṛin*) associated with youngsters, the commuter codes and slangs, and pejorative ethnic vocatives, among others. The urban and youth language connection is more pronounced when we examine the language of youth groups within the city. One group that is conspicuously connected to street life in Lagos is the group known as "area boys".

"Area boys" rule the streets of Lagos and the underworld. They are mostly school dropouts and folks who, at least in popular perception, either lack opportunities for social advancement or have opted to live outside the constraining structures of conventional society anyway (see also Heap, 2010; Momoh, 2000; Omitoogun, 1994). In reality, quite a number of fairly educated or even college educated but jobless youths are sometimes bracketed as "area boys", and some soon actually acquire the traits of the traditional area boys. Thus, there are mimic individuals and groups to be found on colleges and campuses.

Before the term "area boys" (whose precise origin is unknown) emerged, the "boys" were simply called *ọmọ ita* on local parlance (literally "child of the outside" in Yoruba, i.e. street urchin or gangster)[13], or *ọmọ amugbo* (consumer of marijuana). The area boys populate the motor parks and marijuana or *kainkain* (local gin) joints, occupy spaces under bridges, roam the night, pimp for and keep prostitutes, and are often unwelcome visitors at parties and "pepper soup joints". Sometimes, the area boys function at higher than jobless levels, as drivers, "conductors" and *agberos* (passenger hustlers) for the ubiquitous, rough riding Danfos and Molues of Lagos.

Sometimes the area boys are seen as hangers on or thugs to political office holders. The "area boys" phenomenon is pervasive. Oloruntoba-Oju (2017) notes their connection to the "criminal milieu", although some of those in the professions do try to lead respectable lives. Wole Soyinka's (1997) theatrical representation, titled *The Beatification of Area Boy: A Lagos Kaledioscope,* also represented the area boys within this milieu. The play, as appreciated by the blurb, is located "amidst everyday racketeering, general hubbub and disquiet, [in which] the police try to clear the area of undesirables" (see the blurb). However, Soyinka tries in the play to ameliorate this negative view of the area boys, presenting them as victims of a warped political and socio-economic structure who are doing their best to survive (See, also, Dunmade, 2001, amongst others, for a critical elaboration).

A distinctive group of the area boys are those referred to as *ọmọ onilẹ* ("heirs of the landowners"). These are usually seen as spoilt or wayward and generally jobless children of core indigenes of "inner Lagos" or their mimics. They often claim ownership of numerous parcels of land in Lagos, on the basis of which, coupled with threats of violence they collect illegal dues from hapless investors. Momoh (2000) puts the percentage of this subgroup at about 26% of the total number of area boys.

---

[13] The term *agbalagbaọmọita* (literally, "elder child of the outside" – "irresponsible adult") is commonly used in Yoruba as a rebuke to an elderly person behaving like a rascal.

While there have been some social science studies of the area boys in Lagos as noted above, there has been no study of their language to date. Soyinka's representation of the language of area boys, in the play referred to above, is not a useful guide to the language. Since he writes in English, he effectively puts English words in the mouth of folks who hardly use English in reality, save for the occasional Pidgin English. Furthermore, part of the "beatification" of the area boys in the play seems to be the use of fairly elevated language by some "lowly" characters. However, Oloruntoba-Oju (2017) has observed that the language of the area boys is to be regarded as "youth language" and that the base of this language is Yoruba. A focused investigation on the language of the area boys is desirable and long overdue. However, only a summary of the associated sociolinguistic profile can be provided here.

The speakers of *Erea* can be formally described as urban male, young (between 18 and 35 years), typically homeless, jobless or otherwise rascally members of the Yoruba community in Lagos. The occasional females, often their consorts, but sometimes independent "Area Girls", would also be found in this group (Momoh, 2000 puts their number at approximately half of the "boys"). Iginla (2007) puts the population of area boys in Lagos at about 35,000 as at 1996, but this estimate seems to be well understated, and the number would have ballooned to over a million anyway, relative to the soaring population of Lagos over the intervening years. They are not a united organization but operate in groups, gangs or as nomadic isolates. They will be found mostly at commuter (motor) parks, along commuter traffic routes, at or around social parties and other places described as "staging areas of youth engagement" (Oloruntoba-Oju, 2017).

Linguistically, the area boys are generally Yoruba monolinguals. Their specific language can be described as a sub-set of Eko, the urban Yoruba spoken in Lagos. I refer here to this language as *Eko Erea* (i.e. the Eko of area boys), or *Erea* for short. This is not only because the name resembles the term "area boys", but also because *Erea* is actually a reference term amongst the area boys themselves. *Erea!* is a vocative by which area boys sometimes call out to each other, or which they use as a cue for some point of note; it is a rallying term. (Alternatively, slang vocatives or noun words used as slangs, such as *Haruba! Omọ! Egbon! Alaye! Baba! Fada!* – "father", etc. are also used.) As a corollary, the beloved music of the various categories of area boys is the Yoruba fuji or *apala*, which they patronize along with thousands of other Yorubas, including several dignitaries who also patronize the music. Hardly does one hear any music other than fuji blaring from the CD collection in the Danfo or Molue. Reference to "Ekoerea" is also common in Fuji music renditions. In some Fuji music renditions, the term *Erea!* is used as cue for a change of tone, music, message or point of emphasis.

In addition to Eko, the Area boys also use the Standard, de-dialectalised variety of Yoruba, while Yoruba is the matrix language in the case of code-mixing. The traditional area boys are not sufficiently versed in English to use it comfortably; they typically have only a smattering command of Pidgin English in addition to the use of Yoruba.

Their language is also marked by aspects of linguistic innovation, vernacular speech as well as in-group interaction already noted earlier in the literature on youth language. In addition, *Erea* is marked pragmasemantically by the use of taboo or curse words and phonologically by a consistent gutturalisation or larhyngealisation. This is a deepening of voice or creaking that functions as an emotive marker of identity plus a manipulative intent (see Henton & Bladon, 1987; Yanushevskaya, NíChasaide & Gobl, 2011).

An extralinguistic marker of area boy identity is the "Twale!" gesture. "Twale!" is an exclamation to convey salutation, praise or obeisance to a superior, or stated in play to a pal. The exclamation is usually accompanied by simultaneous raising of both hands and stamping one foot, usually the right foot, on the ground. However, prior to popularization of the word "Twale" by a Nigerian gospel singer, Flo Ezeadichie Emmanuel, the gesture has long been associated with area boys, who usually accompanied it with words addressed to the object of obeisance, such as: *Baba alaye* (Superior), *Mo/mi tuba* ("I offer respects"); *Mi/mo o sako o* ("I am not boastful"); *mo/mi gentle* ("I am gentle", i.e. submissive), etc.

Again, while a full inventory of the linguistic and sociolinguistic characteristics of *Erea* awaits a much more focused research, the brief survey above does establish it as a bonafide urban and youth language in Nigeria.

## 5. Conclusion

The colonial language trajectory looms large in the classification and analysis of urban and youth languages in Africa. This has led to the privileging of languages or language practices with substantial colonial language infusions in the identification, characterization and analysis of urban and youth languages on the continent. The projection of code-switching and code-mixing of indigenous and colonial languages as a principal evaluative criterion for African urban languages appears to be a major manifestation of this orientation. This apparent fixation with the colonial trajectory has also led to the invisibility or sidelining of indigenous African languages in several African cities, especially Nigerian cities, in the consideration of candidates for urban and youth language classification and analysis. The foregoing survey has provided prima facie evidence of the existence of indigenous urban and youth languages that are not defined or primarily identified by their relationship to colonial languages.

In establishing that indigenous Nigerian languages do exist and merit classification as urban and youth languages in Nigerian cities, the foregoing survey has drawn close attention to languages or dialects such as *Hausan Kano, Otu Onitsha,* and *Yoruba Eko* as the urban Hausa, urban Igbo and urban Yoruba in the Nigerian cities of Kano, Onitsha and Lagos respectively. Like similar languages in other African cities, these urban varieties have existed over time, literally hidden in plain sight, and suppressed in notable critical practice. Youth languages exist openly in these cities as well, but have also been undetected by western scholarly radar so far. Attention has been drawn in the foregoing to *Erea,* language of the area boys of Lagos in Nigeria as an example of this scholarly omission. These revelations provide impetus for the reevaluation of the criteria for determining urban and youth languages in Africa, and for a more balanced view of the development and role of indigenous African languages in African cities.

## References

Abdulaziz, M. H., & Osinde, K. (1997). Sheng and Engsh: Development of mixed codes among the urban youth in Kenya. *International Journal of the Sociology of Language*, 125, 43–63.

Adedun, E. A., & Shodipe, M. (2010). Yoruba-English bilingualism in Central Lagos, Nigeria. *Journal of African Cultural Studies*, 23(2), 121–132. https://doi.org/10.1080/13696815.2011.637882.

Adegbija, E. E. (2004). The candidature of Nigerian Pidgin as a national language: Some initial hurdles. *International Journal of Applied Linguistics*, 105/106, 1–23.

Adesanya, A. (1997). From film to video. In Haynes, J. (Ed.) *Nigerian Video Films*. Jos: Nigerian Film Corporation, 13–20.

Agheyisi, R. N. (1984). Minor languages in the Nigerian context: Prospects and problems. *Word*, 35(3), 235–253.

Ahmed, U., & Daura, B. (1970). *An introduction to classical Hausa and the major dialects*. Zaria: Northern Nigeria Publishing Company.

Ajetumobi, R. O. (2003). The Benin factor in the history of Lagos. In Ajetumobi, R. O. (Ed.) *The Evolution and Development of Lagos State*. Lagos: A–Triad Associates, 46–62.

Akere, F. (1972). Language use and language attitudes in a Yoruba suburban town: A sociolinguistic response to the factors of traditionalism and modernity. *Anthropological Linguistics* 24(3), 344–362.

Akere, F. (1978). Grammatical competence and communicative competence in relation to the users of English as a second language. *Lagos Review of English Studies*, 1, 1–22.

Aladejana, F. O., & Odejobi, C. O. (1999). Effects of mother tongue on JSS students' performance in integrated science, *Ife Journal of Behavioural Science*, 1, 1–12.

Ambrose, N. Read, M. J., & Webb, A. (Eds.) *Workshop Papers: The Role of the African Languages in Democratic Africa*, University of Pretoria.

Auer, P. (1998). Introduction: Bilingual conversation revisited. In Auer, P. (Ed.) *Code–switching in conversation: Language, interaction and identity*. London and New York: Routledge, 1–24.

Auer, P. (1999). From codeswitching via language mixing to fused lects: Towards a dynamic typology of bilingual speech. *International Journal of Bilingualism*, 3, 309–332.

Auer, P. (2000). Why should we and how can we determine the 'base language' of a bilingual conversation? *Estudios de Sociolingüística*, 1, 129–144.

Ayeomoni, M. O. (2006). Code–switching and code–mixing: Style of language use in childhood in Yoruba speech community. *Nordic Journal of African Studies*, 15(1), 90–99.

Bamgbose, A. (1998) Language as Resource: An African Perspective. In Ambrose, N., Read, M. J., &Webb, A. (Eds.) *Workshop Papers: The Role of the African Languages in Democratic Africa*, University of Pretoria, 5–21. http://www.up.ac.za/academic/libarts/crpl/1998–03–05–Bamgbose.pdf.

Beck, R. M. (2010). Urban languages in Africa. *Africa Spectrum*, 45(3), 11–41.

Blom, J. P., & Gumperz, J. J. (1972). Social meaning in linguistic structures: Code switching in Northern Norway. In Gumperz, J. J., & Hymes, D. (Eds.) *Directions in sociolinguistics*. New York: Holt, Rinehart, and Winston, 407-434.

Bosire, M. (2006). Hybrid languages: The case of Sheng. In Arosanyin, O.F. and Pemberton, M.A. (Eds.) *Selected proceedings of the 36th annual conference on African linguistics*. Somerville, MA: Cascadilla Proceedings Project, 185–193.

Brook, J. *(6 September 1987)*. Brazilian houses in Nigeria are a legacy of thousands of freed slaves. New York: *Chicago Tribune*. https://www.chicagotribune.com/news/ct–xpm–1987–09–06–8703080006–story.html.

Brown, S. H. (1964). *A history of the people of Lagos:* 1852–1886. Ph.D. Dissertation, Northwestern University, Evanston, Illinois, USA.
Brown, S. H. (1992). Public health in Lagos, 1850–1900: Perceptions, patterns and perspectives. *The International Journal of African Historical Studies*, *25*(2), 337–360.
Chamo, I. A. (2011). Hausa–English code–switching in Kanywood films. *International Journal of Linguistics*, *4*(2), 87–96.
Datumbishi, M. A. (2013). Language, style and register in contemporary Hausa environment. *Journal of the Linguistic Association of Nigeria*, *16*(1&2), 115–126.
Demographia (2017). *World urban areas*. 14th Annual Editions. http://www.demographia.com/db–wor dua.pdf.
Dunmade, O. I. (2006). *Understanding Wole Soyinka: The beatification of area boy*. Ilorin: Integrity Publishers.
Eades, J. S. (1980). *The Yoruba today*. Cambridge University Press.
*Ethnologue* (n.d.) (a)). Languages of Nigeria. Accessed on 16 Aug. 2017 at https://www.ethnologue.com/country/ng/languag-es.
*Ethnologue* (n.d.) (b)) Hausa. https://www.ethnologue.com/language/hau
Eze, E. A., & Odo, D. C. (2017). Sociolinguistic analysis of youth language in Igbo. *Journal of Languages, Linguistics and Literary Studies (JOLLS)*, *5*, 197–208.
Ezuoke, C. O. (2018). Languages of wider communication, globalization and the Igbo language vitality. In Mbagwu, Ezeodili, S., Asadu, O. F., Ezeafulukwe, O., Nkamigbo, L. C. *Apostolate of Language and Linguistics: A Festschrift in Honour of Professor Emmanuel Okonkwo Ezeani*, 17-23. http://www.jmel.com.ng/books/profezeani/downloads.html
Ferguson, C. F. (1959/1972). Diglossia. In Gigliolo, P. (1972) (Ed.) *Language and social context*. Harmondsworth: Penguin, 232–252.
Fosudo, S., & Ademeso, A. A. (2001). Contemporary Lagos: A study of the people, literature and culture of Lagos State. In Fakoya, A. A., & Osoba, G. (Eds.) *The English Compedium 1 & 2*. Lagos: English Department, Lagos State University, 425–434.
Heap, S. (2010). Their days are spent in gambling and loafing, pimping for prostitutes, and picking pockets: Male juvenile delinquents on Lagos Island, Nigeria, 1920s–60s. *Journal of Family History*, *35*(1), 2010, 48–70.
Henton, C., & Bladon, A. (1988). Creak as a sociophonetic marker. In Hyman, L. M., Fromkin, V., & Li, C. N. (Eds.) *Language, speech and mind*. London: Routledge, 3–29.
Hurst, E. (2017). African (Urban) youth languages. *Oxford Encylopaedia*. DOI: 10.1093/acrefore/9780199384655.013.157. Accessed 16 Aug. 2017.
Iginla, S. L. (2007-04-11). "Area boys' activities: An underground economy". *The Punch (Lagos)*. Punch Nigeria Limited. Retrieved 08 May 2008.
Ikekeonwu, C. I. (1987). Igbo dialect cluster: A classification. In *University of Nigeria, Nsukka: Linguistics Departmental Seminar Series*.
Isola, A. (2010, March 24). Yoruba, other Nigerian languages on the verge of extinction. *The Vanguard* (Lagos). Retrieved from https://www.vanguardngr.com/2013/03/yoruba–other–nigerian–languages–on–the–verge–of–extinction–prof–akinwunmi–isola–warns/
Jones, J. F. (2015). *Army Special Forces Language Visual Training Materials – HAUSA*. Fort Lewis: Corps Foreign Training Centre.
Kerswill, P. (2010). Youth languages in Africa and Europe: linguistic subversion or emerging vernaculars? *Presentation at African Linguistics School: Contact/Sociolinguistics* Accessed on 16 Aug. 2017 at https://tinyurl.com/yxsk8dvl.
Levtzion, N. (1980). *Ancient Ghana and Mali*. New York: Africana Publishing Company.
Losi, J. B. (1967). *History of Lagos*. Lagos: African Education Press.
Mann, C. C. (1990). Choosing an indigenous official language for Nigeria. *British Studies in Applied Linguistics*, *6*, 91–103.
Mann, C. C. (2009). Attitudes toward Anglo–Nigerian Pidgin in urban, southern Nigeria: The generational variable. *RRL, LIV*, *3–4*, 349–364.
Mazrui, A. (1995). Slang and code–mixing: The case of Sheng in Kenya. *Arbeitspapiere*, *42*, 168–179.

McLaughlin, F. (2001). Dakar Wolof and the configuration of an urban identity. *Journal of African Cultural Studies*, *14*(2), 153–172.

McLaughlin, F. (2009). Senegal's early cities and the making of an urban identity. In McLaughlin, F. (Ed.) *The languages of urban Africa*. London: Continuum, 71–85.

Momoh, A. (2000/2003). Yoruba culture and area boys in Lagos. In *Jega, A. J.* (Ed.). *Identity transformation and identity politics under structural adjustment in Nigeria*. Stockholm: Nordiska Afrika institutet in collaboration with Centre for Documentation, Kano, 181–204.

Mous, M. (2003). Loss of linguistic diversity in Africa. In Janse, M., & Sijmen, T. (Eds.) *Language death and language maintenance: Theoretical, practical and descriptive approaches*. Amsterdam: John Benjamins, 157–170.

Musa, R. I., & Altakhaineh, R. M. (2015). An application of optimality theory (OT) on syllable structure within reduplication in Hausa spoken in Kano. *International Journal of English Language and Linguistics Research*, *3*(1), 32–44.

Myers–Scotton, C. (1993). *Social motivations for code–switching: Evidence from Africa*. Oxford: Clarendon Press.

Nassenstein, N. (2015). The emergence of Langila in Kinshasa (DR Congo). In Nassenstein.N., & A. Hollington (Eds.) *Youth language practices in Africa and beyond*. Berlin: De Gruyter Mouton, 81–98.

Nassenstein, N. (2017). Kirundi slang—youth identity and linguistic manipulations. In Ebongue, A., & Hurst, E. (Eds.) *Sociolinguistics in African contexts: Perspectives and challenges*. Berlin: Springer, 247-267.

Nassenstein, N. (2017). Rural youth language practices: Linguistic creativity and the globalised African village. In Seale, E., & Mallinson, C. (Eds.) *Rural Voices: Language, Identity, and Social Change across Place*. Lanham, Maryland: Rowman, & Littlefield, 105–123.

Nkamigbo, L. C. (2015). Conceptual metaphor analysis of Igbo youth language. *Creative Artist: A Journal of Theatre and Media Studies* *9*(1), 84–102.

Nkamigbo, L. C., & Eme, Amaoge, C. (2011). Igbo Slang in Otu–Onitsha: Towards Enriching the Igbo Language. *African Research Review: An International Multidisciplinary Journal*, *5*(6), 83–94.

Obadan, M. I., & Okolo–Obi, B. C. (2017). Aspects of Igbo dialectology: Exploring the between Nri and Ogwashi dialects of Igbo. In Bewaji, J. A. I., Harrow, K. W., & Omonzejie, E. E. (Eds.) *The Humanities and the dynamics of African culture in the 21st century*. Cambridge: Cambridge Scholars Publishing, 342–355.

Oloruntoba–Oju, T. (1994). Communication and the colonial legacy in Nigeria. In Obafemi, O., & Lawal, B. (Eds.) *Issues in contemporary African Thought* 2. Lagos: Academia Publications, 109–125.

Oloruntoba–Oju, T. (1999). Sociolinguistics: An overview. In Adegbija, E. E. (Ed.). *The English language and literature in English: An Introductory handbook*. Ilorin: Department of Modern European Languages, University of Ilorin, 121–142.

Oloruntoba–Oju, T. (2007). Irreducible Africanness and Nigerian postcoloniality from drama to video. *West Africa, Issue 7, 2007*.

Oloruntoba–Oju, T. (2017). Contestant hybridities in African urban/youth languages". In Hurst–Harosh, E. and Erastus, F. (Eds.) *African youth languages: New media, performing arts and sociolinguistic development*. London: Palgrave, 151–170 (forthcoming).

Omitoogun, W. (1994). The *Area Boys* of Lagos: A Study of organized street violence. In *Albert*, I. O., Adisa, J., Agboola, T., Herault, G. (Eds.) *Urban Management and Urban Violence in Africa, Urban Management and Urban Violence in Africa*. Ibadan: IFRA.

Omolo–Okalebo, (2011). *Evolution of town planning ideas, plans and their implementation in Kampala City 1903–2004*. Doctoral dissertation, Royal Institute of Technology, Stockholm, Sweden. Accessed on 16 Aug. 2017 at https://tinyurl.com/y5z4yx4p.

Omoniyi, T. (2006). Hip–hop through the world Englishes lens: A response to globalisation. *World Englishes*, *25*(2), 195–208.

Onumajuru, V. C. (2017). A contrastive study of Onicha and Central Igbo varieities of the Igbo lannguage. Accessed on 16 Aug. 2017 at https://tinyurl.com/y2thzo6p.

Paden, J. (1968). Language problems of national intetgration in Nigeria: the special position of Hausa. In Fishmane, J. C., Ferguson and J DAS GUPTA (Eds.) *Language problems of developing nations*. New York: John Wiley.

Phaahla, P. (2014). Indigerous African languages as agents of change in the transformation of higher education institutions in South Africa. *Nordic Journal of African Studies*, *21*(1), 31 – 56.

PMnews (2017, November 9). *Okunnu faults Akiolu, says Lagos a Yoruba State*. Accessed on 16 Aug. 2017 at *https://www.pmnewsnigeria.com/2017/11/09/okunnu-faults-akiolu-says-lagos-a-yoruba-state/*

Poplack, S. (1980). Sometimes I'll start a sentence in Spanish Y TERMINO EN ESPANOL: Toward a typology of Code–switching. *Linguistics*, 18, 581–618.

Ritchie, W. C., & Bhatia, T. K. (2004). Social and psychological factors in code–switching. In Bhatia, T. K., & Ritchie, W. C. (Eds.) *The handbook of bilingualism*. Oxford: Blackwell, 437–459.

Rudd, P. W. (2017). The invisible niche of the AUYL. In Albaugh, E., & de Luna, K. M. (Eds.) *Tracing language movement in Africa*. Oxford: Oxford University Press, 196–209.

Schindler, M., Legendre, C., & Mbaye, A. (2008). Violations of the PF interface condition in urban Wolof. *Proceedings from the Annual Meeting of the Chicago Linguistic Society*, *44*(2), 169-184.

Scotton, M. C. (1975). Multilingualism in Lagos: What it means to the social scientist. *Patterns in Language, Culture, and Society: Sub–Saharan Africa. OSU WPL 19*, 78–90.

Shillington, K. (2005). *History of Africa*. New York: Palgrave.

Soyinka, W. (1997). *The beatification of area boy: A Lagosian kaleidoscope*. London: Methuen.

Taiwo, R. B. (2009). The functions of English in Nigeria from the earliest times to the present day. *English Today*, 98, 25(2), 1–10.doi:10.1017/S0266078409000121.

Tamba, K. (2014). *Clausal nominalization in Wolof*. PhD dissertation, Linguistics and the Graduate Faculty of the University of Kansas. Accessed on 16 Aug. 2017 at https://tinyurl.com/yxjerrxzf.

Thelander, M. (1980). *De–dialectalisation in Sweden*. Uppsala: Institutionen för Nordiska Sprak vid Uppsala Universitaet.

Ugot, M. (2010). Language choice, code–switching and codemixing in Biase. *Global Journal of Humanities*, *8*(2), 27–35

Wardhaugh, R. (2006). *An introduction to sociolinguistics*. Malden, MA: Blackwell Publishing.

World Atlas (n.d.). Biggest cities in Africa. Accessed on 16 Aug. 2017 at www.worldatlas.com/articles/15–biggest–cities–in–Africa.html.

World Population Review (n.d.). Lagos Population. Accessed on 16 Aug. 2017 at http://worldpopulationreview.com/world–cities/lagos–population.

Yanushevskaya, I., NíChasaide, A. & Gobl, C. (2011). Universal and language–specific perception of affect from voice. *Proceedings of the XVII International Congress of Phonetic Sciences*, Hong Kong, China, 2208–2211.

# Rural and urban metaphors in Sheng (Kenya) and Tsotsitaal (South Africa)

*Fridah Kanana Erastus* (Jomo Kenyatta University, Nairobi, Kenya)
*Ellen Hurst* (University of Cape Town, South Africa)

## 1. Introduction

Research into youth languages in Africa has focused primarily on urban forms springing up in the large urban centres such as Nairobi (Kenya) and Johannesburg (South Africa). Language practices such as Sheng from Kenya and Tsotsitaal from South Africa have received significant attention in terms of the multilingual resources drawn on by youth in their performance. However, recent research has indicated that these practices are also prevalent in what could be considered as 'rural' areas. Authors such as Kioko (2015) and Hurst (2017) have considered the spread of these forms from urban centres into rural areas; simultaneously, Hurst (2016) suggests that urban youth language also draws on rural practices in its resources.

Metaphor is an important aspect of these youth language practices, and can highlight the interchange between rural and urban language, as well as the types of indigenous knowledge drawn on in the practices of urban youth. This paper will present data on isiXhosa-based Tsotsitaal from Cape Town, isiZulu-based isiTsotsi from Kwa-Zulu Natal, and Swahili-based Sheng from Nairobi, as well as data from rapidly urbanizing rural towns in Kenya, to illustrate how urban youth do not only draw from modern/ European paradigms and languages in their linguistic performances, but also draw from archaic and rural forms to create layers of meaning in their constructions of African modernity.

The dichotomy of 'rural' and 'urban' arises from a particular conceptualization of modernity. According to Roth-Gordon and Woronov (2009: 136), modernity assumes a set of oppositions:

> [...] between, for example, the 'center' and the 'periphery,' 'black' and 'white,' 'traditional' and 'modern' – [that] structure both our everyday ways of thinking about difference [...] the process of identifying and locating social practices and social actors in binary categories constitutes a hallmark of modernity. At the same time, everyday common sense and scholarly analyses assume that the modern world is also teleological: that people and societies inexorably move from the 'traditional' to the 'modern,' from the 'local' to the 'global,' and from the 'rural' to the 'urban.'

This dichotomy of urban and rural plays out in many domains of life. According to Mudimbe (1988: 4), this dichotomizing system is a result of the colonizing structure and leads to oppositions such as traditional versus modern, oral versus written and printed, subsistence versus growth economies, and rural/agrarian versus urban/industrialised civilization. Mudimbe states that "In Africa a great deal of attention is generally given to the evolution implied and promised by the passage from the former paradigms to the latter" (1988: 4). As Hurst (2017: 210) points out,

In Africa, the teleological drive towards modernity has resulted in rapid urbanization, and one of the effects of the rapid movement of people towards the urban centres, primarily for work, has been expanding peri-urban areas and large informal settlements on the margins of many African cities. Within these contexts, language has been impacted in specific ways. Different language effects from processes of urbanization can be seen in the global North and South. In Europe, urbanization may have resulted in dialect leveling and koineised (mixed, levelled and simplified) new dialects (Kerswill, 2006). However, 'In the developing world, rural-urban mass migration is a phenomenon of the latter part of the 20th century, with Sub-Saharan Africa the latest region to be affected... In West Africa, the dominant sociolinguistic effect appears to be an increase in individual multilingualism and the spread of lingua francas (Kerswill, 2006).

There has been a recent surge in interest in African Urban Youth Languages (AUYLs) in sociolinguistic literature. Some AUYLs include Sheng in Kenya, Nouchi in Ivory Coast, Luyaaye in Uganda, and Camfranglais in Cameroon. One of the interesting features of African Urban Youth Languages across the literature appears to be their link to a 'modern', urban identity. Roth-Gordon and Woronov (2009: 136) explain that youth '…must be understood as specifically modern subjects, in Foucault's sense of the term, including how they both utilize and trouble the binary categories associated with modernity'. This chapter aims to outline if and how the rural-urban dichotomy manifests in language. The chapter will present data from Zulu-based Tsotsitaal from Kwa-Zulu Natal, Xhosa-based Tsotsitaal from Cape Town, and Swahili-based Sheng from Nairobi, to unpack how this rural-urban split manifests in the urban youth languages themselves. To further understand the rural-urban nexus in youth language practice, data from rural towns which are rapidly urbanizing will be discussed. The paper will illustrate how urban youth do draw from not only modern/European paradigms and languages in their linguistic performances, but also from archaic and rural forms to create layers of meaning in their constructions of African modernity.

## 2. African Urban Youth Languages

AUYLs can be conceptualized not as 'languages', but rather practices, styles or registers, used by youth within the contexts of African cities. They share some features in common with slang use. According to Allen (2001), while older forms of folk speech are associated with rural society and with the oral tradition, newer forms of folk speech, particularly slang, are associated with cities, modern society and the mass media: "Sociologically speaking, slang is the urban part of popular speech and has historically found many of its incentives and referents in the socially diverse urban setting" (Allen, 2001: 266).

AUYLs have arisen in contexts of, and perhaps partly as a result of, processes of rural-urban migration over the last century. In South Africa for example, Tsotsitaal arose in the 1940s during a period of contestation over land and urban settlement for Africans. Ntshangase explains that tsotsitaal marks "permanence in black urban settlement" (1995: 292) within a context of African land dispossession and urbanization. In different countries, different contexts have resulted in different ways that these phenomena have emerged. Multilingualism, urban-rural migration, and language attitudes and ideologies relating to urban and rural dynamics have all impacted on AUYLs.

The dominance of particular languages in urban centres has led to some AUYLs utilizing European languages as their base language (the language which provides the grammatical frame), although this is not always the case. In one of the more well-researched examples, Sheng in Kenya was initially based on Swahili, yet Sheng is now widespread in Kenya, and has spread to less urban regions, and incorporates different languages. As Kioko (2015) explains:

> What is commonly referred to as Sheng is purely a complex of highly unstable and everyday-changing urban varieties and rural registers, some of which become key identity and group markers and the first language of some speakers especially in Nairobi and other urban centres in Kenya. Furthermore, ethnic mother tongues are increasingly forming part of these registers as the over 50 mother tongues in Kenya contribute to the formation of grammatically unstable grassroots codes, often comprehensible only to speakers of the particular mother tongues from which many borrowings are made. (Kioko, 2015: 119)

Sheng appears to have originated in the slum areas of Eastlands in Nairobi, although it was not one coherent code even in that context – "Eastlands is a vast area encompassing 25 distinct estates whose residents constantly create unique words to form specific 'Shengs' that identify their *bazes/mitaa* (Sheng: 'residential areas/estates')" (Kioko, 2015: 120). This leads to different styles (or possibly varieties) of Sheng that speakers identify with.

The concept of African Urban Youth Languages cannot be conceptualized in the sense of homogenous languages. Instead, these codes are utilized for particular social purposes, to construct social groups and spaces in which different images of 'we' vs. 'them' are negotiated (Githinji, 2006). These youth language practices involve strategies, particularly coining new words that "draw and enhance categorical boundaries" (Kioko, 2015: 128).

Due to rural-urban migration, many youth in Kenya, who are born and socialized in 'multi-ethnic urban settings', grow up speaking the urban Kenyan Swahili and/or Swahili based Sheng as a first language. This has resulted in a loss of ethnic 'mother tongues'. In the rural areas, meanwhile, ethnic languages remain dominant, but rural areas are also subject to urbanizing and modernizing principles. Thus, larger towns in areas traditionally considered rural are impacted by language practices from larger nearby urban centres, and from Nairobi. Kioko (2015) describes the situation regarding Kamba, an ethnic language from Machakoscounty:

> Though popularly known to be a rural County, Machakos encompasses some areas that are more rural and remote than others and usage of English and Swahili varies widely with respect to closeness to urban centres (especially Machakos town). In this case, the areas close to urban centres have a higher usage of these languages than most remote areas, where Kamba dominates almost all forms of socio-cultural, political and economic interactions. (Kioko, 2015: 143)

Kioko describes how Kamba becomes the base language for a new form of Sheng, 'Shengnised Kamba', which spreads urban forms to more urbanized centres in rural areas: "Kamba speakers living or working in areas of Eastlands where varieties of Sheng are spoken… are important agents in the spread of Sheng lexemes from these urban varieties to their rural backyards where such lexemes are used to enrich their register" (Kioko, 2015: 143). The dichotomy between rural and urban is therefore permeable, and not as absolute as the concept 'Urban Youth Language' would suggest.

In fact, while rural-urban migration and the resultant multilingualism in urban centres appears to be at least partly the cause of the emergence of AUYLs, reverse or circular migration from urban to rural areas can be credited for their spread. In Kenya, for instance, urbanization of the rural towns is on the increase due to the expansion of higher education coupled with the devolved governance system which was enacted in the Kenyan constitution in 2010. The devolved governance system has seen massive movements from large metropolises like Nairobi, as people take up employment in the counties (federal states). Moreover, the expansion of university education in the last decade saw the government upgrade previous tertiary colleges to universities with students admitted in these new universities coming from all over the country. The growth in higher education has led to a massive growth of rural towns and this growth directly impacts on language use and youth language practices. Towns that were predominantly monolingual with occasional use of English and Kiswahili in more formal settings have seen an upsurge of people who do not understand the regional local languages. The immediate outcome of these movements is multilingualism in all domains of language use. The youth who move into these towns for purposes of work and study carry with them aspects of youth language practices which are quickly adopted by the local youth as a way of expressing modernity, urban-ness and elitism.

Technology can also play a role in blurring the urban-rural boundaries, as more African youth become connected to online social networks which transcend traditional geographical restrictions, and expose them to urban and global language practices (cf. Hollington and Nassenstein, 2015: 352).

## 3. Modernity

The use of AUYLs is commonly explained as a desire by youth to connect to a 'modern' lifestyle. As Bogopa (1996: 113) explains: "[The urban youth] like to live a life which is modern in orientation, and their thinking as well as their lifestyle is based on modern technology; for example the clothes and the hairstyle they wear and the music they play and so on". Kiessling and Mous (2004) suggest that AUYLs function as an interethnic bridge and "it is the modernity and urban status of youth languages that dissociate them from ethnic associations" (Kiessling and Mous 2004: 316). They argue that AUYLs are part of a project of identity building amongst African youth, and that these identities do not arise from traditional identities, which are characterized as confined to rural settings, ethnic and linguistic minority communities, and "emblematic of a way of life that is felt to be incompatible with modern challenges" (Kiessling and Mous, 2004: 330). Instead, the "source material" for these new identities "is taken from the totality of cultural features to be found in the urban setting of the large African cities" (Kiessling and Mous, 2004: 330). This includes the influence of the "information society", in Castells' (1997) terms – the worldwide spread of information technology enabling access to youth cultural norms such as hip hop and rap along with their associated linguistic emblems (Kiessling and Mous, 2004: 331). They posit that the cultural communities of African urban youth are primarily construed as:

> ...reactions against the traditional way of life in a rural setting, dominated by patriarchal family structures and networks of obligations towards elders and the community, and as an identity-creating reaction towards globalization, seeking access to and partaking in the possibilities and prospects of globalization. (Kiessling and Mous, 2004: 331-2)

Referring to the rejection of 'mother tongues' in favour of AUYLs, Kiessling and Mous suggest that these vernacular languages are representative of traditional ways of life, which is in "sharp contrast to the urban setting and to these youths' general outlook on modern life" (Kiessling and Mous, 2004: 333). The identity they wish to project is "the identity of an urban cosmopolitan, constituting the new identity of urban progressiveness" (Kiessling and Mous, 2004: 335).

This identity of an urban cosmopolitan has taken particular forms in many urban contexts which manifest AUYLs. In South Africa, the original identity invoked by Tsotsitaal, that of an urban criminal (a 'tsotsi', hence the name *tsotsi-taal*, where *taal* is Afrikaans for 'language'), has been replaced by that of the young and 'urban-wise', which, according to Ntshangase, "distinguished itself from the rural identity of migrant workers" (Ntshangase, 1995: 292-293). He continues:

> An important aspect of both Iscamtho and Tsotsitaal is that they embody salient features of black urban culture. These languages and the urban culture they support, ironically, involve an acceptance of the townships as 'home', even though they were created by the apartheid state to serve its own interests. (Ntshangase, 1995: 295)

The identity of the 'urban-wise' who accepts the urban or peri-urban township as home, is embodied in the figure of the 'clever' (sometimes 'kleva') in South Africa. Glaser (2000: 107) explains that clevers are "streetwise city-slickers", and may also be gangsters, but that non-gangsters may also aspire to the style. Using similar terminology, Brookes (2014: 63) describes how "[s]killful use of gesture and speech is a symbol of being *clever* in the sense of 'streetsmart' and 'city slick'". The use of the AUYL is intimately associated with this streetwise identity. Bogopa (1996: 108) explains how '[t]alking 'tsotsitaal' in 'Nicaragua' [a township in Gauteng province, South Africa] is associated with cleverness.'

In Kenya, Sheng has also developed a similar connotation. While traditionally it was viewed as a street language, a language of the ghetto and an argot used by thugs and young *matatu* touts from low income neighbourhoods (Muaka, 2011; Kariuki, Kanana & Kebeya, 2015), today it is perceived as the language of cleverness and cunningness. The youth will often describe it as *luhga ya mtaa* ('language of the hood'), where *mtaa* is used in the sense of urban sophistication, or *lugha ya ujanja/wajanja* (the language of cleverness/clever ones), *language ya base* (language of the base[1]), *kubonga kibase* (talking the base way), etc.

The identity of being 'streetwise' assumes a particular understanding of the 'street', which may have links to the sense of 'street' used in African American popular culture (and links to other references to locality and to authenticity such as being from, belonging to or being born in the 'hood', or 'ghetto'). Hollington and Nassenstein explain of African youth languages that youth language communities of practice consider themselves to be 'street-based': people whose range of agency is related to the social topos of the street where they work, carry out their social practices such as socializing, and experiment with language (Hollington and Nassenstein, 2015: 16).

The opposite of being 'streetwise' is being rural. Makhudu explains: "In addition to its 'male' connotations, Flaaitaal [his preferred name for tsotsitaal in South Africa] carries overtones of urban life, as evidenced by the superior attitude of Flaaitaal speakers to non-users, who are stigmatized as 'country bumpkins'" (Makhudu, 1995: 301). Bogopa agrees that in South Africa's townships most of the youth from both sexes consider themselves better than rural youth in many ways, for instance "in terms of social behaviour" and "mastering the environment (being streetwise)" (Bogopa, 1996: 108). This dichotomy is upheld in Sheng: "[In Kenya] tribal languages are associated with ethnic ties but are also socially tied to traditional values and lack of modernization and/or education" (Karanja, 2010: 1).

## 4. Urban-Rural Lexical Items, Discourse and Metaphor in AUYLs

The rural-urban dichotomy manifests in the lexicon of many African Urban Youth Languages, for example in the naming of these varieties. Sheng has been described as a language of urban-ness by use of words such as *lugha ya mtaa* (language of the neighbourhood) by its users and those who do not speak it are considered *washamba* (rural and remote) which is derived from *shamba* (farm) in Kiswahili. *Ushamba* is therefore a demonstration of the inability to be urban, cool and wise. Other expressions used to describe the rural folks and the youth who lack the linguistic capability to perform in a cool urban/city-wise way include: *fara* (stupid), *dandi* (dunderhead) etc

Similarly, in the case of Tsotsitaal, it was earlier known by the name Flaaitaal. Ntshangase explains the derivation of this term where '*Flaai* means 'citywise' and *tsotsi* means "city-wise and slick" (Ntshangase, 1995: 292). Makhudu expands:

> [...] the word *fly/flaai* itself denotes 'city-wise, urbane, slick'. This dichotomy fly/not fly is represented by such terms for authentic Flaaitaal persons as *die main ou* 'the main man' or group terms like *die autis, die ouens* and *majitas,* and on the other hand terms for foolish, dim-witted or 'slow' persons, e.g. *mugu* [muxu], *bari, mumish, pop, kashu* [xaʃu:]. (Makhudu, 1995: 301)

---

[1] Base/baze – is used to mean 'home' or hood in this context

Within the lexicon of these phenomena we also find words and discourse that enhance the sense of a rural-urban dichotomy. For example, in tsotsitaal, *Cowza* means "someone from rural areas" (Bogopa, 1996: 126); and *Jambok* refers to "a foolish guy especially from rural areas" (Bogopa, 1996: 129). Brookes also gives the following example:

> If a young man does not display sufficient communicative skill to hold the attention of his peers, they describe him as boring and label him a *bari* 'a stupid', which is the label township dwellers give to people from rural areas who are considered backward and tribal. (Brookes, 2014: 63)

The use of language in a particular style therefore creates a separate communicative space for the youth and is understood as modernity by the youth themselves, and it also indexes the identity of a modern African youth.

In some research with township youth in South Africa in 2006 (Hurst, 2008), the interviewees, some resident in peri-urban townships, some from suburbs close to a university, were interviewed about rural-urban migration and language. Different orientations to rurality and urbanity emerged from the interviews. Some speakers were negative about rural speech which was seen as slow, while some young speakers exhibited positive attitudes towards city talk. They distinguished a 'style' of speaking associated with the city. The following extract illustrates this:

1)
F1: We don't have time to say [said really slowly]: *Ndingu Nomthunzi mna* ['Me, I am Nomthunzi']. Eyo!
[laughter]
Q: So what do you say in the city?
F1: *Ndingu Nomthunzi* [I'm Nomthunzi] *qha* [only]!
F2: Yah, I think that's...
F1: *Ndingu Nomthunzi mna* ka, yoh... That's five seconds of our life gone, Joe! We don't have the time.
F3: It's that *mna ka* that's the difference.
(Hurst, 2008: 116)

This example reflects another aspect of the urban identity – as the speaker says, 'that's five seconds of our life gone, Joe!' indicating a faster pace of life in the city, while the slowness of rural speech is exaggerated.

Meanwhile, some respondents represented the urban style and language, including Tsotsitaal, as less respectful than rural speech. The following illustration gives an instance where Tsotsitaal lexis is seen as inherently disrespectful. Tsotsitaal words are highlighted in bold in the example.

2)
M1: Kaloku zezi zinto zoo**tsotsi** ezi zoku**vaya**, thina kaloku sithi umntu utshabile.
['These are these things of Tsotsis these of 'vaya' we say a person 'utshabile''.]

M2: Siyifumana kuni kaloku, siyifumana kuni.
'We get it from you, we get it from you.'
Q: Bona bath'a uvay-
['They say he is 'uvay-'']
M1: Uvayile.
[''Uvayile.'']
M2: Kuthiwe hay'ela **thayima** livayile.
['They say no that thayima livayile [old timer has gone].']
(Hurst, 2008: 119)

In this example, *utshabile* is a respectful way of saying a person has died, while *uvayile*, derived from the Tsotsitaal *vaya* 'to go'[2], is disrespectful. In the final sentence the speaker is mimicking Tsotsitaal: *thayima*, from English 'old timer', is also a Tsotsitaal term.

So far in this section we have seen the ways in which the rural-urban dichotomy is created in lexical items and discourse in Sheng and Tsotsitaal, and we have looked at how urban and rural speech is represented in different ways by youth from urban areas. Urban speech is fast while rural speech is slow; rural speech is respectful while urban speech can be disrespectful. In this way, African Urban Youth Languages are constructed as being aligned to a streetwise, modern identity of the city, while 'mother tongues' are represented as rural, and as upholding traditional values. However, as discussed earlier, categories of rural and urban are porous and the simple dichotomy is challenged in practice.

Deumert (2013: 63) describes the language use of rural migrants to Cape Town in South Africa including "the use of urban slang (Tsotsitaal) which indexes a streetwise and hip urban persona", signaling a shift towards emblems of modernity by rural-urban migrants. However, she (2013: 70) argues that:

> The link between city/modernity and village/tradition is never fully severed, and although new arrivals work hard at establishing and presenting an urban self, there remains [...] continuity with the place of origin. A consequence of this is that the linguistic resources associated with the rural home continue to play a role in the urban environment.

Thus Deumert describes how speakers use 'deep' isiXhosa as a way of evoking traditional authenticity.

Roth-Gordon and Woronov (2009: 137) describe recent scholarship on European youth which shows that 'young people in Paris suburbs are both North African and French, traditional and modern', and conclude that 'the categories of 'modern' and 'traditional' are not mutually exclusive but instead are constantly co-constitutive'. In agreement, Karanja (2010) describes how Sheng in Kenya opens avenues for Kenyan urban youth to re-negotiate their identity and cultures, which moves them...

---

[2] Either based on Portuguese 'to go' or Afrikaans 'to blow, to go (slang)'.

...beyond unitary, fixed identities and binaries of traditional versus urban, and local versus global, to a third hybridized space that is fluid and shifting. The 'hybrid' identities that *Sheng* has enabled have presented these youth with the opportunity to view themselves as urbanized by internalizing the popular cultural artifacts and behavior while at the same time keeping in touch with their ethnicity, since *Sheng* allows them to add words from their tribal languages as it evolves and develops. (Karanja, 2010: 1)

In Kenya, the Sheng phenomenon is a sociolinguistic evidence of how the youth carve out identity using varied semantic processes. According to Gibbs and Nagaoka (1985), growing linguistic practices such as Sheng strongly rely on heavy metaphorical communication which cannot be understood without determining the non-literal meanings. As such, metaphorical utterances are considered more convenient due to the secret meanings associated with them. In the words of Mutiga (2013), almost all Sheng words have, to a great degree, a correspondence with either an African language or English/Kiswahili. Therefore, the link between the words is maintained through metaphorical mappings which take forms such as *propositional, metaphoric, metonymic, and symbolic* (Lakoff, 1987). Further, because youths in the urban areas have migrated from different rural backgrounds, certain lexical gaps may be filled using words from the indigenous forms of expression. In Kenya, the urban youth borrow from both city codes[3] and local tongues to communicate both attitudes and propositional contents in different set-ups.

The contribution of Kenyan languages in the composition of Sheng is significant in metaphorical references. Notably, as Ogechi (2005) observes, most Sheng coinages are heavily influenced by the dominant languages, like the Gikuyu dialects which border on Kiswahili. He also notes that in order to comprehend these metaphors, it is important for one to investigate certain pragmatic properties of the utterances. This argument corroborates Kioko's (2015) observation that "...events or happenings could lead to the birth of the next Sheng word". For example, after several cases of marital conflicts in Nyeri, a town in Central Kenya, where several men were assaulted and severely injured by their spouses (women), a new term was coined to describe husband battering. Thus, the words *'nyeriosis, nyeriyad'* have been used as euphemistic coating to describe any cases of husband battering in urban circles today. Other words include *'kideriosis'* which describes woman battering in Nairobi after the Governor of the county of Nairobi, slapped a female politician publicly; *mututho* (the name of a politician who introduced the law that bars drinking from a certain time of the day), *lei* (truncated from lesbian to *lei*), used to describe lesbian(ism) which is still considered a taboo in Kenya, among others. The socio-political occurrences in Kenya have therefore provided a key ingredient to innovation of Sheng words.

---

[3] According to Ogechi (2005), there are certain major towns in Kenya where African languages are widely spoken. Therefore, the urban youth heavily borrow these codes for the creation of hybrid languages in pursuit of either secrecy or prestige.

In Kenya, it is quite common for youngsters to go out to drinking joints and buy each other 'rounds' of drinks. Expressions like *'waiter chafua meza'* or *'kuchapwa na machupa'*, which would be translated literally as 'waiter make the table dirty' and 'to be beaten with bottles' respectively, are commonly used. The Sheng translation of these innovations is to buy a lot of drinks, in the sense fill the table with bottles of beer, and to be drunk respectively. In describing the physical appearance of women, expressions such as *'kubeba'*, *'haga'*, *'haga inatokoka'* would be used. *Kubeba* is a Kiswahili word which means to carry but in this context it means a big bum, buttocks or behind; *haga* has the same connotation but *haga inatokoka* is used to describe a shaking bum (kutokota means to boil strongly/heavily in Kiswahili). The lexical innovation and the metaphorical use of language as exemplified above clearly shows that the youth are alert and conscious of their environment and this consciousness constantly rejuvenates their language practice.

The inventive nature of the Kenyan urban youth sees the ongoing metamorphosis of coinages. Githiora (2002) opines that the link between the old and new coinages keeps changing depending on sociological occurrences. This is the idea that is echoed by Momanyi (2009) who notes that metaphorical language in Sheng involves different linguistic processes.

An example from Hurst (2016) to illustrate the use of metaphor from both 'modern' and 'indigenous' contexts comes from a video recording of three young people speaking tsotsitaal. They utilized various metaphors during their speech, and the following section is drawn from the transcript. The speakers are describing a scenario in which speaker B2 is going to be beaten up by a woman:

3)
B3: Mfethu, ukumbone umntu **oxovayo intlama**? **Akwenz'intlama** Khazi Ucinge wena ubethwayi-outie. Mfethu, uyakungombasani. Uyakungomba. Ndithi buphel'ubu-outie. Uyakungomba. Uyava? Bakuphel'ubu-outie my broer.
'My brother, have you seen someone **kneading dough**? She would make you her **dough**. Cousin and you would think that you are beaten by a young man. My brother, she's thrashing you severely sonny. She's thrashing you until your manhood expires. She's thrashing you severely. Do you hear me? I'm saying until your manhood expires, my brother.'
...
B1: Utsho uba ukugcine phantsi kwenywantsi. Yinambari eyi-one. Iyakusika qha
'You mean if she keeps you held down. She does one thing. She just stabs you persistently.'
B2: Yes. Qha mfethu.
'Yes. Like that my brother.'
B1: **Delete**.
B2: **Delete**.
B1: **Delete**. Yinambari eyi-one uyabo. Iyavela iyakuformata, uyabo? Ukwenz'i**memory card**; uyaku**formata** – format. Kungaphinde kililwe ngawe.

'**Delete**. She's doing one thing, you see. She would just format you, you see? She's making you her **memory card**; she's formatting you – **format**. So that there won't be any mourning for you.

In this example, both a 'traditional' and a 'modern' metaphor are present – firstly, the metaphor of 'kneading dough' to illustrate how B2 will be pummeled with the fists of the woman. The metaphor was accompanied by a gestural demonstration in which B3 showed how to knead dough with your fists. The second metaphor involves a modern technology, the memory card, and B1 explains how B2 will be 'reformatted' or 'deleted' by the woman, and here, the linguistic resources are derived from English. Here we can see how the youth involved are drawing from all of their linguistic and social resources to create these metaphorical scenarios.

The following excerpt is drawn from a conversation recorded at a popular joint in Eastlands, Nairobi where young men meet to play pool and socialize. The conversation is about one of them whose female friend (assumed to be his girlfriend) visits the joint and wanted to have airtime and chips from him. Notably, there are interesting metaphors used to describe love which are exemplified and discussed below.

4)
A: Lakini hakujileta, ni wewe ulimwendea
'but she did not bring herself you went for her'
B: Ha! Sikumwendea. Hebu uliza **mzae** ndio huyu hapa. Mimi niliendeanga huyu **gala**? Najua hujui. Tulipata nangatu hivi
'(excl!) I didn't go for her. Please ask the guy, he is here. Did I go for this girl? I know you don't know. We just met'
C: Eheheee**mkakufiana**tu,
'(laughter), then you just fell in love'
A: **Mnakufiana**aje? Ile love *yakuimpres*t first
'how are you falling in love/loving each other?, is it the love to impress first?'
(is it the love at first impression?)
C: Hata huyu demu anakutambua. **Alipigwa** hug **mbaya mbaya**
'even this girl appreciates/recognizes you. He was given a big/passionate hug'
A: Mpaka tukalia, Woooi!
'Until we cried, wooooi'
C: **Cheki, alipigwa** hug?
'see, he was given a hug'
All: Kwanza ile **noma noma**
'firstly, a passionate hug'
A: **Unamkalia mende** labda
'you are fooling her probably'
All: laughter
B: Zii! Mimi sina doo yachipo. 60 bob nimaziwaya **mokoro**
'no, I do not have money for (to buy) chips) 60 shillings is (enough to buy) mother's milk'

Words such as *Mzae, -kufa (kufiana), -pigwa hug, cheki, noma* and *mbaya* (reduplicated), *-kalia mende* and *mokoro* are all used in a metaphorical sense. Love is described as death or dying for each other (*kufiana*), the boy is also hit/beaten with a hug (*kupigwa hug*) and a bad or serious hug for that matter (*mbaya mbaya* and *noma noma* respectively). *Cheki* is borrowed from the English word 'to check' but used to mean 'see' emphatically in the context of this conversation. Other words borrowed from English are girl (*gala*), impress (*yakuimprest*) and chips (*chipo*). There are also words borrowed from Kiswahili and other Kenyan languages such as *mzeiya* (mzee) and *mokoro* (elderly person in Gikuyu). The sense in which these words are used in this conversation differs from their meaning in the source language; *mzee* and *mokoro* for instance, mean an elderly or respectable person in both languages but in the context of this conversation the words refer to urban males, usually peers, and mother respectively. The use of the expression '-kukaliamende', is quite intriguing. This expression would literally mean 'sitting on cockroaches' but is used in this context to mean 'fooling someone or taking them for a ride'. Clearly, the understanding of these metaphors requires a pragmatic approach which provides the background entailments, but it appears from this initial analysis that the metaphorical constructions are built on indigenous linguistic forms and knowledge, yet at the same time, signal 'modernity'. In this conversation, we also note that Kiswahili is the matrix language and most of the metaphors are drawn from Kiswahili with sprinklings from English and Gikuyu.

The following examples are recordings from rural towns in Kenya which are rapidly urbanizing due to presence of universities that attract student and workers from all over Kenya. Example 5 was recorded in a rural town in Central Kenya (Karatina) town where Gikuyu is the dominant local language in the area. The conversation was between two people in a public transport vehicle, who apparently moved to the area recently to do transport business and particularly targeted university students and staff.

5)
X: Is vipi? 'How are you?'
Y: Fiti fiti oratne 'I'm very fine my brother'
X: **Fuom** za siku? 'What are you up to today?'
  ('What is the form of the day?')
Y: Kupiga maround mtaa afu kuna *mresh* Fulani anadai tumeet 'Just doing rounds in the estate, then there is a certain girl who wants us to meet up'
X: haina ile, **bytha mathena** zimetokea phase 2
  'it's ok. By the way problems have arisen at phase 2'
  ('there are problems in phase 2')
Y: zipiizo? 'which ones?'
X: Izzo **alidedi** kwa nyumba ya kina Melisa, sema budeng'deng wa Izzo kuzua! 'Izzo died at Melisa's home, say (emph) Izzo's father caused trouble!'

Y: wololo izo **riba nimeziget**. Venye hao wawili walikua **issa ya each other**, kwani kuliendaje? 'Wololo I received the news. The way those two were fond of each other/were easy with each other. What happened?'

X: uyo mkoba alikua **anacheza mafuom za madree** but alikuwa **akicheza magrounds kidiva**. Saa si **akavuta Izzo izo story za kushikisha**. Naye hakuwa anawezana but **kukanyagia tu**. Saa ndo io day **wakikush ikamzidia akadedi** 'that girl was handling drugs but she was not exposing it, she was playing (using the drugs) like a diva. Then she pulled (influenced) Izzo to start smoking (bhang) but Izzo could not handle it, he remained silent (did not disclose how he felt). So that day as they were smoking, it (bang) overwhelmed him, he died'

Y: waah! Izza kwake 'I'm sorry for him/easy for him'

X: aarif mi nimeishia hivi kutafuta **kiroma** si **tuchekiane maarea** 'my friend, am going to look for food, see you later'

X: ata **kasolar** kameshika si tuchekiane 'it's getting hotter, see you later' (Lit: 'the solar is strong, let's check on each other in the area – used to mean the sun is hot, let's see each other later')

In this conversation there is a mix of modernity, traditional language use and youth innovation which are blended to create metaphors that describe the daily lives of the participants. The conversation involves two people who live in the same 'hood' who are discussing the death of a young man who was recently introduced to drugs by a young woman. There is a blend of English, Kiswahili and Gikuyu, which is the vernacular commonly spoken in the area, and Sheng. Clearly, there is dominance of English and Kiswahili in the blending to generate Sheng words and this could be attributed to the socialization of the participants in this particular conversation. We noted earlier that the interlocutors moved from Nairobi to this rural town to do business. In the process, they carry the youth language practices to the rural areas and continue to innovate through borrowings from the local language. In this discourse, commonly used Swahili and English expressions gain new meanings to create a metaphorical sense of the intended meanings in the context in which they are used. Hence, *fiti fiti* is borrowed from English 'fit' (in this context used to mean 'very fine'), *or at the* is 'brother' and *fuom*is 'form' in English. Other words used to express meaning in a metaphorical sense include: *kupiga maround* – 'to wander', *mathena* – 'problems' in Gikuyu, *issaya each other* – 'easy on each other', *cheza mafuom za madree* 'trade/use drugs', *cheza magrounds kidiva* – 'professional" underground drug peddler', *akavuta story ya kushikisha* – 'attract to use (drugs)', *kanyagia* – 'step on/to be silent' (the correct Swahili word would be *kanyangia* but in this context there is a clear influence of Gikuyu pronunciation), kasolar – 'heat', etc. Consider the following example:

6)
(Context: Rural Town (Kirinyaga) in Central Kenya)
X : Aje aje arif? 'How are you friend?'
Y: Sina ngori kakren, nchapie 'I am ok. Talk to me'

X : Riba ziko kibao. Ka sa hii **denge** Fulani **ametuuchapia** za **mukoro** wake
'There are many stories, like right now, a girl has just told us about her mother'
Y : Akadai? 'What was she saying?'
X : Vile **mukoro** wake ni **ATM mbovu** 'The way her mother is daft' (a faulty/non-functional ATM)
Y: **Sekta gani?** 'on what issues/ in which sector?'
X : Kaa ile maneno ya Jaymo **kuchafua rada** juzi afu **akabambwa na mosanse**.
'Like the issue of Jaymo messing up things the other day then he got (himself) arrested'

Again, the traditional vs. modernity is expressed in words such as *mokoro* – 'old woman', *denge* – 'bird', where the former is an archaic Gikuyu form for 'woman' and the latter is from the Kiswahili word 'dege' (bird) which is also given a Gikuyu pronunciation with a prenasalized stop; *sekta* – 'sector' and *ATM* (Automatic Teller Machine) are an indication of modernity but all used in a metaphorical sense.

In the final example, from a peri-urban township near Durban in Kwa-Zulu Natal, South Africa, the speaker is asking about a friend, and how he travels home with no money:

7)
Hey **baba** manje u**F**ingo **udala** kanjanikeke eseko Suncoast engena**nyuku** makumele aye **edladleni**?
'What is it that Ringo does, living/working at Suncoast with no money, when he is supposed to go home?'

The words in bold, *baba*, *-dala*, *-nyuku*, and *–dladleni* are drawn from isiTsotsi – the name for the Tsotsitaal register in Kwa-Zulu Natal. The matrix language for isiTsotsi in the Durban area is isiZulu, which is the main language of the province. In terms of the tsotsitaal lexical items, all of them originate from isiZulu, so there is no borrowing from other languages such as English in order to confer modernity in this example; rather, the tsotsitaal register is achieved through semantic or metaphorical shift. For example, *-dala* in isiZulu means 'to make' or 'to create', while in isiTsotsi it means 'to do'. Similarly, *baba* means father in isiZulu, but in the context of this conversation taking place in isiTsotsi between peers, it means 'friend' with respectful connotations. This example indicates that AUYLs are not reliant on colonial languages to confer modernity or urbanity, but that this can be achieved solely through metaphor and semantic shift, enabling the performance of youth identities to take place in indigenous languages without requiring access to language resources more closely associated with the cities.

## 5. Discussion and conclusions

The data provided in this paper has therefore illustrated that there is no simple binary between rural/urban youth language resources or practices and what we are witnessing in the African cities and towns (whether rural, urban or peri-urban) is the infiltration of rural forms to urban areas and vice versa. Needless to say, the examples provided from both Sheng and Tsotsitaal further show how urbanization and its effects, rural-urban migration, creation and expansion of peri-urban areas have impacted on language. Forms that may be considered old and archaic and/or traditional in youth language do not necessarily die; they find their way into rural towns and vice versa. In many instances, forms re-surface with a metaphorical meaning. Would we then be right to redefine the rural-urban dichotomy as *rurban* to encompass both and use it more inclusively in youth language studies? With these insights, should the focus also shift from African Urban Youth Language (AUYL) to African Youth Language (AYL) to challenge the dichotomizing discourse?

Metaphor in youth language use is neither 'figure of speech' nor just a 'poetic fiction or decoration', but can be regarded as underlying the structure and evolution of human thought and language (Nerlich and Clarke, 2001). Metaphors are thus seen as necessary for growth of human thought and language. According to Lakoff and Johnson (1980) metaphor does not only passively exploit pre-existing similarities via comparison; it can actively create new realities. Metaphor is thus seen as 'a means of structuring our conceptual system and the kind of everyday activities we perform'. Lakoff (1993) argues that basic level conceptual metaphors are grounded in human experience and are therefore likely to be found widely across different languages and cultures although mappings are culture-governed. This is in line with Charteris-Black (2007) who says that a metaphor that works in one society may be preposterous in another. Our concepts structure what we perceive, how we get around the world and how we relate to other people.

Steen (2011) notes that metaphor apart from being a matter of language and thought also has a communicative aspect. Thus metaphor arises in language use to address particular and often specific communicative needs and functions. Metaphor, as an important aspect of youth language practices, and as exemplified with naturalistic occurring data in this paper, cannot therefore be overemphasized. The use of metaphor in youth discourse further highlights the interchange between rural and urban languages as well as the indigenous knowledge drawn on in the practices of urban youth. The metaphorical use of the language is context bound and understood only by the in-group members until it becomes conventionalized and new metaphors are generated.

Researchers investigating youth language need to begin to look more holistically at youth practices and how they draw on resources across the rural-urban binary. The use of metaphors, as evidenced in this paper, complicates the urban-rural dichotomy; both 'modern' and 'traditional' concepts are drawn on in the meaning making of these youth; and both European and indigenous languages contribute the source material. This research has begun to outline the complexities of an emergent African modernity, and suggests that youth language can provide a window on this emergence.

# References

Allen, I. L. (2001). Slang: Sociology. In Mesthrie, F. (Ed.) *Concise Encyclopedia of Sociolinguistics*. Oxford: Elsevier, 265–270.

Bogopa, D. (1996). *The language and culture of the youth in the 'Nicaragua' section of Tsakane in Gauteng*, MA Thesis University of Durban-Westville.

Brookes, H. (2014). Gesture in the communicative ecology of a South African township. In Seyfeddinipur M. and Gullberg, M. (Eds.) *From Gesture in Conversation to Visible Action as Utterance: Essays in Honor of Adam Kendon*. Amsterdam: John Benjamins, 59–73.

Castells, M. (1997). *The Information Age: Economy, Society and Culture*. Volume 2: The Power of Identity. Oxford: Blackwell Publishers.

Charteris-Black, J. (2007). *The Communication of Leadership: The Design of Leadership Style*. London: Routledge.

Deumert, A. (2013). Xhosa in Town (revisited) – Space, place and language, *International Journal of the Sociology of Language*, 222, 51–75.

Gibbs Jr, R. W., & Nagaoka, A. (1985). Getting the hang of American slang: Studies on understanding and remembering slang metaphors. *Language and Speech*, 28(2), 177-194.

Githinji, P. (2006). Bazes and their Shibboleths: Lexical variation and Sheng speakers' identity in Nairobi. *Nordic Journal of African Studies*, 15(4), 443–472.

Githiora, C. (2002): Sheng: Peer Language, Swahili dialect or emerging Creole? *Journal of African Cultural Studies*, 27(2) 229-246.

Glaser, C. (2000). *Bo-tsotsi: The youth gangs of Soweto, 1935-1976*. Oxford: Heinemann.

Hollington, A., & Nassenstein N. (2015). Youth languages in Africa (and beyond). In Nassenstein N. & Hollington A. (Eds.) *Youth language practices in Africa and beyond*. Berlin: De Gruyter Mouton, 345-356.

Hurst, E. (2008). *Style structure and function in Cape Town Tsotsitaal*. PhD Thesis, University of Cape Town, South Africa.

Hurst, E. (2016). Metaphor in South African Tsotsitaal. *Sociolinguistic Studies*, 10(1-2) 151–173.

Hurst, E. (2017). Rural/urban dichotomies and youth language. In: Ebonguè, A. & Hurst, E. (Eds.) *Sociolinguistics in African contexts - perspectives and challenges*. Springer.

Karanja, L. (2010). 'Homeless' at home: linguistic, cultural, and identity hybridity and third space positioning of Kenyan urban youth. *Education Canadienne et Internationale*, 39(2), 1-19.

Kariuki, A., Kanana, F. E. & Kebeya, H. (2015). The growth and use of Sheng in advertisement in selected businesses in Kenya. *Journal of African Cultural Studies*, 27(2), 229-246.

Kerswill, P. (2006). Migration and language. In Mattheier, K., Ammon, U. & P. Trudgill (Eds.) *Sociolinguistics/Soziolinguistik: An international handbook of the science of language and society*. 2nd ed. Vol. 3. Berlin: De Gruyter.

Kiessling, R. & Mous. M. (2004). Urban youth languages in Africa, *Anthropological Linguistics*, 46(3), 303–341.

Kioko, E., (2015). Regional varieties and 'ethnic' registers of Sheng. In Nassenstein, N & Hollington, A. (Eds.) *Youth language practices in Africa and beyond*. Berlin: De Gruyter Mouton, 119-148.

Lakoff, G. (1987). *Women, fire and dangerous things. What categories reveal about the mind*. Chicago: The University of Chicago Press.

Lakoff, G. (1993). The contemporary theory of metaphor. In Ortony, A. (Ed.) *Metaphor and Thought* (2nd Edition). Cambridge: Cambridge University Press, 202-251.

Lakoff, G. & Johnson, M. (2003[1980]). *Metaphors we live by*. Chicago: University of Chicago Press.

Makhudu, D. (1995). An introduction to Flaaitaal. In Mesthrie, R. (Ed.) *Language and social history: Studies in South African Sociolinguistics*. Cape Town: David Philip, 298-305.

Momanyi, C. (2009). The effects of 'Sheng' in the teaching of Kiswahili in Kenyan schools. *The Journal of Pan African Studies*, 2(8), 127-138.

Muaka, L. (2011). Language perceptions and identity among Kenyan speakers. In Bokamba, E. G., Shosted, R. K. &Ayalew, B. T. (Ed.) *Selected proceedings of the 40th Annual Conference on African Linguistics*. Somerville, MA: Cascadilla Proceedings Project, 217-230.

Mudimbe, V. Y. (1988). *The Invention of Africa: Gnosis, Philosophy, and the Order of Knowledge (African Systems of Thought)*. Indianapolis: Indiana University Press.

Mutiga, J. (2013). Effects of language spread on a people's phenomenology: The case of Sheng in Kenya. *Journal of Language, Technology & Entrepreneurship in Africa, 4*(1), 1-15.

Nerlich, B. & Clarke, D. D. (2001). Mind, meaning and metaphor: the philosophy and psychology of metaphor in 19th-century Germany. *History of the Human Sciences, 14*(2), 39-61.

Ntshangase, D. (1995). '*Indaba yami i-straight*': Language and language practices in Soweto. In Mesthrie, R. (Ed.) *Language and Social history: Studies in South African Sociolinguistics*. Cape Town: David, 291-297.

Ogechi, N. O. (2005). On lexicalization in Sheng. *Nordic Journal of African Studies, 14*(3), 334-355.

Roth-Gordon, J., & Woronov, T. E. (2009). Youthful concerns: movement, belonging and modernity. *Pragmatics 19*(1), 129-143.

Steen, G. (2011). The contemporary theory of metaphor-now new and improved. *Review of Cognitive Linguistics 9*, 26-64.

# The Grammar of Indigenous Languages in African Urban Youth Languages: Questioning in Camfranglais in Cameroon

*Comfort Beyang Oben Ojongnkpot* (University of Buea, Cameroon)

## 1. Introduction

The phenomenon of presenting ambivalent selves by urban youth in general and those of Africa, in particular, through their languages, commonly referred to as AYULs (African Youth Urban Languages) has been an attraction to researchers over the years, more so because there is an implication for getting insight into the youth in the urban space, who have been considered as rebellious and poised to "disrupt the natural order of things" through language use. Such languages are exemplified by: Indoubil in the Democratic Republic of Congo, Nouchi in Ivory Coast, Camfranglais in Cameroon, Tsotsitaal in South Africa and Sheng in Kenya (Goyvaerts & Kabongo-Mianda, 1988; Kiessling & Mous, 2004; Ojongnkpot, 2017, Hurst 2017). These phenomenal languages have often been described in terms of the bending of rules, mixing of linguistic structures, lexical borrowings from other languages such as colonial languages or African languages, and making use of dominant European languages as the grammatical base, such as French in the case of Camfranglais (Hurst, 2017). Inspired by Halliday (1985), Hurst (2017) refers to them as 'relexicalised' languages used by young people for creativity and entertainment, to have fun with peers, to affirm in-group relations, and to indicate status. Little wonder why AUYLs have been described as 'antilanguages' that instantiate resistant identity "exclusion of the excluders by the excluded" (Castell, 1997).

In this research, we adopt a divergent perspective from the foregone. Our premise is that these languages do not only communicate ideas, strengthen their ties and create their identities as an in-group, but also link them to their indigenous roots as they appropriate in them an African identity that redefines their position in society. Thus, they portray a double voice (Bakhtin, 1981) that emanates from the urban youths' shift norms, which Kiessling and Mous (2004) refer to as 'paradox of norms'. On the basis of this premise, AYULs users stand astride two linguistic norms: the community of AYUL on the one hand, and that of exoglossic languages and base languages (indigenous African), on the other. Silverstein (1998) calls this the normativity of a shared grammar. This study will then explore the interplay of these languages in the context of question patterns.

## 2. Camfranglais Use

Early studies have described Camfranglais as an antilanguage as it exhibits traces of hybridity and transcultural interaction wherein the users explicitly "reject ascriptions of cultural identity with the intention of concealing meaning from the outgroup through the conscious play with words". Maher (2005: 83) used the term "metro-ethnicity" to explain the situation whereby language users attempt to reconstruct ethnicity. This reconstruction of ethnicity is understood by Otsuji and Pennycook (2009) as a hybridized "street ethnic" metrolingualism, whereby the urban youth attempts to hide meaning, and exclude the 'others'. Others maintain that users of Camfranglais adopted this urban noble slang for prestigious purposes as well as to hide meaning from the out-group (Ojongnkpot, 2015). The foregone explanations are in line with Camfranglais users' speech in the Cameroon cities, which is marked by such mixing and shifting, making use of exoglossic and indigenous expressions. Inasmuch as they endeavor to keep the 'others' out, by adopting certain linguistic practices, the questioning pattern of Camfranglais is argued to be in conjunction with that of Ejagham. This research contends that there should be an explanation of the presence of an African identity in the linguistic practices of Camfranglais. It is, therefore, the aim of this study to demonstrate the value of Camfranglais as an embodiment of African identity.

In the case of Camfranglais online chats, there is evidence of adoption of grammatical characteristics of dominant languages in the aspect of question formation, which engenders multiple simultaneous social identities of the speakers in the aspect of questioning. In this way, there is an important aspect of interethnic bridging of differences. An observation of the questioning pattern of Camfranglais as used in the online chats of speakers finds similarities with Ejagham. Although Camfranglais, like other AYULs, has been considered as an imperfect language, 'antilanguage', language of the streets used by adolescents in informal contexts (Kiessling and Mous, 2004 ), Camfranglais, on its part, has also been observed to be related to Cameroon Pidgin English (CPE) and some African indigenous languages in terms of question pattern. It is for this reason that we embarked on investigating the question pattern of this novel urban youth language vis-à-vis a Cameroonian indigenous language, Ejagham. Although Camfranglais has been considered as having a very restricted amount of rules, this study aims to demonstrate that Camfranglais uses structures from indigenous languages. The linguistic material that emanates from the base languages may be different to make the outcome incomprehensible, but it is composed of structures that are related with African indigenous languages.

It was important to carry out empirical analysis of the questioning pattern of Camfranglais as used online, since it has been observed that there is some relationship in the question pattern. Moreover, it is essential to determine the various types of questions used by Camfranglais online chatters. In this way, we have been able to account for the African identity of the Camfranglais users.

As established thus far, the grammatical focus of this study is to explore questioning by Camfranglais speakers so as to figure out indigenous language trends (Appendix A). The current study aims at comparing question patterns of Camfranglais to Ejagham. The study thus hypothesizes that there is no significant difference between the questioning pattern of Camfranglais and Ejagham, but there is a significant difference between the questioning pattern of Camfranglais and English. In order to address this hypothesis, the study draws on Bourdieu's (1991) *Theory of Cultural Reproduction*, which posits that language is not merely a method of communication, but as well, a mechanism of power. Based on this theory, the language one uses is designated by one's relational position in the field of social space. Linguistic interactions are a manifestation of the participants' respective positions in social space and categories of understanding, and thus tend to reproduce the objective structures of social field. He then concludes that the representation of identity in forms of language is subdivided into language, dialect and accent. This theory thus underscores that the way one chooses to present one's social space to the world depends on the internalized dispositions, which, according to Bourdieu, are internalized by children early enough such that they are guided by them towards their appropriate social positions. He emphasises the dominance of cultural capital through the habitus syndrome. He therefore contends that people inherit their cultural attitudes as read to them by the elders. Consequently, cognitive structures are internalized, as 'embodied' social structures become a natural entity to the individual (Bourdieu, 1984 468).

## 3. Camfranglais as Embodiment of African Identity

The premise here is that the questioning pattern of Camfranglais signals an African identity in the youth. Particularly, it is argued that the question structure of Camfranglais ties with that of Ejagham. Identity is the condition of being a certain person, including those characteristics that make a person aware of the group to which he or she belongs. Indeed, identity is a connecting factor between language use by the youth and the Ejagham people. It cannot be gainsaid that identity indicators are crucial in getting understanding of people's behavior, which of course, is manifested in various ways such as gender, linguistic, and ethnic, to rural-urban identities (Adedeji, 2017). Simply, identity is being oneself and not another. It is a matter of distinction that spells out who one is. Identity directs one to a state he/she wants to be in – which means that identity placement most of the time is by choice, (Bourdieu & Passeron, 1970) at the background of an intent or purpose. Newman (1990) postulates that identity is one of our most essential and personal characteristics as it comprises our membership in social groups (race, ethnicity, religion, gender, etc.), the traits we exhibit, and those others ascribe to us. We are located in the social world through our identity and we are actually affected by it in the way we feel, say, do and think throughout life (Adedeji, 2017). Language is undeniably a chief bearer of identity. Al-Saleem (2011), states that languages are ways of expressing and recognizing the many identities people have. It is for the same reason that Ngugi (1986: 4), argues that "the choice of language and the use to which language is put is central to a people's definition of themselves in relation to their natural and social environment". The grammar of a language is the building block that enables us to figure out the relationship between communication and the identities signaled therein. In fact, it is the pivot of values and beliefs. Thus, in this study, it is the spectrum through which we view the African in urban youth language. We are able to lay open the fact that grammar is more than just an aid to communication. In this study, we argue that apart from serving as a means of communication, language provides a means through which people's identities are signaled to make them unique as belonging to a specific group. Identity is here negotiated through language use. Thus, the connectedness of language use and identity is one of the key issues in this study. Other studies have proven that the SVO structure runs through all Bantu languages (Guthrie, 1948; Watters, 1981), which implies, therefore, that, by extension, African identity is revealed in this study. Even though the subjects were not necessarily Ejagham, they are shaped by the African root and culture – the way one thinks, the things one does, one's affiliations and contacts reflect the community one belongs to (Bourdieu, 1990, 1997; Adedeji, 2017). In that way, Camfranglais speakers are exhibiting what they are – the internalized African identity.

## 4. Related Studies

The view of the discursive practices in language and sense of belonging is fundamental in Applied Linguistics. Watters (1981) did a comprehensive study on Ejagham interrogatives and illustrated that Ejagham makes use of the same questions that are found in the English language, but with a different structure (SVO), unlike the VSO structure found in the latter. Watters' study has been the basis of the present one in that it has worked elaborately on Ejagham interrogatives. Myers-Scotton (1993) worked on structural similarities in English–Swahili code-switching in Nairobi and Dakar Wolof, and found out that it shares many functional properties with urban youth languages as reported by McLaughlin (2001). Town Bemba and Dakar Wolof have been described as being closer to the languages on which urban youth languages are based. This study contends Kiessling and Mous (2004), who affirm that speakers separate the grammatical base from the lexical deviations and associate the deviations with the language. However, Kiessling and Mous (2004), in a comparative article on AYUL phenomena, illustrate the connectivity of AYULs to identity and maintain that urban languages may represent new identities for young Africans in rapidly modernizing cities. They also add that these new identities cut across 'obsolete boundaries' of ethnicity, and signal multiple cultural allegiances. Omoniyi (2006: 204), on his part, is concerned with rap as an aspect of AYUL, as he illustrates that irrespective of the exposure of Nigerian Hip hop to the outside world, the linguistic strategies portrayed in Nigerian music follow their "glocal selves rather than 'other' based on his tracing the origin of Hip hop right back to the 'pre-slavery African cosmic space'". Referring to that phenomenon as a "Boomerang Hypothesis", Gbogi (2016: 172), relates Omoniyi (2005, 2009)'s assertion about Hip hop in Africa as a re-appropriation, rather than an appropriation or imitation. Gbogi (2016) believes that Omoniyi (2009) makes a pertinent and interesting case, not only for Nigerian Hip hop, but also, by extension, Africa, in general. Auer (2005, 2007) and Auer & Wei (2007) investigated the connection between language and identity – sense of belonging, and resolved that the very effort by the youth to keep themselves away from the languages of the elders ironically traps them down to it, through one way or the other. In the same line, Perullo and Fenn (2009) describe as the ill-literacies of the urban youth. As concerns languages appropriated through mixture and fusion, Pennycook (2007) addresses the question of transcultural flows – how cultural forms are moved, changed or reused to fashion new identities in diverse contexts. Pennycook (2007) believes that Hip hop is one of those media expressions that help to convey aspects of identity across other languages as he illustrates thus:

> Whether is Kaneka music, in Calcedonia, Libraville rap or Aboriginal rap, the flows around and between English and other languages open up domains beyond fluid identities…, often addressed of its linguistic features or elements of which languages get appropriated, mixed or fused (36)

The foregone is in line with the present study in the way the questioning pattern of Ejagham is taken up by Camfranglais users to ascribe to them the African identity.

Talking about the influence of Yoruba as an African language on youth language, Adedeji (2017) demonstrates that the Hip hop genre among Nigerian youth emanated from their American counterparts in response to diffusing economic tension created by the austerity measures that characterized the West African country in the 1990s during the military regime at that time. He further explains that it was a way of expressing their anger and disgust towards the ruling class. Adedeji thus posits that the transformations characterized by Hip hop have earned the users fame in the use of indigenous languages in place of African-American "Ebonics" rapping. This has contributed greatly in imprinting Hip hop on Nigeria's music landscape, especially, with the juxtaposition of well-known musical styles such as Highlife and Juju, thereby, "nigerianizing" the genre while creating the sub-culture now called 'Afro Hip hop'.

From the foregone, these scholars seem to argue that AYULs are influenced by global popular culture that specifically emanates from African diaspora practices such as cultural Hip hop. As for Mous (2004), the linguistic innovations of AYULs are not different from less modern phenomena of the complex linguistic landscape of the African continent and the richness of repertoire of its speakers. In this vein, AYULs deserve to be compared to 'registers of respect'. Otsuji (2008) investigated the processes of constructing language, culture and identities in respect to macro and micro levels of society. In order to achieve the goal of the study, data were analyzed from four workplaces in Australia. The focus on trans-institutional talk deals with people from varied linguistic and cultural backgrounds. He illustrates that transcultural performances display a relationship between idiosyncratic individual performances and the construction of transcultural linguistic and cultural phenomena within globalization. The point of convergence between our study and

Otsuji's lies in the construction of identities through linguistic practices. Hybrid linguistic practices by Camfranglais online chatters are instrumental in constructing them an indigenous identity. Sirsa and Redford (2013), making use of global perceptual analysis, investigated the similarities and differences between Indian English and native languages. In addition, acoustic measurements were used to investigate group differences in the production of Indian English as well as the similarities and differences between Hindu and Telugu. Part of the findings of this study indicated perceptible effects of L1 on Indian English.

The aforementioned studies demonstrated the impact of grammatical aspects on other languages, and their findings will be considered in the following. Although different studies have been carried out on the impact of linguistic practices on other languages, little or nothing has been done on Ejagham and Camfranglais question patterns. Therefore, examining the question pattern of Camfranglais vis-à-vis Ejagham provides us with the opportunity to add to the existing body of knowledge and to discern African identity trends.

## 5. Questioning Pattern in English

Asking and answering questions remains an arduous task. In conversation, interlocutors find difficulties not only in asking, but also in answering questions appropriately. A well-known case is the Garden story in Genesis 3:9. After perceiving that Adam and Eve had gone wrong, the Lord asked, "Adam, *where art thou*?". Instead of answering the question accordingly, Adam responded, "*I am naked*". This indirect answer demonstrates the difficulties in the asking-answering communication process. In order to have a mastery of the art of questioning, there is a need to understand the questioning pattern of any language. Questioning depends on the situation: is it a polite request? Is it to confirm what is already known? Is it to gather information about a subject? For example, in English, direct questions ask for both simple and complex information and are usually structured as follows: *Question-word + Auxiliary + Subject + Verb Form + Objects + ?*, although not all constituents are obligatory. For example, *when do you get to work?* Direct questions in certain situations can sound impolite, especially when posed to a stranger. Therefore, to make them polite, phrases like *'excuse me', 'could you',* and *'would you'* are added (which may alter the word order). To illustrate the concepts of Subject and Object Questions, it is important to consider the following examples:

*Ex: wh? + (aux) − verb + object*

Q: *What does Ebot like playing? A: football.*
Q: *Who likes playing football? A: Ebot.*

Direct questions beginning with question words are thus usually followed by the auxiliary when asking about the object. Contrarily, when asking for the subject of the action, the auxiliary is omitted and instead the question-word *(Wh-)* is used as the subject in the question.

Ex:   Wh-? + (aux.) + verb + object?
      Who plays the piano?

English has a plethora of question types that have a particular way of asking and answering. We were able to review 12 types of questions in the English language: Yes/No (Auxiliary + Subject + Verb Form + Objects + ?), *Wh-* questions, Tag questions, Hypothetical, Alternative, Echo, Embedded, Leading, Hypophora, Rhetorical, "Like" questions, and Suggestions.

Asking and answering questions is an integral aspect of communicating, and more specifically, is a form of active learning. In a social setting, asking a question is the best way to start a conversation. When questions are well asked, it is possible to get appropriate answers because understanding is evoked. Consequently, questions can be inserted in different parts of the sentence or can constitute sentences of their own (Quirk et al, 1985). The study of questioning here has to do with analyzing the grammatical utterances of speakers in the course of making certain inquiries. The study thus aims at investigating the questioning pattern of Camfranglais vis-à-vis Ejagham.

## 6. The Ejagham and their Language

The Ejagham live in the Cross River Basin along the border between Calabar and Ikom, in Nigeria and Mamfe, in Cameroon. In Cameroon they occupy the heart of the Equatorial rain forest, at the Western part of the Mamfe–Central Subdivision of the Manyu Division, in the South West Region of Cameroon. In Nigeria, they live in the south-western part of Ikom local government, the eastern portion of Akampka local government, and the northern portion of Calabar, but all within the Cross River State (Watters, 1981, 2010; Ojongnkpot, 2015). The Ejagham people make up a population of 49,394 (Grimes, 2005) and live in approximately 145 villages. They also constitute an overwhelmingly large population in the diaspora.

The Ejagham language is referred to as the Ekoi dialect cluster (Westermann and Bryan 1952); Williamson (1971) and Richardson (1957) prefer to call it Keaka. Other terms used to refer to variants of the language are: 'Ejagham', 'Ekwe' (Ekoi), 'Keaka', 'Obang', 'Etung', 'Edjagam', 'Kwa' and 'Eyafin' (Grimes, 2005). According to Ruel (1969), the term 'Keaka' originated from the Kenyang-speaking people to the east of the Ejagham. The Obang are located in the south-eastern dialect area. The Etung are people of the north-western dialect area, especially in Ikom. Kwa refers to the southern Ejagham dialect. Eyafin is the term used by the Obang speakers to refer to the north-eastern dialect area or Keaka. However, the term 'Ejagham' is used with wide coverage to refer to the people and the language spoken by them (Ejagam), the culture (Élûk̞-Éăjàgàm), and the area (ÊβàréÉjâghâm). In the Eastern Ejagham dialect, the term 'Éjâghã', also refers primarily to the language. Thus, 'ŋjâĥâ' (singular), refers to a person who speaks the related dialects of Ejagha, and 'âjâĥâ' (plural), to people who speak Ejagha. But the variant used in this study is Obang (Ôβâŋ). Williamson (1971) classifies Ejagham as follows: Niger-Congo, Benue-Congo, Bantoid-Bantu, and Nigerian

Bantu-Ekoid dialect Cluster (Ejagham). The language has a literacy rate of 10% for first language speakers and 30% for Second Language (L2) speakers (Grimes, 2005). Being one of the 286 indigenous languages, it is used informally in education, literature and radio broadcast (Ojongnkpot, 2015). Just like most African languages, Ejagham belongs to the Niger-Congo phylum. Ejagham in Cameroon has just been introduced in primary and secondary schools within the past five years or so.

### 6.1. The Grammar of Ejagham

The language typology of Ejagham comprises prepositions, genitives, articles, adjectives, relatives after noun heads, question word final and maximum prefixes. It is a noun class language with SVO structure, whereby a noun phrase may consist of a noun as head, followed by modifiers such as adjectives or determiners. The question pattern of Ejagham takes the Subject, Verb, Complement (SVC) (Watters, 1981, 2010).

    Subject + Verb + Complement

1. *βô[you] kélé[gave] wî-â? [her/him]?*
'Did you give her/him?'
'Have you given her?'

2. *βô [you] ké¹é [gave] â- ŷî? [who]?*
'Whom did you give to?'

Interrogatives in Ejagham have various forms, which do not occur at the beginning of sentences, unlike in English. They rather maintain the same positions as in declarative sentences, as is the case in Camfranglais (Table 2 below).

6.1.1. Yes/No Question is formed with the adjectival interrogative

Examples for these question patterns are:

3. R2.3) *βô* -[you]-rŭκ [came] Yaounde?
'Are you from Yaounde?'
'Tu comot Yaounde?'

4. R2.5) *βô*-[yɔu]ƒô[have]-mbîκ-â?[money]?
'Do you have money?'
'Tu have les dos'

5. R8.1) wî[ycu]ô-rî[are]kâ[in]-ŋjôr-â? [trouble]?
'Are you in trouble?'

## 6.1.2. Wh- Questions

i) The 'what'? interrogative asks about things and has both a simple and a complex form. The simple form is 'zî' ('what?'), while the complex form derives from the adjectival interrogative 'βâ-ghé?' ('which?'). So there is 'é-zîm' ('thing') and βâ-ghé –é-zîm ('what?'). This is used when a specific thing is asked for.

    6. Wî [you]-ô-châké[played]-zî?[what?]
       'What did you play?'
       R30.14) Tu as game quoi ?

ii) The 'where' (*place*) interrogative has a simple form, a complex form and an adjectival form. The simple form is 'fâ?' (where?) and is generally used as a locative interrogative whose meaning is non-specific.

    7. βô-[you]zîk[go] –fâ['where'] nâ-tûk?[in the night?]
       'Where are you going at night?'
       R28.11) Gar t'es go ou la night?

The complex form is derived from the adjectival interrogative 'βâ-ghé?' (*which?*) and the noun 'é-zîk' ('place') - βâ-ghé - é-zîk? (Where?). In that way, the complex form has a specific locative meaning of: 'which specific place?' which could be substituted with 'fâ?'.

    8. Bô [you]-zîk [go] fâ? ['where?']
       'Where were you?'/ 'Where did you go?'
       R2.14) Tu es go ou...?

iii) The time question word *'when'* is formed with the adjectival interrogative βâ-ghé (which) and the noun é-βûk 'time'.

    9. ŋ-yié[mother] wâ[your] βâ-zîk[go]-étŭm[work] βâgé-é-é-βûk?[when?]
       'When does your mother go to work?'
       R34.12) Ta mater go au work quand?

If the time in consideration is in terms of days, the noun 'ôfûk' ('day') is substituted for the noun é-βûk ('time') in the complex form to give the expression βâ -ghé-ô-fûκ ('when?'), which means 'which day?'.

    10. wî [He] â-[will]-βâ[come] βâĥé-é-βûκ?[which day?]
       'When will he come?'
       R2.15) Le gar come kel day?

iv). The question word *how?'* has the meaning of manner. It has just a simple form 'nâ?', which asks about the condition or manner of something or a person. It has no complex form.

    11. ô[you ]-rî[are]-nâ?[how?] (asking about a person's condition of health)
    12. é[things]-rî[are]- nâ?[how?] (a form of greeting, to establish phatic communion)
    13. ékî[we]-yî[do]nâ?[how?] or tchôŋ-é[we]-yî[do]-nâ?[how?]
        'How are we going to do it?'
    14. R52.1) on do how? (a suggestive question on how to address a problem)

This question word also makes use of quantity ('how many/how much'), which relates to a number adjective of quantity. It is a simple form that varies according to noun class, so 'â-βéκ' and 'é-βéκ', denoting countable and uncountable respectively, are added after the subject (complement).

    15. βô[you]-fô [have]-â-βô[children] â-βéκ?[how many?]
        'How many children do you have?'
        R56.13) Tu get combien de mounas?

    16. βô[you]-rîκ ate] –ŋsîŋ[mango] – â-βéκ?[how many?]
        'How many mangoes have you eaten?'
        R4.17) Tu as tcop combine du mango?\Tu as tchako les mango combine?

    17. βô –[you]-fɔ[have]-ŋ-κôp[cups of] erîsî[rice]é-βéκ?[how much?]
        How much riz do you have?
        R55.13) Tu as tchoko kel kantite du riz?

v) The reason/purpose interrogative *(why)* is used in different ways:

Often, it is expressed in a complex interrogative clause, which is introduced with the interrogative pronoun 'zî' ('what?'/'why?'), and includes the verb root 'yî' ('to do'/'make'). The conjunction 'yî' ('then', 'but', 'or') is required to introduce the following clause. 'Zî' means 'why', though it can be equally used as 'what'.

The interrogative 'zî' occurs immediately after an intransitive verb without ambiguity in some instances. Nevertheless, after a transitive verb, there is the possibility for ambiguity when the direct object is deleted.

    18. βô[you]-βâ[come]-zî?[why?/what?]
        'why did you come?'
        R6.9) Tu came why?

19. zî['what']- wî[you] ô[did] -rîκ[eat] é-rîκ é-zâ?[my food]?

Surprisingly, this question word can be used at the beginning or end of a question. Another way of asking 'why' is by using a pseudo-cleft construction (Watters, 1981).

    20. É-chîk[head]-é-zî[why]-ŋ-jîk ô βâ?[that you come?]
        Why did you come?
        R57.12) Tu es come pourqoui?

The *why* interrogative has a variant 'βâ-ġĥé-zûm', as in:

    21. βâ-ġĥé-zûm [what thing] wî[you]-ô[did]-rîk[ate]-é-rîk-é-zâ?[my food?]
        'Why did you eat my food?'
        R19.8) Tu grope ma tchop pourqoui?

vi) The interrogative possessive '<u>nî</u>?' ('whose') is expressed when the noun is put in association with the interrogative forms for 'nî' ('who').

    22. m-bîk[money] βâ-ġĥé[which]-nî?[person?]
        R57.12) Les dos de qui?
        'Whose money?

### 6.1.3. *Alternative (Choice) Questions*

Choice questions are asked in two ways:
The first way is to use 'βâ-gĥé', the adjectival interrogative ('which') and a noun consisting of root 'βâ-ġĥé':

    23. βâ-ġĥé -[which] ŋ- njŭk[house] é-*f*é-méĥ?[burned?]
        'Which house got burned?
        R54.16) Kel piol et brule?

The second way is to use one set of specific referent adjectival interrogatives ('which one'), which are similar to the locative ('where') that has been discussed earlier. So this is achieved through 'n-jén' or the variant 'm-bén'.

    24. étîk[stick] n-jén?[which one?]
    25. βésî[Pot] βé-ré[like] m-bén?[which one?]

### 6.1.4. *Indirect Questions*

Indirect questions are formed with relative clauses that have a generic term as the head noun phrase.

> 26. ŋ-kâ[I don't]- mé-ĥé[know]n- nî-ŋû[person who] â-rî[eat] é-rî?[food]

Nouns like 'n-nî' [person], 'é-zûm' [thing], 'é-zîk' [place], 'é-βŭk' [time], 'é-kpâk' [type], and 'é-chîk' [head] act as generic terms for constructing indirect questions.

### 6.1.5. *Rhetorical Questions*

Ejagham makes wide use of rhetorical questions, which usually have pragmatic effects as they lay emphasis on the interlocutor's emotional reaction.

> 27. wî-ô[you] kɛ̂[have not] yî[seen]-â-βâ-chî [women] kâ[in]-n-sîk- â?[world?]
>    'Have you not seen women in the world?'

This is very explicit because the speaker begins by directing the interlocutor to see that 'there are women in the world'. It thus refers to a common truth. However, this is not the aim of the question. We realize that rhetorical questions maintain the same structure as other questions (SVO).

### 6.1.6. *Leading Questions*

Ejagham also makes use of leading questions, without a change in structure.

> 28. Wî-o-[you] kî [are]-bâ?[coming?]
>    'Are you coming?'
>    Tu come nor?

Based on the data presented above, we can safely assert that Ejagham uses a wide range of questions just like the English language and Camfranglais. Moreover, from the preceding, it has become evident that the questioning patterns of Ejagham and Camfranglais are characterized by the SVO structure.

## 7. Methodology

### 7.1. Design

This study made use of a mixed-methods design, which is essentially descriptive: data were collected, first from archival material and field data of Ejagham. Secondly, data were gathered from naturally-occurring online chats of Camfranglais users. The third type were data collected face-to-face from Ejagham and Camfranglais informants who had been previously contacted. This follow-up data comprised interviews and questionnaires relating to the informants' bio-data. The choice of the archive data was to enable the researcher to have a baseline of the use of questions, given that all the participants were L2 users. It was therefore important to illustrate the questioning pattern of English, also because English is one of the lexifier languages for Camfranglais, with a significant impact on **L2 users** academic achievement (Ojongnkpot, 2017).

## 7.2. Sample

A total of 90 participants (30 Ejagham speakers and 60 Camfranglais online chatters of francophone background) constituted the sample. The mean age of Ejagham speakers was 35.25 years (range 21-60 ), that of Camfranglais speakers 23.5 (range 19-26).

## 7.3. Instruments

The study made use of online chats of Camfranglais users, sent from their phones to that of the researcher. 30 Ejagham speakers, both from urban and rural areas, provided data through structured and unstructured interviews. Two sets of questionnaires collected bio-data from all respondents during follow-up sessions. All in all, the data gathered from the chat conversations comprised 740 questions of various types and levels.

## 7.4. Procedure

The purpose of research as explained to the respondents was to help address language issues. It was made clear that their participation was voluntary. They were requested to forward all the questions they had asked in their chat forums within the previous nine months. The informants were met three times as a group in the course of collecting the data. The focus was to investigate trends of indigenous language structures in terms of questioning patterns in Camfranglais in comparison with Ejagham and English. To complement the data collection procedure, the same respondents were requested to engage in pair questioning while the research team moved round to ensure that the exercise was well carried out. In order to enhance the understanding of the investigated structures, another exercise subjected respondents to the interpretation of a number of questions into English. Finally, another exercise had questions in English read out to the respondents, where they were asked to provide the Camfranglais equivalents in writing.

## 7.5. Data analysis

Data were analyzed manually, making use of the Content Analysis procedure, following Holsti (1969) and Krippendorff (2004: 413), where questions were grouped under umbrella terms (quotes), whose frequency was established and normalised.

The questioning structure used in Camfranglais was then compared to English and Ejagham (Table 1). This was done in order to gain results for the use of questions by Camfranglais chatters (independent variable) in the established indigenous language (dependent variable).

## 8. Results

Data collected from the Camfranglais expressions of the respondents were first examined in relation to the English language and then compared to parallel structures in Ejagham. After assessing evidence, it was revealed that the question pattern of Camfranglais was more in line with that of Ejagham than that of English (Tables 1&2).

| Question Type | Camfranglais | | English pattern | | Indigenous pattern | |
|---|---|---|---|---|---|---|
| | N | % | N | % | N | % |
| YES/NO | 297 | 40.1 | 8 | 1.0 | 289 | 39.1 |
| WH- | 402 | 54.3 | 6 | 0.8 | 396 | 53.5 |
| TAG | 2 | 0.3 | 0 | 0 | 2 | 0.3 |
| SUGGESTION | 1 | 0.1 | 0 | 0 | 1 | 0.1 |
| RHETORICAL | 1 | 0.1 | 0 | 0 | 1 | 0.1 |
| LEADING | 37 | 5.3 | 0 | 0 | 37 | 5.3 |
| CHOICE (ALTERNATIVE) | 0 | 0 | 0 | 0 | 0 | |
| Total | 740 | 100 | 14 | 1.8 | 726 | 98.3 |

Table 1 Questioning Pattern by Camfranglais vis-a-vis Ejagham and English

In order to present the differences in the structures of the question types in the three languages, Table 2 juxtaposes Camfranglais examples from the corpus with their Ejagham and English equivalence.

| Type | Camfranglais | Ejagham | English Equv. |
|---|---|---|---|
| YES/NO | R2.3) Tu comot de Yaounde? | ô-rûk-Yaounde? | 'Are you from Yaounde?' |
| WH | R4.14) Tu etais go ou yesterday? | ô-zîk- é fããhéh-ã? | 'Where did you go to yesterday?' |
| LEADING | R47.13) Tu wanda sur les ways de la mater la nor? | βô-ko̧t é-lûk n-ŋ-κîŋûhäh? | 'Are you surprised by that ladies atitude?' |
| TAG | R3.14) n'est-ce pas tu as reach? | Tchang-bo-sik-a? | 'You have reached, haven't you?' |
| SUGGESTION | R48.1) on go ou le soir? | é-zikfã né-wûk? | 'Where do we go this evening?' |
| RHETORICAL | R60.4) Tu boscha lorsque ton voisin va tchoko les ans? | wî ô-pâ- n-jwîdnjî-kî n-tîé-wâjôŋ â-sé-réwâ? | 'Why are you studying 'when your neighbor will provide the answers for you?' |

Table 2: Camfranglais sentences with indigenous pattern

This study focuses on questioning in social settings, with common themes related to the typical concerns of the modern youth. Examples are in the domain of food, sex, stealing, playing study, playing pranks at home, partying, travel and ownership. Questions transgressed some standard rules in English. Yes/No questions started with subject rather than auxiliary (Tu a tchpo le dos la? 'Have you spent that money?'). In like manner, *Wh-* questions started with subjects rather than question words.

Table 1 confirms the expected relationship between questioning patterns in Camfranglais and Ejagham. This is because out of a total of 740 questions used by Camfranglais chatters in their online and face-to-face communication, just 17 (2.3%) made use of the English pattern, while an overwhelming number of 736 (99.4%) used the Ejagham pattern. From the same analysis, it is observed that Camfranglais made use of just 7 types of questions, with a wider margin of use of Yes/No, scoring 297 (40.1%) and 402 (54.3%) for *Wh-*questions, and the third most used (Leading question), scored 37 (5.3%), while the rest scored very minimal percentage use of < 1%. Of interest is the fact that out of a total of 37 (5.3%) Leading Questions used, all the 37 followed the Ejagham question structure. As for Rhetorical and suggestive questions, just one item each was registered, and both adopted the Ejagham pattern.

Based on the Content weightings for the items, which comprised question types, we can safely conclude that Camfranglais is related to Ejagham in terms of question pattern. Hence, we uphold the study's hypothesis, which stated that there is no significant difference between the question pattern of Camfranglais and Ejagham. It is evident that the effect is high in cases where scores are compared with English and Ejagham, implying that the Camfranglais users who are English L2 learners used Ejagham structures significantly more than their English counterparts (Table 1). Consequently, the tenability of the hypothesis leads us to maintain that there is an African identity signaled in the linguistic practices of Camfranglais. These results are in line with Maher (2005); Pennycook (2007, 2009); Otsuji (2008), and Adedeji, (2017), who have proven that the linguistic practices of AYULs are influenced by indigenous languages.

## 9. Discussion

The results of this study reveal that both Camfranglais and Ejagham are related in question structure. For example, out of the 740 questions asked, 736 (99.4%) followed the Ejagham structure, while just 17 (2.3%) were in line with the English pattern. In this way, we maintained that the grammar of Camfranglais is found in that of Ejagham. It is worth noting that there was significant difference with respect to the questioning pattern of English. More so, there were some types of questions that are common in English, but not exploited by the chatters. Whereas, it was revealed that all the type of questions used by Ejagham speakers were also used by Camfranglais online communicators, making use of SVO structure. These results are in line with Watters (1981); Myers-Scotton (1993) and McLaughlin (2001).

This leads us to assert that the grammar of indigenous languages is prevalent in that of AYULs, thus meeting the second objective of the study; investigating the aspect of identity through language use. This is in consonance with the work of Otsuji (2006, 2008) who argues that culture and identities are constructed in language use. Such uses were seen to be as a result of a link to cultural roots, thus, carving out African identity for the urban youth, following Pennycook (2007), Makoni & Pennycook (2007), McLaughlin (2009) and Adedeji (2017), who all attest that indigenous languages impact the speech of the urban youth to avail the users of African identity. This is consistent with the findings of Sirsa and Redford (2013), who have proven that such similarities and differences are the effect of L1 on Indian English. These facts point to the fact that Camfranglais is not just a street language, language of miscreants that has nothing to offer; it is an embodiment of the indigenous African identity. Indeed, we have proven that a certain grammatical consensus exists between Camfranglais and Ejagham. Based on this congruity, we hold that there is an indigenous identity that is engendered in the linguistic practices of Camfranglais online chats, which prompts us to conclude that there is an African value in the urban youth language.

## 10. Conclusions

The present study, arguably, is the first to have empirically linked the linguistic practices of Camfranglais to social identity given that association between in-group speakers of Camfranglais and Ejagham has been illustrated. All in all, the data suggest that questioning pattern is a marker of in-group identity, as the use of it may foster a bond by the mere fact that they are in line with the indigenous languages as represented by Ejagham. It prompted us to ask questions and engage in investigations concerning the grammar of AYULs in indigenous languages; the question pattern of Camfranglais in Ejagham and how the linguistic practices of Camfranglais carve an identity in the online questions of the respondents. The research found conformity between the questioning structure of Camfranglais and Ejagham, which made us to conclude that though Camfranglais users try to keep off the 'others', they find themselves being in parity with the indigenous languages through the questioning pattern of indigenous languages, represented by Ejagham (SVO), instead of the one in the exoglossic English.

## References

Adedeji, W. (2017). Nigerian hip hop and the Yoruba influence:"RuggedyBaba" and the negotiation of national identity. *Saudi Journal of Humanities and Social Sciences2(1),* Scholas Middle East Publishers. Dubai, United Arab Emirates, 34-42.

Al-Saleem, B. I. (2011). Language and identity in social networking sites. *International Journal of Humanites and Social Science.* 1(19), 196-202.

Auer, P. (2005). Dialect change: The convergence and divergence of dialects in contemporary Europe. Cambridge: Cambridge University Press.

Auer, P. (2007). Multilingualism and multilingual communication. *Handbook of Applied Linguistics.* 5 Berlin: Mouton de Gruyter.

Auer, P. & Wei, L. (2007). *Handbook of multilingualism and multilingual communication.* Mouton de Gruyter.
Bakhtin, M. M. (1981). *The dialogue imagination: Four essays.* In Michael H. Trans. Caryl Emerson. Austin and London: University of Texas Press.
Bourdieu, P. (1984). *Distinction: a social critique of the judgement of taste.* London: Routledge.
Bourdieu, P. (1990). *The logic of practice.* Stanford: Stanford university press.
Bourdieu, P. (1997). *Outline of a theory of practice.* Cambridge: Cambridge University Press.
Bourdieu, P. & Passeron, J. (1970). *Reproduction in education, society and culture.* Beverly Hills.Sage
Gbogi, M. T. (2016). Language, identity, and urban youth subculture. *Pragmatics. Quarterly Publication of the International Pragmatics Association (IPrA), 26*(2), 171-195.
Goyvaerts, D. L., & Kabongo-Mianda, K. (1988). Indoubil: A Swahili hybrid in Bukavu. *Language in Society, 17*(2), 231-242.
Grimes, B. (2005). (Ed.). *Ethnologue.languages of the world.* (16th ed.) Dallas: SIL International.
Guthrie, M. (1948). Gender, number and person in Bantu languages. *Bulletin of the School of Oriental and African Studies, 12*(3-4), 847-856.
Halliday, M.A.K. (1985). *An introduction to functional grammar.* London: Edward Arnold.
Holsti, O. R. (1969). Content analysis for the social sciences and humanities. Reading: M.A. Addison-Wesley.
Hurst, E. (2017). African (Urban) youth languages. *Oxford Research Encyclopaedia of Linguistics.* DOI:10.1093/acrefore/9780199384655.013.157. Acessed, 15.08.19
Kiessling, R. & Mous, M. (2004). Urban youth languages in Africa.*Anthropological Linguistics. 446*(3), 303-341.
Krippendorff, K. (2004). Reliability in content analysis. *Human communication research, 30*(3), 411-433.
Makoni, S. and A. Pennycook (Eds.) (2007). *Disinventing and Reinventing Languages.* Clevedon: Multilingual Matters
McLaughlin, F. (2001) Dakar Wolof and the configuration of an urban identity. *Journal of African Cultural Studies, 14*(2), 153-172.
McLaughlin, F. (2009). Introduction to the languages of urban Africa. In F. McLaughlin (ed) *The languages of urban Africa.* London and New York: Continuum, 1–18.
Mous, M. (2004). The grammar of conjunctive and disjunctive coordination in Iragw. In Haspelmath M. (Ed.) *Coordinating Constructions.* Amsterdam: John Benjamins, 109-122.
Myers-Scotton, C. (1993). Social motivation for codeswitching: Evidence from Africa. *Oxford Studies in Language Contact.* Clarendon Press.
Newman, P. (1990). *Nominal and verbal plurality in Chadic.* Dordrecht: Foris.
Ngugi wa Thiong'o. (1986). *Decolonising the mind: the politics of language in African literature.* Nairobi: East African Educational Publishers.
Ojongnkpot, C. B. O. (2015). Assessing the nature and degree of endangerment: The case of Manyu indigenous languages. *Unpublished PhD Thesis in Applied Linguistics,* University of Buea, Cameroon.
Ojongnkpot, C. B. O. (2017). Urban youth language use in social media in Anglophone Cameroon: A morpho-syntactic analysis of camfranglais among University of Buea students. In Ebongue, A., & Hurst, E. (eds.) *Sociolinguistics in African Contexts: Perspectives and Challenges. Multilingual Education.*Springer international Publishing, 20, 287-300.
Omoniyi, T. (2005). Toward a re-theorization of code-switching. *TESOL Quarterly, 39*(4), 729-734.
Omoniyi, T. (2006). Hip hop through the world Englishes lens. A response to globalization. *World Englishes, 25*(2),195-208.
Omoniyi T. (2009). "So I choose to do I am Naija style": Hip hop, language and postcolonial identities. In Alim, H. S., Ibrahim, A., & Pennycook, A. (Eds.). *Global Linguistic Flows: Hiphop cultures, youth identities, and the politics of language.* New York: Routledge, 113-135.
Otsuji, E. (2008). Performing transculturation: Between/within' Japanese' and 'Australian' language, identities and culture. *Unpublished PhD, University of Technology,* Sydney.

Otsuji, E. & Pennycook, A. (2010). Metrolingualism: Fixity, fluidity, and language in flux. *International Journal of Multilingualism,* 7(3), 240-254.

Pennycook, A. (2007). *Global Englishes and transcultural flows*. London: Routledge.

Pennycook, A. (2009). Refashioning and performing identities in global hip hop. In Coupland, N., & Jaworski, A. (Eds.) *The new sociolinguistic reader*. Basingstoke: Palgrave Macmillan, 326-340.

Perullo, A. & Fenn, J. (2009). Language ideologies, choices, and practices in Eastern African hip hop. In Berger, H., & Carroll, M. (Eds.). *Global pop, local language*. Jackson, MS: University of Mississipi, 19-52.

Quirk, R., Greebaum, S., Leech, G. & Jan, S. (1985). *A comprehensive grammar of the English language*. London: Longman.

Richardson, I. (1957). *Linguistic survey of the Northern Bantu*. London: Oxford University Press for International African Institute, 2.

Ruel, M. (1969). *Leopards and leaders*. London: Tavistock Publications.

Silverstein, M. (1998). The improvisional performance of culture in realtime discursive practice. In Sawyer, K. (Ed.). *Creativity in performance*. Greenwich. CT. Alblex Publishing Corp, 265-312.

Sirsa, H., & Redford, M. (2013). The effects of native language on Indian English sounds and timing patterns. *Journal of Phonology University of Oregon,41(6),393-406 USA*.

Watters, J. R. (1981). A Phonology and Morphology of Ejagham.*A Dissertation for the Degree of Pholosophy in Linguistics*. University of California, Los Angeles.

Watters, J. R. (2010). Focus and the Ejagham verb system. In Fiedler, Ines & Anne Schwarz (Eds.) *The expression of information structure: A documentation of its diversity across Africa Typological studies in Language 91*. Amsterdam: JohnBenjamins, 349-376.

Westermann, D., & Bryan M.A. (1952). Languages of West Africa. *Part 2 of Handbook of African Languages*. London: Oxford University Press for International African Institute.

Williamson, K. (1971). The Benue-Congo languages and Ijo. In *Current Trends in Linguistics*. The Hague: Mouton, 7, 245-306.

# Sheng as Fractal Language Practice[1]

*Philip W. Rudd* (Pittsburg State University, USA)

## 1. Introduction

In the glare of monoglot ideology, scholarship on African languages sometimes blindly attempts to push the square "master narrative" of colonial contact in Australia and the Americas (McLaughlin, 2008) onto round African linguistic ecologies. Swahili in contact with local indigenous languages led to the development of Sheng, non-standard "ghetto dialects" in the Eastlands area of Nairobi. This postcolonial reality of Kenya's capital leads to the misconception that Sheng is not a real language. This paper presents a brief history of Sheng and likewise proposes a reconceptualization of African Urban Youth Language or AUYL as practice rather than as object. Language usage in the postcolonial context can be depicted as "fractal practice" (McLaughlin, 2015: 144). In linguistic fractal fashion, speakers at the level of discourse "mimic" what they do at the morphological level. Viewed through the prism of the metaphor of fractals, Sheng, along with other varieties of AUYL, reveals its code-mixing, code-switching, and borrowing as reflections of the practice of having an ex-colonial language (English), a local lingua franca (Swahili), and other indigenous languages, merely as the refraction of actual practice at different levels, in the daily linguistic repertoires of urban Africa. Any controversy spawns from monolingual ideological misconception. Languages are not rigidly demarcated, and though Sheng is fragmented and continually changing, it is not broken, nor deserving of dismissal for being illegitimate. On the contrary, its hybridity emanates from the diverse realities in which cosmopolitan speakers find themselves.

The term *fractal* derives from the Latin adjectival *fractus*, meaning "fragmented" and applies to mathematical sets but also extends to patterns in nature. Put more simply, they are "mathematical models of self-similarity and self-resemblance: objects whose parts mimic the whole" (Rotman, 2013: 13). Fractal geometry explains chaos wherever it occurs because it discloses recognizable features at different levels of magnification. The perimeter of an informal settlement is fractal for it reflects self-similarity at each degree of magnification. Language usage too may be put into better focus from a fractal perspective. Based on Edmund Husserl's philosophy, Ludwig, Mühlhäusler & Pagel (2017) present a reformulation of the model of linguistic ecology that incorporates a fractal-like concept in which language in the communicative situation is part of a complex socio-historical-cultural whole. Further, McLaughlin (2015: 144) proposes that language usage in the postcolonial context should be depicted as "fractal practice".

---

[1] Key Words: antilanguage, identity, fractals, language ideology, mandala, reflectaphors, stylistic practice

Colonial language legacy has held such hegemony over indigenous African languages that shade is cast and misconception prevails on African Urban Youth Language or AUYL,[2] a term first used at a Cape Town conference in 2013 to describe the slang, argot, and register usage across the African continent (e.g., Bayankee, Nouchi, Camfranglais, Isicamto, and Sheng). Of course, academic attention to African youth language practices has come, but it was slow to focus primarily because of the social stigma associated with these varieties (Hollington & Nassenstein, 2015: 1). Over the last two decades concentration on language practices in Africa has exploded in the field of linguistics. For excellent examples, see the collected works in Ebongue and Hurst (2017) and in Nassenstein and Hollington (2015). However, linguistics is a discipline often uncovered and unknown to nonlinguist institutions and laypersons, who frequently need convincing, part of the point of this paper.

This paper has the following organization. Section §1 discusses the coming of Sheng to Nairobi and explains that second language interference features contributed to the varieties that eventually jelled into a language of wider communication. Section §2 explores language ideology, contact and conflict between the colonial language and indigenous languages, and the paradigmatic shift of focus from language object to linguistic practice. Section §3 identifies six levels of magnification to observe fractal structures in the morphosyntax of African urban youth languages and applies five of these scales to language examples from Sheng. Section §4 considers the Jungian concept of the mandala to the idiolect as part of the socio-historical-cultural whole context of Nairobi. Finally, the conclusion summarizes the concept of fractal mimesis of morphosyntax in language practice and calls for further application of the paradigm to other African urban youth languages.

## 2. The Advent of Sheng

Prior to arriving in hinterland Kenya, Swahili was a trade language like Kituba (Mufwene, 2009) and Wolof (McLaughlin, 2009). Its spread throughout east Africa has been compared to the diffusion of Vulgar Latin (Rudd, 2017b). The "Manyema hordes," in the fashion of Roman soldiers, became "transmitters of a nonnative, nonstandard variety of language" (Mufwene, 2008: 5). They punctuated their vast array of trade networks with *Kiungwana*, their Swahili dialect (Page, 1971). The coming of European colonialism, however, transformed this variety from a language of slave trade to one of mining and missionary education. Seeking work in the Belgian *shaba* 'copper' mines, migrants from rural communities dispersed along these old Arab-Swahili routes spoke a pidgin-like *Kiungwana* that, because of its being perceived as ethnically neutral, became the most prominent lingua franca (Kusters, 2003: 314), symbolizing to the residents in and around Elisabethville (i.e., Lubumbashi) in southern Katanga "a shared experience of an urban

---

[2] Transposing the second and third letters as in [əjul] makes this acronym much less unwieldy.

life-style" (Fabian, 1986: 110). It was not until early in the 20th century that this variety started to seep into rural Kenya via a dusty path from Tanzania (Wald, 1981). The real catalyst was the carving up of the "magnificent African cake" (Davidson, 1986: 173) at the Berlin conference so that a zigzag gave Mt. Kilimanjaro to the Germans and a coastal strip ten miles deep to the Sultan of Zanzibar, leaving Mt. Kenya and the rest to the British. Rather than an army, the Brits employed a railway to subdue and colonize Kenya. When that railroad reached mile 327 on the 30th of May, 1899, a half-way point depot was constructed. That depot displaced Mombasa as the Protectorate Headquarters two years later. It became the capital of British East Africa six years subsequent to that, and the capital of the colony thirteen years after that. Finally 43 years later Nairobi became the capital of the republic. During this evolution of depot into powerhouse capital of a sovereign independent nation, migrants to the city were bringing with them from the hinterland a variety comparable to *Kiungwana* (Kusters, 2003: 315) that became known as Kenya Pidgin Swahili or KPS (Heine, 1973).[3] The interference features of the individual speakers' first languages differentiated this erstwhile Up-country Swahili. Europeans spoke a "master-slave" connotative *Kisetla* (Vitale, 1980: 53), Asians a heavily Hindustani-influenced *Kihindi* (Neale, 1974), and Africans a rural variety known as *Kishamba* (Duran, 1979: 131). This mingling of varieties is what migrants met informally upon arrival and constitutes the whorl that would become Nairobi's urban vernacular, Sheng. Such mingling cannot properly be called Swahili. In fact, Hymes (1971: 519) labeled the *Kisetla* contribution "perhaps the most aberrant variety." Of course on such an analogy, Middle English could be viewed as aberrant French, and French itself just aberrant Latin. Even Myers-Scotton concedes that Up-country Swahili spoken in Nairobi sometimes causes "a definite breakdown in mutual intelligibility" (1979: 122). The amount of interference and mixing of codes required in Nairobi likely hybridized and caused "the convergence of all dialects …" (Hinskens et al., 2005: 47). Over time across Africa, new urbanites began to desire to accommodate to and become part of the whole of their new African metropolis, opening ecological corridors gestating new forms of wider communication from which AUYLs like Sheng emerged. Section §4 discusses how this background of social milieu provides the contrast that illuminates and motivates the linguistic deviation so prevalent in the language practices of the urban youth of Africa.

## 3. Contact and Language Ideologies

Europeans brought their worldview to Africa. Colonialism applied invented traditions and molded Africa to fit the perspective. At the close of the colonial era, rural Africa was defined as traditional, tribalism primordial, and urban life corrupt (Lüpke, 2015). The "master narrative" of monolingualism that explains language

---

[3] Heine (1979: 89; 1973) labeled Kenyan Up-country Swahili a pidgin because it fit the characteristics of African–based pidgins.

endangerment in Australia and America does not fit the African scenario. In other words, linguistic ecosystems in Africa tend to be polylectal and therefore no one language indexes identity. Social practices, such as age, classes and peer groups, maintain and transmit linguistic diversity and explicate the salience of youth languages and registers in Africa. However, this fact does not imply that language ideology has no foothold. A colonial hangover is hard to shake off. Language ideology can be effectively inculcated as moral obligation (Rudd, 2017a).

Fractals as a concept have been employed before to explain language ideologies. Irvine and Gal (2001: 36-37) identify three semiotic processes in which language ideologies "recognize" linguistic differences: iconization, erasure, and fractal recursivity. In iconization, certain linguistic features are attributed to a certain social group. Perhaps a particular pronunciation is considered an icon or the inherent nature of good breeding. For instance, if "the linguistic expression of Arabism in Kiswahili became an element of sophistication which came to be partly measured by one's ability to articulate any known Arabic borrowing as articulated in Arabic speech" (Mazrui, 1978: 229), a similar level of sophistication could be affected in Sheng by articulating an Anglicism as closely as possible to the articulation perceived to be in English. Considering that speakers create a mixed language as "a symbol of their emerging ethnic identity" (Thomason, 2001: 11), it should be contemplated why the name Sheng in its closed monosyllabicity, seemingly shouts, "We are different!" The name may be marked to show how much the speakers feel that they are their own speech community—a group separate from the communities of the Swahili speakers, the English speakers, and the vernacular speakers. As Abdulaziz & Osinde (1997: 62) point out,

> [t]he main characteristics of the ecology of Sheng and Engsh are that they developed, not because of lack of other means of communication, but rather as varieties serving as peer languages of the youth that assert their subcultures, identities, and group solidarities.

Moreover, speakers form distinct inter-communities (shibbolets) and separate them through lexical variation, as it can be inferred from Githingi's 2006 study of lexification, which accounted for a large number of lexeme variants (e.g., 52 variants for 'fool' and 45 for 'girl' (453)) across distinct Sheng shibbolets in several local bazes (hang out joints). In erasure, the ideology admits no exception, so that certain speakers or sociolinguistic phenomena are rendered invisible (see Amnesty International, 2009; and see Rudd, 2017a for an exploration of the othering of AUYL). In fractal recursivity, the third semiotic process, a mosaic of features is projected at different levels of relationships to maintain opposing roles (e.g. for gender or national identities). McLaughlin (2015) describes how speakers of urban Wolof in linguistic fractal fashion "mimic" at the level of discourse what they do at the level of morphology. The point is to encourage a move away from the conventional language Manichaeanism of the institutions and education of the non-linguist layperson. The linguistic hybridity of African urban centers is neither ex-colonial nor traditional; rather the whorl of the two is something new. One concrete linguistic set of language practices triggered by the rejection of societal norms and standard language ideology and an avenue to recontextualization of language is morphological manipulation. As fractal recursivity in AUYL morphosyntax is salient, it may well be the tool to leverage conventional thinking into a more receptive mode. It is not lost here that one motive for linguistic deviation is to be highly flexible and dynamic to prevent those of the "established" world (Halliday, 1978) from acquiring access. This has been discussed with regard to lexical variation in Sheng shibboleths (Githingi 2006) and the language's "overwhelming" (Ogechi 2005: 353) diachronic change. Nevertheless, the ultimate goal may actually be to create a new norm via "the powerful manifestations of the linguistic system in the service of the construction of reality" (Halliday, 1978: 181). This reconstruction is the resocialization of the milieu into a world in which the speakers belong. One recent example of this is found in Hurst (2017: 181-182), an acknowledgement that "the line between urban forms and tsotsitaals may become increasingly blurry, and may ultimately necessitate a reconsideration of th[e] 'standard'." This paper embraces the paradigmatic shift to language reconsideration and resocialization and analyzes examples of Sheng as postcolonial language practices.

## 4. Scales of Magnification

Fractal geometry is the science of roughness. Though the sands of time may hone the world, much of nature is rough-edged. Today, finding fractals in nature is as easy as stumping one's toe on the bedstead. In the wake of Mandelbrot's (1983) simple equation for transforming the roughness of natural fractals into fantastical visions on computer screens, one cannot help but be curious as to how such beauty in nature could have remained hidden for so long. However, the square, the cone, the cube, and the circle are the abstract ideals of Euclidian geometry. They have no reality in the natural world. Of course, these shapes do occur with ubiquity in the world, but they, like standard languages, are merely human-made.

A metaphor paints a picture with words, and a painting too consists of smaller strokes. The word "reflectaphor" is a term for a recurrent shape or form in a painting (Briggs, 1987). This creative device allows the viewing of fractals in a painting at different scales of magnitude. Being able to observe reflectaphors at different levels provides a "sense of unity, diversity, and wholeness" (Briggs, 2015: 173) that would otherwise remain unobserved. Fractal scaling in language comes into focus once it is realized that poetic devices, such as the metaphor, pun, paradox, synecdoche, simile, and irony, tie similarity to difference and therefore qualify as reflectaphors (Briggs & Peat, 1989: 196). Of course, "[t]he equation isn't the plot of a shape as it is in Euclid. Rather, the equation provides the starting point for *evolving* a shape that emerges out of the equation's feedback" (Briggs & Peat, 1989: 104). The poetry of Gary Snyder, "the poet laureate of deep ecology" (Oelschlaeger, 1991: 437), reverberates with these fractal shapes. Romesburg (2010) offers a template for revealing the fractal basis of such evolving complexity. To uncover fractal structure and clarify the complexity of the language, six levels or scales of magnification undergird an analysis, exposing "self-similarity, wholeness emerging from fragmentation, order and chaos, and other traits of fractal geometry" (7). Vierke (2015) contends, "Sheng can also be considered to be conditioned by the poetic function [(Jakobson, 1981)]: the speakers' concern for form and meaning for their own sake" (227). Drawing on these works, this paper proffers six scales of magnification to identify the fractal structures in African urban youth language: the whole text, clauses, phrases, words, morphemes, and phonemes.

A microscope may serve as metaphor for the approach. The field of view in the eyepiece presents the "circle" seen when one is looking in the microscope. Though the circular field of view seems to be the same no matter which level of magnification is being used, this appearance is not the case. The circular area actually being viewed decreases as the magnification increases.

Texts can be broken down into sentences, and sentences may be broken down further into clauses. As neither the naked eye needs (i.e., magnification is unrequired) nor the scope of this paper permits (i.e., space is limited), the whole of the text will not be examined but stands as ground zero, the starting point. The analysis, however, begins with the clause, the lowest level of magnification and the largest field of view. The Sheng pattern of self-similarity characteristic of fractals is evident even in clauses. In the sentence in (1), a Swahili clause is subordinated to an English main clause. In the dependent clause is found also a lexical item (i.e. *shaggs*) known only in Sheng. This whole is the language Sheng itself and the intermingled language interactions that occur in the speakers' daily lives.

(1)  Sheng Clauses
Keep them safe coz **naenda shaggs**.

| keep | them | safe | because | na- | | end | -a | shaggs |
|---|---|---|---|---|---|---|---|---|
| | | | | SBJ.1SG.PRES- | | go | -FV | |
| V | Pro | Adj | C | Pro.TAM- | | V | | -TAM |
| | | | | N | | | | |

Keep them safe because **I am travelling upcountry**.
(SWH-W_DAO1-BEC.180)
(Marlo et al., 2015)

An "eco-purist" might argue that this sentence is an example of code-switching and code-mixing. However, Ludwig, Mühlhäusler & Pagel (2017) explain that these terms are "metaphorically misleading" for the donor language loses no lexical organ, and the borrower accumulates no extravagantly indebted lexicon. McLaughlin (2015: 144) further points out that African urban speakers "communicate in a heteroglossic fashion" by taking advantage of all the resources in their linguistic practices. "If a dog lives in the same house as a bird," writes Kibbee (2003: 51), "it does not grow wings, nor does the bird sprout paws. If two languages are in contact, they create a new language." What is seen in example (1) is a Sheng word inside of a Swahili clause inside of an English sentence. This alternation is mirrored at the phrasal level as well.

(2) Sheng Phrases
Ni kama ako **ready kubite**
| ni | kama | a- | | ko | ready | ku- | bite |
|---|---|---|---|---|---|---|---|
| COP | if/whether | SBJ.CL.1- | COP.Cl.17 | | ready | INF- | bite |
| V | C | Pro- | V | | Adj | TAM- | V |

It's like he is **ready to bite**
(SWH-W_DAO1-BEC.214)
(Marlo et al., 2015)

Here in (2) can be seen that the same pattern of alternation occurs. The bold-faced phrase begins with English *ready* and ends with a Swahili infinitive, albeit the infinitive has the English base verb *bite* preceded by the Swahili infinitive *ku-* prefix. An English base verb is in a Swahili infinitive structure in an English adjectival phrase as a complement to a Sheng locative. A whorl within a whorl wrapped in a whorl.

(3) Sheng Words
**Ndo** naona!
| ndo | na- | on | -a |
|---|---|---|---|
| so_that | PRES- | see | -FV |
| C | TAM- | V | -TAM |

**D'oh** I can see!
(SWH-W_SCR-GS.006)
(Marlo et al., 2015)

At the level of words in (3), the self-similarity is a bit more perplexing with sundry potential sources. First, the word *ndo* does not exist in Swahili, but perhaps it could be a truncation of *ndiyo*. Second, the word *ndi* exists in Luhya, yet that would require deletion of the vowel [i] and affixation of [o], which is not uncommon in Sheng as will be demonstrated below. A third possibility is that it derives from American slang *d'oh*, which has been popularized by the character Homer in the television series *The Simpsons* (OED 2017; American Slang Dictionary 2017). Perchance it is just a coinage, but it could be a combination of all three. Recall that a lexeme may be a combination of several morphemes or just one. Multimorphemic, this word not only mirrors the self-similarity characteristic of fractals, but also designates no clear source of origin. Monomorphemic, the lexeme demonstrates Sheng's potential to structurally represent a linguistic verticil with neither start nor end. Despite extensive descriptions of Sheng lexicalisation and lexification processes in the literature (Ogechi, 2005; Githinji, 2006), this excerpt provided evidence of Sheng lexemes of unknown origin.

As the magnification power increases, the field of view gets smaller and discloses in (4) a single morpheme, a minimal unit of meaning that cannot be broken down further semantic-wise. In Swahili, the morpheme *ko* is a noun class 17 locative marker. The example here employs it with the preposition *na* to indicate possession. In standard Swahili, one would never say, "Nikona Rösti" even if in Basel.[4] Rather one should say, "Nina Rösti." Nonetheless, Duran (1979) shows that when it is prefixed with the class nine subject marker, as in *iko*, it is ubiquitous in the L2 Swahili of east Africa. It may be generalized as a fossilized form in Kenya Pidgin Swahili (KPS), which is also attested by both LeBreton (1936) and Heine (1973). Furthermore, Drolc (2004) argues that the locative form *iko* may have been functionally expanded by Asians because of first language interference. That is, their substratal influence affected how other speakers used the language, giving Sheng yet another whirl in the whorl.

(4)     Sheng Morphemes
Btw nikonadondoo
btw    ni-    ko      na    dondoo
by the way SBJ.1.SG- COP.Cl.17    with/and agenda_item
By the way, I have news.
(SWH-W_DAO1-BEC.015)
(Marlo et al., 2015)

Narrowing the view to the highest power of magnification discloses that the phoneme in (5) again has the whorl structure of the whole text and other subaltern scales. The word *weddo* appears to be a borrowing, or code copying from English *wedding*. However, evidence of clipping (i.e. the inflectional *–ing* has been lopped off) and suffixation (i.e. the vowel or phoneme /o/ has been added) support a view that the copying is covert, not overt (Ludwig, Mühlhäusler & Pagel 2017). Truncation and affixation are common methods of creating AUYL neologisms. Such distortions engender an argotic spin, making the usage appear to be an anti-language (Halliday, 1978), an anti-society variety used as a counter to the established or privileged language.

(5)     Sheng Phonemes
Fanya weddo
fany    -a           wedd      -o
do/work -FV       wedding    Ø
V     -TAM         N          dummy suffix
Do a wedding
(SWH-W_DAO1-BEC.058)
(Marlo et al., 2015)

Conventional and established wisdom views these manipulations as a method to disguise meaning and deny comprehension to all but a covert few. Equally

---

[4] An earlier version of this paper was presented at the 7th European Conference on African Studies (ECAS 2017) in Basel, Switzerland. Rösti is a popular Swiss potato dish that is like hash browns.

plausible, however, is that rapid turnover of vocabulary is a linguistic display of "urban belonging" (McLaughlin, 2015: 140). In Eastlands, speakers "walk a linguistic tightrope, balancing between the labels *mshamba* ('rube') and *Mswahili* ('slick talker'). However, Sheng provides a sociolinguistic embodiment symbolizing what nuances their existence" (Rudd, 2008). To illustrate this point, consider an anecdote from this author's past when he as a volunteer teacher, who had been living in Kenya Eastern Province, first traveled to Nyanza Province.[5] Somewhere along the route between Kisumu and Homa Bay, a *manamba* or conductor on a *matatu* (public transport vehicle) addressed him as *Odiero*, a term he had never heard before. Though the word's denotative meaning is *Lanius collari* or the African pied crow, in this context it reflects the legacy of Livingstone's only capitalized letter in his mantra of three: Christianity.[6] The first Europeans to travel to and reside on the banks of Lake Victoria were missionaries dressed in black and white garb and inspired by Livingstone's call. The name became associated with the *mzungu* or European because of the attire of the missionary: white shirt, black jacket. Sounding distinctly Luo and non-bantu may be the appeal in Sheng. Other words have been similarly manipulated. For instance, the Swahili word *duka* or shop in Sheng is *oduko*. This foreignness has given Sheng a way to sound inclusive of other languages, and now the affixation of an [o] to the end of a lexeme creates the air of cosmopolitanism displayed in *weddo*. As Swahili already has the mid, back, rounded vowel, this is not an addition to the phonemic inventory, rather it is a special marking of a noun. In fact, it may well be prosodic in that the stress seems to move to the final vowel from the penult. It should be noted here that at least one Sheng word (i.e. *budaa* or toothless old man) receives final stress as well but without the final [o], suggesting further research is required. Incidentally on the level of graphemes, Sheng speakers reject the Swahili trigraph <ng'> and embrace the English digraph <ng> for the velar nasal /ŋ/, perhaps another effort to mark distance from *Kiswahili sanifu* albeit orthographic. This final, looser spiral of reflectaphors could be read as the fractal practice of intertwining linguistic sources in a flashier fashion, thus encapsulating the multiple levels of symbolism whirling at work in African urban youth language.

## 5. The Fractal Mandala Paradigm

Nairobi is a fractal city. Like all cities, it manifests disorder and chaos reflecting its fractal qualities, but it was designed on the concept of the garden city (K'Akumu & Olima, 2007). Seen on a map, from the air, or in the eye of the colonial, the city was an image of Euclidean beauty. Striations of settlements based on social status and ethnic group were manifest in its very layout like a mandala, a Sanskrit word

---

[5] Nyanza and Eastern were two of eight administrative provinces that existed before the new constitution of 2010.
[6] The three Cs were Christianity, commerce, and civilization (Etherington & Maxwell 2004). They were from Sir Thomas Fowell Buxton of the Society for the Extinction of the Slave Trade and for the Civilization of Africa, but they inspired David Livingstone and the Scramble for Africa.

meaning "circle" that is a schematic visual of fractals nested within fractals representing the universe and the self in several Asian traditions. Such "idealized geometric plans produced without any regard to urban functioning are not likely to resolve any ... urban ills" (Batty, 2008: 771). The mandala design cut the city into a three-tier social class ladder. As government officials and plantation owners, the Europeans were on the highest rung in the North and West of the city. As the clerks, manufacturers, and traders, Asians perched on the middle rung in the East and South of the city. As farmhands and short-term casual laborers, indigenous Kenyans, forbidden any official location, were left at the bottom with no true rung on the outskirts of the city in the East and South in informal settlements. On the one hand, British aviator and writer, Beryl Markham (1942), daydreamed about Nairobi as one of the utopian cities detailed in *Garden Cities of To-Morrow* (Howard & Osborn, 1965). On the other hand, "Jomo Kenyatta generally referred to Nairobi, or indeed, any town, as *Gecombaini*, a place of strangers" (Lonsdale, 2002: 211). The mandala then did not square with everyone.

Let it be granted that slums existed in Nairobi before the nation's independence and that indigenous Kenyans from the colonial perspective were temporary residents. Moreover, there were no official areas for Africans until 1923 (Bujra, 1974) and no family housing until 1957, with Maringo, Jerusalem and Jericho as part of the Ofafa developments (Hake, 1977). Nevertheless, it was not until after the departure of the colonial that slums greatly "enlarged, densified and proliferated" reaching 60% of the urban population in 2006 (Githira, 2016: 2-3). In other words, Nairobi is a maelstrom of shanties with the capital at its core (Anderson, 2002: 154). Regardless, over these past fifty years Kenya has become the largest economy in East Africa (Balistreri et al., 2009) and has started providing government-funded "free" primary education. Still slum dwellers, who, it should go without saying, are the meekest of the meek, are not reaping the benefits (Oketch & Mutisya, 2012; Ngware et al., 2009: 605). If as stated earlier, they consist of around two million people today (and will exceed three million by 2025), they have to be living in a whorl of a world of their own. The ecological pressures from the socio-economic system are local because Westernization reaches only the elite (Mufwene and Vigouroux, 2008: 23). National language policies mean little for the ex-colonial language, along with perhaps any standard language, is but an elite entitlement (See Laitin and Eastman, 1989: 52).

All language change is "externally motivated" (Mufwene, 2001), but the change occurs in the idiolect in an attempt to accommodate to other idiolects on the communal level, where "cross-idiolectal patterns of evolution emerge" (Mufwene, 2008: 32). The communal labyrinth is a fractal mandala through which the idiolect is trying to find itself. In Jungian theory, the self is the part that seeks to find the whole, a reverberation of Husserl's philosophy and Mandelbrot's fractals. During difficult times and challenges, the self seeks balance with the whole. Sometimes an ecology develops a swing out away from equilibrium, such as the mass exodus of migrants from rural areas to urban areas in post-independence Africa (Tarver, 1994). Just as the need for balance in nature searches for harmony in the ecology, the disequilibrium in the self seeks harmony too. To explain this search for harmony, Jung took the Asian concept of the mandala and applied it to the self.

Jung (1968: 715) perceives the mandala as "an archetype of wholeness" because it has the fractal ability to bring order out of chaos. The process of finding the path to the whole is called the "quaternity" or *quadraturacirculi*, "squaring the circle" (713). For geometry, this phrase could mean looking at a three-dimensional structure from four different perspectives, such as from the center, corners, edges, and faces, or as areas, lines, volumes, and points (Schneider, 1995: 63). "The quaternity can appear as a geometric figure of square or sometimes rectangular shape, or it will have some relation with the number four...," writes Ellenberger (1970). "Often it is a matter of completing a triadic figure with a fourth term, thus making it into a quaternity" (712).

In the world exist several sets of four, for which, if one were missing, the fourth would be sought. The directions are four (north, south, east, and west). The winds are known to be Boreas, Eurus, Notus and Zephyrus. Seasons, as life, have the four stages of spring, summer, autumn, and winter. The mandala that is the ecology of Nairobi has to be squared as well. Section §2 explored and enumerated what languages exist in the newly independent capital of Kenya. There were the ex-colonial language English, connoting elitism, Kenya Pidgin Swahili with the mark of being a master-slave language, and the first language of the various indigenous migrants having both ethnic and rustic affinities. Recall that speakers are endeavoring to be accommodating. Choices can be conscious or unconscious in the individual, and often unrecognized. The languages were in a constant state of fluctuation, and idiolects were emerging in this community. With no one noticing, the dynamics of this linguistic process remained unseen as an "invisible hand" cast the die making the city residents "unwitting agents" of linguistic change (Mufwene, 2008: 14-18) in a new "invisible niche" (Rudd, 2017b) and "hybridized space" (Karanja, 2010: 2). Quaternity for Nairobi emerged when the parts became the whole, when the resident was able to move beyond being just a colonial subject, just a tribal member, just a speaker of a former slave language to become a cosmopolitan, one who belongs despite ethnicity, income, and geographical origin as long she or he speaks Sheng.

Bucholtz and Hall (2005) adumbrate a sociocultural linguistics framework that anchors the construction of self or identity to social interaction. If all of one's friends, neighbors, and colleagues are of different ethnicities, tribal affiliation is not much of a card to play. A neighbor has more in common with a neighbor than with a clansman. One must necessarily adopt a more cosmopolitan identity when "ethnic essentialization" (Makoni et al., 2007: 44) is a drawback. Therefore, traditional thinking about ethnic, cultural, regional, national and linguistic status is wrongheaded (Blommaert, 2010: 7). Identity is negotiated in the social milieu and emerges in the mind. The neighborhood has become glocalized. "Coming to more recent, post-colonial times one cannot help but wonder," ponders Lonsdale (2002: 213), "whether one of the reasons for Tom Mboya's assassination in 1969 was that, for an otherwise rurally-based political elite, he had a disturbing ability to appeal, trans-ethnically, to Nairobi's townsmen and women." Another more recent example is that of a businessman from Nyanza province who understandably in one breath refuses to speak Swahili but in another happily conducts affairs in Sheng (Beck, 2010: 31). Whereas Swahili reeks of the master-slave interactions of colonialism and the tribal-favoritism of independence-era politics, Sheng whirls past both by overturning hegemonic language ideology, creating a safe haven on the social ground, and encouraging a postcolonial identity to emerge.

It will be recalled that traditional thinking about the neologisms in AUYL is that the manipulations are to hide what is being meant. However, speakers could be flavoring their language to make it more distinct from the national and official languages[7] or code-switching between the two. As Halliday (1978: 181) clarifies, "The modes of expression of the antilanguage, when seen from the standpoint of the established language appear oblique, diffuse, metaphorical; and so they are, *from that angle*" [italics in original]. However, Sheng and other AUYL should be observed from a different perspective, that of the speakers. On this last point, an example of how this occurs in fractal fashion in the language itself should suffice as evidence. Take the name of Nairobi's AUYL. Conventional thinking dismisses Sheng as a blend of the letters <s> and <h> from **Swah**ili and the <eng> from **Eng**lish (Spryopoulos, 1987). However, from the angle of a fractal perspective, the appellation comes from a transposition of the syllables from *Eng-lish* to *lish-Eng*. The *li-* is reanalyzed as a class five CL5 Bantu prefix (being too Bantu, it is dropped), and the *sh-* as the phoneme /ʃ/ is reanalyzed as an onset for the remaining syllable. The resulting name, *Sheng*, is an inversion of the old colonial order, "a tactical reversal of domination—a resistance-through-appropriation…" (Pollock, 2000: 625). As reflectaphors go, the parts of the name Sheng readily exemplify how fractal self-similarity in the whorl emanates the diversity, sense of unity, and wholeness of African urban youth language.

## 6. Conclusion

In response to McLaughlin's (2015) call to describe postcolonial languages as "fractal practice" (144), this article has employed the distinction between part and whole to draw out the differences between language usage conceived as regular or standard on the analogy of Euclidean geometry and language perceived as fragmented or irregular on the analogy of Mandelbrot's geometry. The attempt has been to draw together a few threads of Sheng artifacts in postcolonial practice as reiterations of fractal forms to suggest that the geometry of chaos fits African urban youth languages in the hope that these examples of reflectaphors or morphosyntactic fractals are salient enough to add to the weight of evidence to convince the established world that the concept of language practice has more human import

---

[7] The 2010 constitution made Swahili co-official with English but before then the latter was official while the former national.

than that of language object. Moreover, it is hoped that researchers of other varieties may elect to take up the baton of morphosyntactic reflectaphors. Prescriptive attitudes are so deeply ingrained that it is difficult to remember that standard language ideology or "language as a delimitable entity" (Hollington & Nassenstein, 2017: 5) is but "a useful fiction" (Haugen, 1972: 335). What one language calls standard, another labels nonstandard. On a map a finger may trace the lines of a coast or the borders of an informal settlement as if they are Euclidean shapes. Yet when shoes walk the shores or eyes see the slums, the smoothness is revealed as roughness. In developing a geometry of AUYL fractals, six scales of magnification unveil the fractal structures of self-similarity. Five of those levels reveal a verticil of hybrid patterns in Sheng of clauses, phrases, words, morphemes, and phonemes. Viewed through the lens of Jungian theory, the whorl discloses the idiolect as the self in search of identity and wholeness in the historical and cultural milieu of the city. Ecology casts the die but fractals control the roll. This vision of language as living flux can be scary. The fear that some may have is that the childlike admiration of language as object will be lost. Without "the primordialization of languages" (Makoni et al., 2007: 26) in which they are perceived as "stable depositor[ies] of culture" (Fabian 1986: 5), society may lose not only a sacred cultural possession (i.e., a reliable standard code) but also a measure of morality (Rudd, 2017a). Fractals then shake us free from the reverie of a master deception that conventional education and culture have striven to paint. Like waves created by the strokes of a brush, standard language is an object that has only the look but not the authenticity of real-life language practices. Such stylistic practice is like the true mandala – temporary, ephemeral, and shifting with the sands of time. Just as grains drift and waves wax and wane, speakers seek the self and negotiate the center.

## References

Abdulaziz, M. & Osinde, K. (2009). Sheng and Engsh: development of mixed codes among the urban youth in Kenya. *International Journal of the Sociology of Language*, *125*(1), pp. 43-64. Retrieved 15 Aug. 2017, from doi:10.1515/ijsl.1997.125.43

Amnesty International (2009). Kenya. The unseen majority Nairobi's two million slum dwellers. London. Retrieved from https://www.amnesty.org/en/documents/AFR32/005/2009/en/

Anderson, D. M. (2002). Corruption at City Hall: African housing and urban development in colonial Nairobi.In Burton, A. (Ed.) *The urban experience in Eastern Africa c. 1750–2000*. Nairobi: British Institute in Eastern Africa, 138–154.

Balistreri, E. J., Rutherford, T. F. & Tarr, D. G. (2009). Modeling services liberalization: The case of Kenya. *Economic Modelling*, *26*(3), 668–679.

Batty, M. (2008). The size, scale, and shape of cities. 08 FEB 2008. *Science 319*(769): 769–771. Retrieved from http://science.sciencemag.org/content/319/5864/769

Beck, R. M. (2010). Urban languages in Africa. *Africa Spectrum*, *45*(3), 11–41.

Blommaert, J. (2010).*The sociolinguistics of globalization*. Cambridge, UK: Cambridge University Press.

Briggs, J. (2015). *Fractals: the patterns of chaos: a new aesthetic of art, science, and nature*. Brattleboro, Vermont: Echo Point Books & Media.

Briggs, J. (1987). "Reflectaphors: The (implicate) universe as a work of art." In Hiley B. J. & Peat, F. D. (Ed.) *Quantum Implications: Essays in honour of David Bohm*. New York:

Routledge & Kegan Paul, 414–435. Retrieved from http://people.wcsu.edu/briggsj/Reflectaphors.html

Briggs, J. & Peat, F.D. (1989).*Turbulent mirror: An illustrated guide to chaos theory and the science of wholeness.* New York: Harper & Row.

Bujra, J. (1974). Pumwani: Language use in an urban Muslim community. *Language in Kenya.* Whiteley, W. H. (Ed.) Nairobi: Oxford University Press, 217–252.

Bucholtz, M. & Hall, K. (2005). Identity and interaction: A sociocultural linguistic approach. *Discourse Studies* 7.4–5: 585–614.

Davidson, B. (1984 [1986]). *The story of Africa.* London: Mitchell Beazley.

d'oh. (n.d.). The dictionary of American slang. Retrieved from Dictionary.com website http://www.dictionary.com/browse/d-oh

"doh, int.". OED Online. March 2017. Oxford University Press. http://www.oed.com/view/Entry/249869?rskey=A9FDup&result=2

Drolc, U. (2004). "Asili ya Matumizi ya Iko katika Kiswahili cha Bara." *Swahili Forum.* Institut für Afrikanistik, U Koln, Germany.Volume 11, 171–178.

Duran, J. J. (1979). Non-standard forms of Swahili in West-Central Kenya. In Hancock, I. F. (Ed.) *Readings in Creole Studies.* Ghent, Belgium: E. Story-Scientia, 129–151.

Ebongue, A. E. & Hurst, E. B. (2017). *Sociolinguistics in African contexts: perspectives and challenges.* Cham: Springer.

Ellenberger, H. F. (1970). *The discovery of the unconscious: The history and evolution of dynamic psychiatry.* New York: Basic Books.

Etherington, N. & Maxwell, D. (2004). Missions and empire. *Journal of Religion in Africa* 34 (1/2).194–199.

Fabian, J. (1986 [1991]). *Language and colonial power: The appropriation of Swahili in the former Belgian Congo 1880–1938.* Berkeley: University of California Press.

Githinji, P. (2006). Bazes and their shibboleths: Lexical variation and Sheng speakers' identity in Nairobi. *Nordic Journal of African Studies*, *15*(4), 443–472.

Githira, D. N. (2016). Growth and eviction of informal settlements in Nairobi. *An Unpublished Master's Thesis.* University of Twente, Enshede, The Netherlands.
Retrieved from http://www.itc.nl/library/papers_2016/msc/upm/githira.pdf

Hake, A. (1977). *African metropolis: Nairobi's self-help city.* London: Chatto and Windus for Sussex University Press

Halliday, M. A. K. (1978). *Language as social semiotic: the social interpretation of language and meaning.* Baltimore: University Park Press.

Haugen, E. (1972). The ecology of language. In Dil, A. S. (Selected and Introduced) *The Ecology of language: Essays by Einar Haugen.* Stanford: Stanford University Press, 325–339.

Heine, B. (1979). Some linguistic characteristics of African-based Pidgins. In Hancock, F. (Ed.) *Readings in Creole Studies.* Ghent, Belgium: E. Story-Scientia, 89–98.

Heine, B. (1973). Grammatische Skizze des Kenya-Pidgin-Swahili. *Pidgin-Sprachen im Bantu-Bereich.* Kölner Beiträge zur Afrikanistik, 3. Berlin, .70–118.

Hinskens, F., Auer, P., & Kerswill, P. (2005). The study of dialect convergence and divergence: conceptual and methodological considerations. In Auer, P., Hinskens, F., & Kerswill, P. (Eds.) *Dialect change: Convergence and divergence in European languages.* Cambridge, UK: Cambridge University Press, 1–48.

Hollington, A. & Nassenstein, N. (2015). Youth language practices in Africa as creative manifestations of fluid repertoires and markers of speakers' social identity. In Nassenstein, N. & Hollington, A. (Ed.) *Youth language practices in Africa and beyond.* Boston: De Gruyter Mouton, 1–22.

Howard, E. & Osborn, F.J. (1965). *Garden cities of to-morrow.* Cambridge, Mass: M.I.T. Press.

Hurst, E. (2017). Overview of the Tsotsitals of South Africa: Their different base languages and common core lexical items. In Nassenstein, N. & Hollington, A. (Ed.) *Youth language practices in Africa and beyond.* Boston: De Gruyter Mouton, 169–184.

Hymes, D. H. (1971). Pidginization and creolization of languages: Proceedings of a conference held at the University of the West Indies, Mona, Jamaica, April, 1968. Cambridge, England: Cambridge University Press.

Irvine, J. T. & Gal, S. (2000). Language ideology and linguistic differentiation. In Kroskrity, P. (Ed.) *Regimes of language: Ideologies, polities, and identities*. Santa Fe: Schoolfor Advanced Research, 35–83.

Jakobson, R. (1981 [1960]). Linguistics and poetics. In Jakobson, R. & Rudy, S. (Eds.) *Poetry of grammar and grammar of poetry. Selected writings, 3*. The Hague, Mouton, 17–51.

Jung, C. (1968). *The collected works of C. G. Jung*. Trans. R. F. C. Hull. Vol. 9.part i, 2nd edition. Princeton: Princeton UP.

Karanja, L. (2010). Homeless at home: Linguistic, cultural, and identity hybridity and third space positioning of Kenyan urban youth." *Canadian and International Education / Education Canadienneetinternationale, 39*(2), Article 2.

K'Akumu, O. A., & Olima, W. A. (2007). The dynamics and implications of residential segregation in Nairobi. *Habitat International, 31*(1), 87–99.

Kibbee, D. A. (2003). Language policy and linguistic theory. In Maurais, J. & Morris, M. A. (Eds.) *Languages in a globalizing world*. Cambridge: Cambridge University Press, 47–57.

Kusters, W. (2003). *Linguistic complexity: The influence of social change on verbal inflection*. Utrecht: LOT.

Laitin, D., & Eastman, C. M. (1989). Language conflict: Transactions and games in Kenya. *Cultural Anthropology, 4*(1), 51–72.

LeBreton, F. H. (1936 [1964]). *Up-country Swahili exercises: For the soldier, settler, miner, merchant, and their wives, and for all who deal with up-country natives without Interpreters*. 15th Ed. Richmond, Surrey: R.W. Simpson.

Lonsdale, J. (2002). Town Life in Colonial Kenya.In Burton, A. (Ed.) *The urban experience in Eastern Africa c. 1750–2000*. Nairobi: British Institute in Eastern Africa, 207–222.

Ludwig, R., Mühlhäusler, P. & Pagel, S. (2017). *Linguistic ecology and language contact*. Cambridge: Cambridge University Press.

Lüpke, F. (2015). Ideologies and typologies of language endangerment in Africa. In Essegbey, J., Henderson, B. & McLaughlin, F. (Eds.) *Language documentation and endangerment in Africa*. Amsterdam: John Benjamins Publishing Company, 59–105.

Makoni, S., Brutt-Griffler, J. & Mashiri, P. (2007). The use of "indigenous" and urban vernaculars in Zimbabwe. *Language in Society, 36*(1), 25–49.

Mandelbrot, B. B. (1983). *The fractal geometry of nature*. W. H. Freeman and Company: San Francisco, CA.

Markham, B. (1983). *West with the night*. San Francisco: North Point Press.

Marlo, M. R., Rudd, P. W., Sifuna, M. & Simpson, S. (2015*). A corpus of electronic messages in Swahili/Sheng*. University of Maryland Center for Advanced Study of Language (CASL).

Mazrui, A. M. (1978). The religious factor in language nationalism—The case of Kiswahili in Kenya.*Studies in African Linguistics*. 9(2), 223–231.

McLaughlin, F. (2015). Can a language endanger itself? Reshaping repertoires in urban Senegal.InEssegbey, J., Henderson, B. & McLaughlin, F. (Eds.) *Language documentation and endangerment in Africa*. Amsterdam: John Benjamins Publishing Company, 131–151.

McLaughlin, F. (2009). *The languages of urban Africa*. London: Continuum.

McLaughlin, F. (2008). The ascent of Wolof as an urban vernacular and national lingua franca in Senegal.In Vigouroux, C.B., Salikoko S. &Mufwene, S.S. (Eds.)*Globalization and language vitality perspectives from black Africa*. London: Continuum, 142–170.

Mufwene, S. S. (2009). Kituba, Kileta, or Kikonko? What's in a name? In Carole de Féral, C. (Ed.) *Le nom des langues III. Naming Languages in Sub-Saharan Africa: practices, names, categorisations*, Louvain-la-Neuve, Peeters, BCILL , 211–222.

Mufwene, S. S. (2008). *Language evolution: contact, competition and change*. London: Continuum.

Mufwene, S. S. & Vigouroux, C. B. (2008). Colonization, globalization and language vitality in Africa: An introduction. In Vigouroux, C. B., Salikoko S. & Mufwene, S. S. (Eds.) *Globalization and language vitclity perspectives from black Africa*. London: Continuum, 1–31.

Mufwene, S. S. (2001). *The ecology of language evolution*. Cambridge: Cambridge University Press.

Myers-Scotton, C. (1979). The context is the message: Morphological, syntactic and semantic reduction and deletion in Nairobi and Kampala Varieties of Swahili. In Hancock, I. F. (Ed.) *Readings in Creole studies*. Ghent, Belgium: E. Story-Scientia, 111–127.

Nassenstein, N. & Hollington. A. (2015). *Youth language practices in Africa and beyond*. Boston: De Gruyter Mouton.

Neale, B. (1974). Kenya's Asian Languages. In Whiteley, W. H. (Ed.) *Language in Kenya*. Nairobi: Oxford University Press, 69–85.

Ngware, M. W., Oketch, M., Ezeh, A. C., & Mudege, N. M. (2009). Do household characteristics matter in schooling decisions in urban Kenya? *Equal Opportunities International, 28*(7), 591–608.

Oelschlaeger, M. (1991). *The idea of wilderness: from prehistory to the age of ecology*. New Haven: Yale University Press.

Ogechi, N. (2005). On lexicalization in Sheng. *Nordic Journal of African Studies, 14*(3): 334–355.

Oketch, M. O. & Mutisya, M. (2012). Education, training and work among youth living in slums of Nairobi, Kenya. In Oketch, M. O. & Ngware, M. W. (Eds.) *Urbanization and education in East Africa*. Nairobi: African Population and Health Research Center, 21–42.

Page, M . E. (1974). The manyema hordes of Tippu tip: A case study in social stratification and the slave trade in Eastern Africa. *The International Journal of African Historical Studies. 7*(1), 69–84.

Pollock, S. (2000). Cosmopolitan and vernacular in history. *Public Culture, 12*(3), 591–625.

Romesburg, R. (2010). The fractal nature of Gary Snyder's *Mountains and Rivers Without End.College Literature 37*(3), 1–25.

Rotman, B. (2013). Techno-sublime: Fractals. Review of Benoit Mandelbrot. *The Fractalist: Memoir of a Scientific Maverick*. London Review of Books, 23–24.

Rudd, P. W. (2017a [Forthcoming]). The AUYL syndrome: A case study of the stigmatized code Sheng. In Nana, O. & Jacob, P. J. (Eds.) *Ufahamu: A Journal of African Studies*.

Rudd, P. W. (2017b [Forthcoming]). Chapter 13: The invisible niche of the AUYL. In Albaugh, E. & de Luna, K. M. (Eds.) *Tracing language movement in Africa*, Oxford: Oxford University Press, 196–209.

Rudd, P. W. (2008). Sheng: The mixed language of Nairobi. *Unpublished Dissertation in Linguistics*. Muncie, IN: Ball State University.

Schneider, M. S. (1995). *A beginner's guide to constructing the universe: The mathematical archetypes of nature, art, and science*. NY: Harper Perennial.

Snyder, G. (1990). *The practice of the wild*. New York: North Point Press.

Tarver, J. D. (1991). Urbanization in Africa since Independence. *African Insight*, 24(1), 75–78.

Thomason, S. G. (2001). *Language contact: An introduction*. Washington, DC: Georgetown University Press.

UN-HABITAT. (2003). *The challenge of slums: Global report on human settlements*. London: Earthscan Publications Ltd.

Vierke, C. (2015). Some remarks on poetic aspects of Sheng. In Nassenstein, N. & Hollington. A. (Eds.) *Youth language practices in Africa and beyond*. Boston: De Gruyter Mouton, 227–256.

Vitale, A. J. (1980). Kisetla: Linguistic and sociolinguistic aspects of a Pidgin Swahili of Kenya. *Anthropological Linguistics, 22*(2), 47–65.

Wald, B. (1981). Swahili pre-Pidgin, Pidgin, and depidginization in Coastal Kenya: A systematic discontinuity in non-first varieties of Swahili. In Highfied, A. & Valdman, R. (Ed.) *Historicity and variation in Creole studies*. Ann Arbor: Karoma Publishers, Inc, 7–26.

# Is the Term "Youth Language" Not a Misnomer?

*Moufoutaou Adjeran* (University of Abomey-Calavi, Benin)
*Gratien G. Atindogbe* (University of Buea, Cameroon)

## 1. Introduction

Adolescents tend to distinguish themselves from adults in speech through specific linguistic productions such as coding, and in sundry mannerisms. Although language practices of youth identities have been studied for long (Ledegen 2001, Trimaille 2004, Bulot 2007), they have recently been established as sociolects in view of their recognition as speech forms that emanate from the emergence of a new economic and social status for the most disadvantaged, and this within the context of an urban progressive ghettoization that either exacerbates or dilutes the consciousness of identity (Kiessling and Mous 2004, Nassenstein and Hollington 2015). The speech of individuals is influenced by their social class; a term such as "youth language" therefore tends to negate the evidence of lexical fluidity or discourse similarities that exist among different generations. Furthermore, since so called youth language practice progressively decreases or enters into decline for the individual youth, it is difficult to predict how the youths will speak once they grow into adulthood and are better integrated into the social situation. This further casts doubts on the validity of the term "youth language."

The goal of this article is to demonstrate that the term "youth language" is problematic once one considers that this purely socio-demographic categorization carries not only a social but also an ethnic coloration in addition to the implied meaning of age-grading. We would argue that the expression "youth language" is also an overstatement, because, on the one hand, belonging to a social group has always implied a certain way of expressing oneself, while, on the other hand the term cannot be generalised to all members of the social group. We retain, instead, the safe enough concept of "youth language practices" while monitoring those features that *appear* to be characteristic of youth speeches at a given point in time. By focusing on a corpus of advertising billboards, viewed both as speeches produced by the marketing companies and as linguistic manifestations of youth practices, we intend to show that the term "youth language" becomes problematic since this purely socio-demographic categorization dissimulates an ethnic social question.

The research focuses on billboards in the Republic of Benin, where they have become more and more an extension of youth sociolect. The questions at the core of the research are:

(i) Does the term "youth language" match the ascribed linguistic standards?
(ii) How and through which variables can youth language be characterised?

Relying on a corpus drawn from some mobile phone network and brewery company billboards in the Republic of Benin, we also aim to demonstrate that the term "youth language" is inadequate. In fact, the thesis that we uphold is that the term "youth language" is quite a misnomer. To develop this argument, this article is divided into five main parts: The first briefly states the methodological approach. The second deals with the difficulty in defining the concept "youth". The third provides an overview of sociolinguistic works on "youth language". The fourth presents some essential traits of "youth languages," while the fifth and last part proposes a discussion subsequent to the analysis.

## 2. Methodology

Urban sociolinguistics addresses the question of billposting from a special angle. Indeed, within the context of this science that deals mostly with the study of "the putting into words of the covariance between the meaningful spatial structure and sociolinguistic stratification"[1] (Bulot, 2002: 94), billposting constitutes one of the diverse epilinguistic speech forms in use that aims at "marking the occupation and the appropriation of urban space by social groups" (Ibid.). It also aims at defining linguistic behaviors and practices and, consequently, discourses on space (Bulot and Veschambre, 2004). In other words, urban sociolinguistics apprehends texts on billboards as speeches around which groups' language practices with regard to the spatial occupation of the city and the definition of space belonging are articulated. We considered our corpus of advertising boards both as speeches produced by commercial companies and as significant indices of the practices of this urban space. "Marking represents a form of identity materialization, both individual and collective."[2] (Bulot and Veschambre, 2004). We first explored the length and breadth of Cotonou, the capital city of Benin Republic. Equipped with a camera, we systematically snapped the signboards that display texts related to the language practices of youngsters. This constitutes the iconographic corpus of the relevant signboards which served as illustrations in this work. Second, we carried out an analysis of the boards from a linguistic perspective with specific emphasis on the study of *figures of speech* (*figures de l'écriture*) as viewed by Millet (1998).

## 3. Defining the Concept of "Youth"

What does it mean to be young? How do speakers perceive the concept *youth*, does that category exist to them? How do they manifest it and recognize it in others? What are its social significance and role, both in the society in which it operates and in the context of the history in which it is registered? It appears that, often blurred or arbitrary and essentially considered from a Western perspective, by speakers as well as by researchers, the *young* category, as Bourdieu (1984) recalls, is not a fact but a construction. It is necessary to define and contextualize it, both from a global point of view – culture, social organization, social stakes, socio-

---

[1] Our translation of « la mise en mots de la covariance entre la structure spatiale signifiante et la stratification sociolinguistique ».
[2] Our translation of « Le marquage représente une forme de la matérialisation de l'identité, à la fois individuelle et collective ».

economic context, living conditions, social practices, etc. – and from a local point of view – the discursive construction of social meanings such as interpersonal positioning, identification or differentiation, etc. Although the temporal limits set on youths are variable, it is commonly accepted in linguistics, as in social science or social psychology (Bourdieu, 1984, Chambers, 1998, Lamizet, 2004) that "youth" is often associated with adolescence and corresponds to a period of transition between childhood and adulthood during which the social subject deprived of responsibility and power is socially "out-of-game" (Bourdieu, 1984: 147, Chambers, 1998, Lamizet, 2004).

Auzanneau (2002), and Auzanneau and Leclère-Messebel (2007), show that, in training centers, youth make sense in roles, relationships, activities and ways of speaking, and this, in a more salient way at some moments of interaction than others. The group also makes sense through the staging of contrasting categories ("old", "young") in speech. In these moments, the speakers render the categories operational and produce differentiations or reconciliations that are interpreted as symbolic marks. On the other hand, Lefort (2013), reporting on new linguistic specificities in certain urban youth, indicates that these features are not shared by all of them and are not socially recognized as identifying characteristics of youth. Moreover, as Auzanneau's (2002, & Fayolle 2004), studies on urban rap in Africa or in France suggest, rappers construct a reproduced and imagined social fabric in which they sometimes positioned themselves as youth, but also in different roles (brother, citizen, enemy of power, etc.). The situations in these studies do not make it possible to predict what happens. Therefore, any categorization with regard to youths can only be evoked by the researcher.

The young category, and thus the language practices of youths, makes sense in the context of the relational spaces within which they evolve in contact with adults. Thus, Auzanneau (2002), Juillard and Leclère-Messebel (2007) report that in the space constituted by a training center, the trainees form a group different from the one constituted by adults, even if the others form a common group sharing space and certain activities. Contextual elements such as those we have just stated can create age-related contrasts that confer a certain social relevance on youth. Likewise, age in research is always associated with social factors whose interdependence cannot yet be measured. Similarly, it remains to study how, at certain times, enunciation makes the age factor more relevant than the other with which it nevertheless coexists: sex, networks or style could be cited as examples. Moreover, the contextual elements are not sufficient to make the concept of youth relevant: this relevance also stems from the activities of the speakers who, in speech, produce social meanings and categories, as shown by Auzanneau, Juillard and Leclère-Messebel.

## 4. "Youth Language" in Sociolinguistics

Since the 1980s, with increasing interest in the origin of migrant populations, studies have been carried out with a variety of objectives, aiming at identifying and questioning the relationship between the multicultural urban environment and the linguistic particularism distinctive of groups of young peers (Billiez, 1985, 1992). Various linguistic mixtures or divergent varieties, among these particularisms inter alia, have been described (Sebba, 1993, Goyvaerts and Kabongo-Mianda, 1988, Kouadio-N'Guessan, 1992). Subsequent to such pioneering works and in their continuity, studies of aspects of youth identity and practices have multiplied since the end of 1990s not only in Europe and in the United States but also in Africa and in the Oceania, and a field of study has emerged. The terms *youth words*, *youth speeches*, *youth languages* or *jugendsprache* (Boyer, 1997, Gadet, 2007, Kiessling et Mous, 2004) owe their existence and standardization to that field of study.

In general, sociolinguistics and linguistics have always been interested in the relationship between age, differences in language use and language change. The age question has been considered in two different ways: on the one hand in terms of age groups, in a strictly chronological way focusing on the language variation and age change in visible time (Labov, 1966, Trudgill 1974, for instance) or, more rarely, in real time (Le Page and Tabouret-Keller, 1985); and on the other in terms of life period that can be associated with status, activities or specific networks (Chambers, 1998, Eckert, 1997). In the perspective of ongoing linguistic changes, some variationists after Labov (1966), sought to refine the relevance of the age variable in the youth period, wishing to find empirical evidence of a linguistic diversity that was not always oriented towards acquisition and control about the normed form of a standard, rather required in adulthood (Trudgill, 1974, Cheshire, 1987).

Similarly, other researchers have raised the question of whether or not young people use the forms (traits, languages, etc.) used by their elders when they become adults (Parkin, 1977, Eckert, 1997). A great number of works have also attempted to determine whether the use of certain traits was specific to youth, if this period of life was a culturally and linguistically marked stage, and if there were specific forms and/or specific registers and therefore not shared by youth. This concern could be grafted on to a limited search, or even interlinguistic limits. The results concur to show in the West that there is a link between the use of non-standard traits and the fact that adolescents participate in a vernacular culture of peer groups (Cheshire, 1982). Under the influence of Labov's (1966) works in Harlem (1972), a number of researchers were thus interested, particularly in the cities, in the grouping of young speakers and their use of language, focusing in particular on identity aspects. Their contributions considered the concerned speakers from the point of view of their groups (Parkin, 1977, Laks, 1977, Eckert, 1989) or as networks likely to promote concomitant linguistic convergence, of which, as in the research, one could not account for the sustainability (Blom and Gumperz, 1972). From the perspective of these ethnographic studies of social networks, age criteria were always considered in relation to other factors such as, the level of education, the social or geographical mobility, the type of relation, etc. According to Milroy (1980, 1992) who worked on speakers' localized networks in the city of Belfast, the age factor was the least relevant in terms of phonic variation and innovative adoption.

A sufficient number of studies have focused on youth pronunciation. Laks (1983) observed a group of five youths of modest origins and poor schooling for a year in a youth house at Villejuif for a year. He regularly spent time with them, sharing leisure activities during which time the tape recorder ran continuously. He conducted interviews at the same time. He studied variable phonological indicators, particularly the fall of the final post-consonantal liquids [l] (*mets la tab,* for "*mets la table*", *i vient,* for "il vient") and [r] (*ferme la fenet* for "ferme la fenêtre").

If this phenomenon was simply related to group belonging, an apparently homogeneous population should not show any variation. Yet, some differences are not confined to the general categorizations and even to analysis in related networks. Laks establishes, through the phonic indicators, the existence of slim differences among group members, which he relates to personal aspirations and social trajectory. Armstrong & Jamin (2002) perform a variationist study at la Courneuve, with youth met in "neighborhood houses". They cross-referenced the usage of two typical traits of the suburbs, the affrication of dental and velar occlusives and the glottalization of r, with four social and demographic variables: sex, social class, ethnic origin and age. These traits appear to be more widely used by youth aged 15-25, even more intensely if they are of modest background and are integrated into ethnic culture, especially for the glottalization of *r* (perceived as related to Arabic). The contexts involved emerge in the process of extension.

Given the stigmatized nature of these traits nowadays, one can speculate on their chance of diffusion beyond the initial group: it depends on their degree of integration into the phonological structure of French (which gives chances to the affrication), and the attraction power of the groups that use it (that are low for the moment). The following features of youth language practices of youth are illustrative of this report.

## 5. Component Traits of Youth Language Practice on Billboards in Benin

Many of the billboards in Benin are not only targeted at youth but also employ what is considered to be "youth language." Component traits of youth language practice are generally more numerous at the level of lexis or vocabulary. While the lexical items are different and seem deployed by the youth, the methods remain the ones of the common language: borrowing, truncating, coding. Some examples from our data (see Appendix) include the following:

- Borrowing:

1. *kif* – "like" (from Arabic) - *kif* can be put in verb form, e.g. *kifer* or *kiffer* (to like)
2. *go* – "girl", "darling" (from African languages)
3. *za* – "food"
4. *kind, lol, now, best, bye, begin, send, day* (from English)

- Truncating: apocope is frequent (example 5), but aphaeresis is also present (6):

5. *biz* – "business"
6. *blèmezon* – "probleme/maison"

- Back slang or putting in reverse, with rapid renewal:

7. meuf – "femme"
8. tof – "photo"
9. soirbon – "bonsoir"
10. jourbon – "bonjour"

As it is typical for vernacular vocabularies mostly with oral transmission, the variability is strong. The formal assessment leads to the observation that, above all, the conventional processes remain active, even if the surface shift changes in a radical way. These features create the effect of something totally new, which is perceived by the speakers. This invites us to observe not only the forms, but also the language practices.

In this context, as the lexical traits of the youth-addressed billboards infer, we have observed, during our fieldwork, some specific manners of speaking amongst the youngsters in Africa and we were thus able to confirm some of the processes taking place in African youth languages, which have been reported in the literature (see e.g. Hurst 2015: 102). However, we did not attach more importance to the *youth* than to other aspects of the speakers' identity, thus presupposing neither the relevance of the *youth* category, nor the existence of specific practices.

It is clear that all those who use the practices known as "youth language" are not always youngsters (Oloruntoba-Oju, 2017). This is precisely what we should understand about the messages of the billboards of mobile phone networks (MTN) and a brewery company (SOBEBRA) which constitute our corpus. The authors of these messages position themselves as youth. Their objective is to capture the attention of the youth who represent a high percentage (55%) of the Beninese population. In short, this practice is for commercial purposes.

In contrast to popular language, "youth language" raises questions that are presented in a paradoxical way: they are given a role to initiate changes, while their ways of speaking are stigmatized, particularly unstable and in constant renewal. One of the most important and more interesting features of language is its ability to change over time. Even if the various tools of linguistic description (grammar, dictionary) appear to fix the language, it is possible, by analogy, to assert that language is alive.

While change in language depends on the individual or a group of individuals, its meaning is determined by the community. The use of the lexemes *blème, zon, kiffer* is for the time considered as an individual variant (word), an exception, and it will remain so until it is accepted in the community (all young French speakers in Benin in this case). According to de Saussure (1972), language is the result of a social convention transmitted by society to individual and on which the latter play only a secondary role. In contrast, speech is the personal use of language (all personal variants possible: style, rhythm, syntax, pronunciation, etc.). Speaking is, in fact, the result of language use, and represents what is produced when one communicates with peers, thus a language practice.

## 6. Discussion

Language practices are generally more open to description. We can recall the definition proposed by Boutet (2002: 459):

> From an empirical point of view, "language practice" refers to the notions of "verbal production", "enunciation", "speech" or even "performance", but it is distinguished from a theoretical point of view by the emphasis put on the notion of "practice": language is part of all social practices, whether production practices, transformation or reproduction. To speak of "practice" is to insist on the praxeological dimension of this activity. Like all social practice, language practices are determined and constrained by the social, and at the same time, they produce effects, they help to transform it. In this perspective, language is not only a reflection of social structures but it is a full component of it. [...] Speaking is not only a representational activity, it is also an act by which one modifies the order of things, and one moves social relations.[3]

Besides the initial postulate (the dimension of language act), we find here an indication of what is empirically a language practice: a set of observable language data in so far as it has social effects. The dimension of "social act" does not, however, seem to be the first object which enables the description of the notion of language practice in its operating character; for Ebel & Fiala (1983: 156), it enables us to:

> [...] describe the processes of the production of meaning as discursive phenomena generated by the relation of social forces in any given situation as well as by factors (grammatical, rhetorical) depending on speech input and of the conditions of the circulation of these speech inputs.[4]

To consider language as agent and social stake is to show how heterogeneous language practices are organized in various forms of verbal interactions (debates, conversations, narrations, publicity) around referents constructed and transformed in the speeches thus produced; these practices are carried out by the social agents, which in exercising language, constitute collective or individual subjects. They are organized according to the force relations that are established in different ways: in producing speech, in bringing into play the rules which regulate the different uses of language, in the constructing and imposing of meanings in speeches, in delivering speeches and achieving the effects produced by this circulation. Indeed,

---

[3] Our translation of « D'un point de vue empirique, "pratique langagière" renvoie aux notions de "production verbale", d'"énonciation", de "parole", voire de "performance", mais ils'en distingue d'un point de vue théorique par l'accent mis sur la notion de "pratique" : le langage fait partie de l'ensemble des pratiques sociales, que ce soit des pratiques de production, de transformation ou de reproduction. Parler de "pratique", c'est donc insister sur la dimension praxéologique de cette activité. Comme toute pratique sociale, les pratiques langagières sont déterminées et contraintes par le social, et en même temps, elles y produisent des effets, elles contribuent à le transformer. Dans cette perspective, le langage n'est pas seulement un reflet des structures sociales mais il en est uncomposant à part entière. [...] Parler n'est pas seulement une activité représentationnelle, c'est aussi un acte par lequel on modifie l'ordre des choses, on fait bouger les relations sociales».

[4] Our translation of « [...] décrire les processus de production du sens comme phénomènes discursifs produits à la fois par des rapports de forces sociauxdans des situations déterminées et par des facteurs (grammaticaux, rhétoriques) relevant de la mise en discours mais aussi des conditions de mise en circulation de ces discours.»

qualifying the linguistic practices of youngsters as "language" will be to over qualify that way of speaking. Youth speeches seem to constitute more of language practices than languages itself. Again it has been observed with regard to youth language in Nigeria, for example, they are "more of sociolinguistic varieties [than] autonomous languages per se" (Oloruntoba-Oju, 2017). This is one of the reasons why "youth language" is an inaccurate name for the caategory.

## 7. Conclusion

Different approaches to youth expressions have culminated in the debate whether "youth languages" exist in the autonomous sense of natural languages or not. This article illustrates the indispensable complementarity that needs to exist between different approaches and viewpoints in the attempt to resolve discursive conflicts. It is important, along the line, to question the categories that one adopts and manipulates as one constantly seeks to refine various observations on and understanding of the facts studied. In the current research, the categories *youth languages* and *youth language practices* conflate but with a tilt towards the latter. The data appropriates what is considered to be "youth language," but this "language" is not known to all youth and it is difficult to say how those youth who do know or speak "it" would behave when they become adults, and are better integrated into the social fabric – just as it is difficult to know if some of the manifestations will continue to occur in common language media such as in the advertising messages mentioned in our corpus. In that regard, the term "youth language" becomes a misnomer.

## References

Armstrong, N., & Jamin, M. (2002). Le francais des banlieues: Uniformity and discontinuity in the French of the Hexagone. In Salhi, K. (Ed.), *French in and out of France: Language policies, intercultural antagonisms and dialogue*. Berne: Peter Lang, 107-136.

Auzanneau, M. (2002). Rap in Libreville, Gabon: An urban sociolinguistic space. In Durand, A. P. (Ed.) *Black, blanc, beur. Rap music and hip hop culture in France and Francophone Africa*. Maryland and Oxford: The Scarecrow Press, 106-123.

Auzanneau, M., & Fayolle, V. (2004). Äußerungsereignis und Sprachvariabilität im senegalesischen Rap. In E. Kimminich (Ed.), *Rap: More than words*. Sonderdruck: Peter Lang, 205-232.

Auzanneau, M., & Leclère-Messebel, M. (2007). *Variabilité linguistique et positionnements dans des interactions de formation. La mise en oeuvre des langues dans l'interaction*. Paris: L'Harmattan.

Billiez, J. (1985). La langue comme marqueur d'identité. *Revue Européenne des Migrations Internationales, 1*(2), 95-105.

Billiez, J. (1992). Le Parler véhiculaire interethnique de groupes d'adolescents en milieu urbain. *Des Villes et des Langues, Actes du Colloque de Dakar*. Paris: Didier Erudition.

Blom, J.-P., & Gumperz, J. J. (1972). Social meaning in linguistic structure: Code switching in Norway. In Gumperz, J J., & Hymes, D. (Eds.), *Directions in sociolinguistics*. New York: Holt, Rinehart and Winston, 407-434.

Bourdieu, P. (1984). *Questions de sociologie*. Paris: Minuit.

Boutet, J. (2002). Pratiques langagières, formations langagières. In Charaudeau, P. ,& Maingueneau, D. (Eds.), *Dictionnaire d'analyse du discour*, Paris: Seuil, 458-460.
Bulot, T. (2002). La double articulation de la spatialité urbaine: "Espaces urbanisés" et "lieux de ville" en sociolinguistique. *Marges linguistiques*, 3, 91-105.
Bulot, T. (2007). Grammaire et parlers (de) jeunes – Quand la langue n'évolue plus... mais continue de changer. *Les Cahiers Pédagogiques*, 453. Accessed 14 Aug. 2017 from https://tinyurl.com/y4u99kop.
Bulot, T., & Veschambre, V. (2004). Sociolinguistiqueurbaine et géographie sociale: Hétérogénéité des langues et des espaces. *Espaces et société aujourd'hui: La géographie sociale dans les sciences sociales et dans l'action.* Rennes. Accessed on 16 Aug. 2017 from http://eso.cnrs.fr/evenements/resumes_10_2004.html.
Chambers, J. K. (1998). *Sociolinguistic theory.* Oxford: Blackwell.
Cheshire J. (1997) *Linguistic variation and social function.* In: Coupland N., Jaworski A. (Eds.) *Sociolinguistics. Modern Linguistics Series.* London: Palgrave. 185-198.
Cheshire, J. (1987). Age and generation specific use of language. In *Sociolinguistics, soziolinguistik: An international handbook of the science of language and society*. Berlin: Mouton de Gruyter, 761-767.
Ebel, M., & Fiala, P. (1983). *Sous le consensus, la xénophobie. Paroles, arguments, contextes (1961-1981).* Lausanne: Institut de Science Politique.
Eckert, P. (1989). *Jocks and Burnouts: Social categories and identity in high school.* New York: Colombia University Teachers College.
Eckert, P. (1997). Age as a sociolinguistic variable. In Coulmas, F. (Ed.) *The handbook of sociolinguistics.* Oxford: Wiley Blackwell Publishing, 151-167.
Gadet, F. (2007). *La variation sociale du français.* Paris: Editions Ophrys.
Goyvaerts, D. L., & Kabongo-Mianda, K. (1998). Indoubil: A Swahili hybrid in Bukavu. *Language in Society, 17*, 231-242.
Hurst, E. (2015). Overview of the tsotsitaals of South Africa; their different base languages and common core lexical items. In Nassenstein, N., Hollington, A. *Youth language practices in Africa and beyond.* Berlin: Mouton de Gruyter, 169-184.
Juillard, C. (1995). *Sociolinguistique urbaine. La vie des langues à Ziguinchor.* Paris: Karthala.
Kiessling, R., & Mous, M. (2004). Urban youth language in Africa. *Anthropological Linguistics, 46*(3), 303-341.
Kouadio, N. J. (1992). Le nouchi abidjanais, naissance d'un argot ou mode linguistique passagère? In Chaudenson, R., & Calvet, L. J. (Eds.), *Des langues et des villes*. Paris: Didier Erudition, 373-384.
Labov, W. (1996). *The social stratification of English in New York City.* Washington: Center for Applied Linguistics.
Laks, B. (1977). Contribution empirique à l'analyse socio-différentielle de la chute des /r/ dans les groupes consonantiques finales. *Langue française, 1*, 109-125.
Laks, B. (1983). Langage et pratiques sociales: étude sociolinguistique d'un groupe d'adolescents. *Actes de la recherche en sciences sociales, 46*, 73-97.
Lamizet, B. (2004). Y a-t-il un "parler jeune"? *Cahiers de Sociolinguistique, 9*, 75-98.
Ledegen, G. (Ed.). (2001). *Les parlers jeunes à la Réunion.* Réunion: Université de la Réunion.
Lefort, J. (2013). Nouvelles pratiques linguistiques dans le Dongxiang: vers une catégorisation d'un parler jeune? *Langage et Société*, 3(141), 71-98.
Le Page, R. B., Tabouret-Keller, A. (1985). *Acts of identity: Creole-based approaches to language and ethnicity.* Cambridge: Cambridge University Press.
Millet, A. (1998). Les figures de l'écriture: Contours, déplacements et métamorphoses des écrits licites. In V. Lucci (Ed.), *Des écrits dans la villes: Sociolinguistique d'écrits urbains: L'exemple de Grenoble.* Paris: L'Harmattan, 57-98.
Milroy, L. (1980). *Language and social networks.* London: Blackwell.
Milroy, L., & Milroy, J. (1992). Social network and social class: Toward an integrated sociolinguistic model. *Language in Society, 21*(1), 1-26.

Nassenstein, N., & Hollington, A. (Eds.). (2015). *Youth language practices in Africa and beyond.* Berlin: Mouton de Gruyter.

Oloruntoba-Oju, T. (2017). Contestant hybridities: African Urban Youth language in Nigerian music and social media. In Hurst-Harosh, E. & Erastus, F. (Eds.) *African Youth Languages: New media, performing arts and sociolinguistic development.* London: Palgrave.

Parkin, D. (1977). Emergent and stabilized multilingualism: Polyethnic peer groups in urban Kenya. In Giles, H. (Ed.), *Language, ethnicity and intergroups relations.* London: Academic Press, 185-210.

Saussure, F. de. (1972 [1916]). *Cours de linguistique générale.* Paris: Payot.

Sebba, M. (1993). *London Jamaican: Language systems in interaction.* London, New York: Longman.

Trimaille, C. (2004). Études des parlers de jeunes urbains en France: Éléments pour un état des lieux. *Cahiers de Sociolinguistique,* 9, 99-132.

Trudgill, P. (1974). *The social differentiation of English in Orwich.* Cambridge: Cambridge University Press.

## Appendix

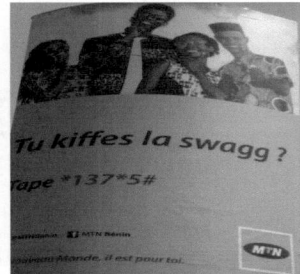

# American English and Urban Nigerian Youth: Investigating the Influence in Tweets from Lagos and Kano

*Matthias Hofmann* (Chemnitz University of Technology)

## 1. Introduction

Few scholars have used Twitter as a resource for the investigation of urban youth English usage in African countries. Even Nigeria has received little attention in this respect, although it is the African country in which most of relative internet users are to be found (Schmied 2015). In the present paper, I hypothesize that Twitter is indeed more than suitable to investigate a very important aspect of youth language, which is its creativeness when used in an online micro-blog. Although its findings may not be generalizable to the whole speech community of urban youth in Nigeria, the paper lays the groundwork for a differentiation between national and sub-national features in such a variety of English.

Traditionally, Hausa English spoken in the North of Nigeria is much more standard than Yoruba English is in the south of the country. Its standard is British English due to its socio-historical development. And yet, some authors have found an increasing influence of American English on several levels of language such as lexis and grammar. They hypothesized that this influence could be due to American broadcasts in Nigeria and contact with American-influenced professionals, which would reduce a differentiation of linguistic features on a sub-national level.

In the next section of this paper, I narrow down the terminology that I find suitable for the present investigation and outline the suitability of Twitter English data for the investigation of youth language and of sub-national features within Nigeria before I introduce the features under investigation that have been mentioned regarding the influence of American English through broadcasts. In Section 3, I describe the corpus compilation using a tool that has been developed by an alumni Master's student at *Chemnitz University of Technology*, briefly summarize data cleaning and annotation procedures, and explain the method of investigation. In section 4, I present and discuss the results of prepositional usage in Northern and Southern Nigeria, contextualize the findings in the Twitter data with those of the Corpus of Global Web-Based English (GloWbE; Davies 2013) for Nigeria and provide additional empirical support for the influence of American English on sub-national orthographic features in Northern and Southern Nigeria. The last section concludes the analysis and provides a brief outlook for further investigations.

## 2. New Sources of Corpus Linguistic Data: Urban Tweets in Nigeria

### 2.1. Relevant Terminologies

Many scholars from various linguistic fields have engaged in investigations of data from the web, using diverse terminologies for situating each of the studies in their respective domains. This development has released a range of terms to choose from when it comes to denote the domain, such as Web as Corpus (WaC), Web for Corpus building (cf. Hundt & Nesselhauf 2007), web linguistics, internet linguistics, etc. I am not concerned with defining concepts and data sources exhaustively in such a way that each of the terms is clear-cut and separable from the next by definitions. Rather, I consider this web/internet-linguistics paper to be of corpus-linguistic nature investigating a highly specialized corpus; a corpus comprised of English tweets from Lagos and Kano, Nigeria.

Other terms have been around to denote the variety of English under investigation, such as Internet English or Cyber(space) English (cf. Heyd & Mair 2014; Mair 2013). Adding to this collection, I am going to introduce a new term – *Twitter English* – that is to loosely include the meanings of the above-mentioned terms as hyponym, but more importantly to capture and reflect the linguistic peculiarities characteristic of tweets that are caused by the limited number of characters allowed per tweet. The difference to English SMS talk, which has a character limitation as well, is obvious in the strong ties or embeddedness of tweet content to or in the internet. That is, unlike the content of conventional text messages, tweets include predominantly pictures links, ads for homepages, and linguistically valuable text in the form of a spread of imminent and short-lived information. Character limitation sets Twitter English also apart from Facebook posts (e.g. cf. Burghardt 2015), although the content and aim of both are more or less similar (cf. Schmied 2012). The variety under investigation in this study can hence be termed Nigerian Twitter English (NiTE).

### 2.2. Twitter and the Youth

Twitter is a rather recent online news and social networking tool that has been implemented in our daily lives in manifold ways. Nevertheless, it has also gained momentum in much more specialized discourses as well. Today, it is not only used for staying up-to-date on opinion-sharing among peers and sometimes even friends or for following a celebrity, but also for communicating with colleagues in academia and with university students in a formalized setting (cf. Schmied 2012). Although Twitter originally started out as an online news service attracting about 30% older adult users three years after its foundation (cf. Lipsman 2009; Kelly 2009), eight years later the service has been established as a standard tool among the youth, as most users world-wide are aged between 18 and 29 (Hutchinson 2017). This may partially be because increasingly more teenager-idol celebrities have joined the social networking service, as a quick-and-dirty look at, for example,

Katy Perry's Twitter profile shows 106 million followers compared to Christina Aguilera's 16.6 million followers – a more experienced celebrity – in November 2017.

Another reason for predominantly young people using twitter may be that 37.6% of tweet content is conversational and 40.1% is "Pointless Babble" (Kelly 2009: 5). Pointless babble refers to "'I am eating a sandwich now' tweets" (Kelly 2009: 4) that I have denoted as imminent and short-lived information above. Mainstream news made only a marginal portion of 3.6% of tweet content in the study (Kelly 2009). I would consider online conversing and babbling an unnatural linguistic behavior in informal styles that requires some acquisition during formative years. Peers of the Twitter founders would still have to get used to the service in terms of substituting natural face-to-face situations in which they learned to converse and babble with such anonymous online situations.

In summary, the language used in Twitter is connected speech by predominantly young people. Although it is written, I consider the language used in tweets likely to be more similar to written-to-be-spoken text types than to formal writing, considering the prominent topics of the majority of tweets. They further have a limited character number, which reduces sentence-length induced complexity of the language.

## 2.3. Twitter and Nigeria

Although Africa's countries do not first come into mind when thinking about the internet and from where its users contribute to it, some of them are home to quite many internet users. As Schmied for example points out, Nigeria's large population causes the absolute number of Nigerian internet users to be higher than that in the United Kingdom and with 70 million users to be highest on the African continent (2015: 190). Nigerian scholars have valued and continue to value the internet as a vital means of communication in Nigeria by contributing to the international academic discussion of digital communication (e.g. cf. Taiwo 2010) and by investigating language and content of discourse data available online (e.g. cf. Opeibi 2011; Sousa & Ivanova 2012). While demographics for Nigerian Twitter usage are scarcely available, Schmied maintains that Twitter is as much an integral part of Nigerian internet usage as Facebook, blogs and other internet fora (2015: 189). As such, Twitter is a rich source of collecting Nigerian English data. Complaints about internet reliability, affordability, and power failures in Nigeria – which by no means reduces the popularity of electronic media – may skew the use of Twitter and other services across the country towards the urban areas. For this reason, I have narrowed the data collection site down to include two of such urban areas, Lagos and Kano. A differentiation into Hausa, Igbo, and Yoruba English (cf. Jowitt 1991) is, however, not possible with this means of data collection, as social meta data is scarcely filled out reliably in Twitter's user profiles (e.g. cf. Bamman et al. 2014; Nguyen et al. 2013). Conjecture suggests, however, that most of the tweets from Lagos are from Yoruba English speakers, representing the fairly Christian south of the country, and that the majority of tweets from Kano is from Hausa

English speakers, representing the principally Muslim north of the country. It would have been desirable to include Igbo English as well, but the number of tweets from Enugu provided by TwitCollect (see below) was just too small to compile a corpus.

## 2.4. American English Influence and the Role of English in Nigeria

As in other former British colonies, English is a high function foreign language with about 4 - 20 % speakers/users in Nigeria (Jowitt 1995). Since 1998, English is the medium of instruction starting grade four in Primary School (Gut 2008). Today, especially among younger speakers, English usage is on the rise in all contexts of daily life except at home, so that its purely elite status (Jowitt 1995) and a somewhat exclusive use of Nigerian Pidgin for domestic functions (Osisanwo 2015) become blurred. More and more speakers of English value the former language of colonialism highly as a potential for material and social gain, a symbol of modernization, and a means of success and mobility (Gut 2008).

The structure of Nigerian English has been well described on all levels of language, e.g. phonology (e.g. Adedeji 2015; Gut 2008), morphosyntax, and lexis (e.g. Alo & Mesthrie 2008), and as a world English variety more generally (e.g. Mesthrie & Bhatt 2008; Schmied 1995; Schneider 2007). Approximately a decade ago, Alo & Mesthrie (2008: 338)[1] have pointed out that Nigerian English becomes increasingly more influenced by American English, allegedly due to American broadcasts (but cf. Stuart-Smith et al. 2013 on the influence of broadcasting media on varieties), music, cinema and contact with American-trained professionals (also cf. Gut 2008: 38, 40; Jowitt 1991). This influence is apparent on several levels of language, including pronunciation, idioms, and lexis. One example of American English influence on Nigerian English is the use of "[…] business terms like *Monday through Friday*" (Alo & Mesthrie 2008: 338), rather than British English *Monday to Friday*. Another example is the use of "[…] verb sub-categorizations like *to protest* + [direct object], rather than *to protest against* (Alo & Mesthrie 2008: 338).

In addition, I am concerned with the analysis of American English prepositions as used for example in phrasal verbs or fixed phrases/idioms. The motivation behind the investigation of prepositions in addition to lexical features is that the latter is usually not as good an indicator of systemic changes in the English language compared to grammatical or phonetic features. Lexical features are quite salient to users of a language, which becomes apparent, for example, in the fast adoption of slang terms or buzzwords among younger groups of people. Likewise, these same terms disappear as fast. None of them really makes it into the register[2] of a speech community. Hence, lexical items alone are not necessarily good features for defining a variety or the influence of another variety. The grammatical features under

---

[1] Please note that the 2008 version is an unaltered reprint of the 2004 version.
[2] I am using the term register in a narrow sense as defined and used by Trudgill (1974, 1999) and Wardaugh (1986).

investigation in the Nigerian English Twitter data set are randomly selected and outlined in Table 1:.

| Feature No. | British English | American English |
|---|---|---|
| 1 | fill in a form | fill out a form |
| 2 | [*Weekday] to [*Weekday] | [*Weekday] through/thru [*Weekday] |
| 3 | get on (with somebody) | get along (with somebody) |
| 4 | at the weekend | on the weekend |
| 5 | haven't had anything for years | haven't had anything in years |
| 6 | in [a street name] | on [a street name] |
| 7 | to protest against | to protest [+ direct object] (DO) |

Table 1: Tabular overview of randomly selected British English and American English prepositions.

Features 1 to 4 are standard examples of British versus American prepositional usage that are cited frequently for illustration and indicate prepositional use in phrasal verbs (*fill in/fill out, get on/get along*), business terms (e.g. *Monday to Friday/Monday through Friday*), and fixed phrases (*at the weekend/on the weekend*). For feature 4, however, it might be the case that the American English variant of the prepositional usage is not derived from American English influence, but cognitive processes of creolization. On its own, it thus may not allow for measuring a direct influence of American English, but as a complement to the other features, it may do so if its distributional patterns are similar to those of the other features. Additionally, the potential origin through processes of creolization of this prepositional usage in NiTE is only confounding, if its frequencies of occurrence outnumber those of the other features by far. Features 5 to 6 are prepositions that do not fall into the above-mentioned categorization. Feature 5 can be generalized as use of preposition *in* in a certain grammatical environment, namely after a negative construction (*have not had*), feature 6 as preposition used before street names, and feature 7 as prepositional verb. The latter three features are certainly used less often when outlining differences between the two native varieties of English in educational settings.

I assume that NiTE neither exclusively uses prepositions from British nor from American English. Rather, it is likely to use prepositions from both, which can also be viewed as empirical support for the question of whether American English influences Nigerian English. If this was not the case, none of the American English prepositions should be in use by Nigerians. However, a parallel use should be complemented by identifying differences in frequency of occurrence that would signal a mix of prepositions from both native varieties versus those that would signal a dominance of one of the two. The literature suggests that an increasing influence of American English should be visible, which I interpret to be represented by a mixed use of prepositions denoting the same concept, rather than a dominance of American English prepositions. Whether a mixed use of prepositions from British and American English differs between the predominantly Muslim north and the rather Christian south of the country remains to be seen in the analysis of the Twitter data.

## 3. Methodology

### 3.1. Corpus Compilation

Using *TwitCollect* (Albrecht & Schmied 2015), a tool developed by an alumni Master's student of *Chemnitz University of Technology* based on *Twython* (by Schettler n.y.), tweets from Lagos and Kano were collected during October and November 2017. The tool uses Twitter's API to download tweets from a certain area, without capturing sociolinguistic meta-information about the authors of the tweets and saves them into a .csv-file by default. Twitter limits the number of tweets downloadable in this fashion to approximately 1% of all tweets (Murthy et al. 2016: 34), yielding an average amount of approximately 1 Megabyte-sized csv-files per 24 hours. This size roughly corresponds to 1000 tweets per file. In terms of corpus size, the Kano sub-corpus totals 849,591 words and the Lagos sub-corpus totals 1,920,578 words. Both corpora contain an amount of not more than two million words, so that the frequency of occurrence will be shown in units of per million words (pmw).

### 3.2. Data Cleaning and Corpus Annotation

Although software is available, "boilerplate" removal (cf. Bernardini et al. 2006: 20; Kilgarriff 2007) from corpus data off the web is typically offered for websites. An example of a discontinued tool as part of a PhD project is *jusText* (Pomikálek 2014), which is designed to remove html code, including navigation bars, headers, and footers, as well as duplicate information from online documents. Such tools are unsuitable to use for tweets, because their content is relatively free of html code, except for hyperlinks. To preserve corpus linguistic data in tweets, hashtag-topics (#category) and addressee-tags (@twitteruser) should be removed in addition to links. However, some tweets contain extremely few characters so that such a removal of text would render the content unintelligible (Kilgarriff 2007). I cleaned the corpus data manually in *MS Excel* to maintain boilerplate when crucial to interpret the semantic meaning of the tweets' content.

Tokenization, POS annotation and lemmatization of the Twitter corpus posed many problems, even after data cleaning. Tweets typically contain relatively great shares of non-standard spelling and a high density of neologisms and acronyms. For this reason, Bernardini et al. (2006: 23) suggest that "POS taggers should be re-trained on Web data". Their suggestion is, however, based on the assumption that the web itself serves as a corpus that needs to be annotated, i.e. a billions-of-words corpus (WaCky corpus). The Twitter corpus is too small to allow for general patterns of investigation that would require POS tagging and the usage of the prepositions outlined in Table 1 can be measured in terms of frequency without grammatical categorization of the lexical items in the corpus.

### 3.3. Method of Investigation

I used *Antconc* (Anthony 2014), Version 3.4.4, for the analysis of prepositional usage and spelling patterns in NiTE-Lagos and -Kano, GloWbE's online search interface (Davies 2013), and R version 3.3.4 for the statistical assessment of the results. Each preposition and orthographic realization was searched for using lemmata of the concordances, e.g. *fill in, filled in, filling in, fills in* are all categorized as instances of *fill in*. The search terms included wild cards (e.g. asterisks) and POS tags as necessary. The search terms for feature 5 in Table 1, for example, included up to four slots for words between the negative and the prepositional phrase *in/for years*: *[v\*] [xx\*] [v\*] \* \* \* \* in years*. The first POS-tag consisting of the small letter *v* plus the asterisk refers to all auxiliary verbs in the corpus, the second tag to negative constructions, and the third tag to auxiliary verbs again. The search for negative constructions followed by *in years* started with one word after the negative and continued with up to four words after the negative. I stopped at a maximum of four because the frequencies of occurrence became too small to include instances with more than four words after the negative construction. The frequencies of occurrence are shown in units of per million words in the respective tables. All the corpus searches were done using a stoplist, which predominantly included single-letter morphemes, abbreviating words like *okay* (short: *k*).

For the statistical assessment, I drew on a chi-squared goodness-of-fit test for the comparison of British versus American English origin of prepositions and spellings. The probability-of-error values $p$ are calculated for a one-tailed test, as the alternative hypothesis is directional: The frequency of occurrence of the British English preposition is higher than that of the American English preposition. For the comparison of tweet content from Lagos versus Kano in NiTE, I applied a chi-squared test for independence with non-directional alternative hypotheses. That is, no direction of the difference between the frequencies of occurrence is provided; they are simply hypothesized to differ between the British and American variants.

The assumptions of a chi-squared test are, first, that all observations are independent of one another, second, that 80 % of the expected frequencies are greater than or equal to five, and third, that all expected frequencies are greater than one (cf. Gries 2013: 166). Although the first assumption is difficult to assure for every single tweet, I made sure that each of the prepositions and spelling variants under statistical assessment was taken from a different tweet. In addition, tweets occurring more than once in NiTE were deleted. Prepositions and spelling variants with expected frequencies smaller than five were disregarded in the analyses and marked with *not tested* in the respective tables.

## 4. Analysis and Discussion

### 4.1. British and American Prepositions in Northern and Southern Nigeria

The results for the investigation of preposition usage patterns in NiTE from Lagos are summarized in Table 2.

| Feature No. | Variants | Occ. of British prep. | Occ. of American prep. |
|---|---|---|---|
| 1 | *fill in : fill out* | 3.64 | 0.52 |
| 2 | [*day] *to* : *through/thru* [*day] | 3.12 | 0 |
| 3 | *get on (with) : get along (with)* | 0 | 0 |
| 4 | *at the weekend : on the weekend* | 0 | 0.52 |
| 5 | [negative] + *for years* : [negative] + *in years* | 0.52 | 1.04 |
| 6 | *in : on* [street names] | 1.04 | 8.33 |
| 7 | *to protest against : to protest* [+ DO] | 3.64 | 18.22 |

Table 2: Frequencies (pmw) of British versus American English prepositional occurrence in the Lagos sub-corpus.

A quick look at the numbers shows that for the first six features investigated the frequencies of occurrence are quite low, suggesting that the corpus is too small despite approximately 2 million words. In more detail, we can discard features 3 and 4. Feature 3 does not occur in the corpus at all and feature 4 does virtually not occur with 0.5 occurrences of the American English variant per million words, respectively. Likewise, the occurrences of feature 5 are negligible, and yet this feature clearly shows a slight tendency towards the American English version of this preposition. Regarding the remaining features, a similarly minor trend towards British English phrasal verbs (feature 1) and business terms (feature 2) is visible and contrasted starkly by a probably significant influence of the American English prepositional usage of *on* before street names and American English *protest* followed by the direct object. Although I used the term significant here, I refrain from implying statistical significance. The amount and distribution of the data violate the assumption of the chi-squared test that the observed frequencies are larger than five and that none of them equals zero (cf. Gries 2013).

A valid interpretation seems to be that both native varieties influence Southern NiTE or have left traces in it. That is, a claim of exclusive use of prepositions from British or American English would be much too strong, except maybe for the British English business term *Monday to Friday*. Although too marginal to generalize, the American English business term *Monday through Friday* is never used in tweets of the Lagos component in Nigerian Twitter Corpus. The same is, however, true for British English *at the weekend*, so that such an exclusive use of a feature is balanced out across all features considered.

| Feature No. | Variants | Occ. of British prep. | Occ. of American prep. |
|---|---|---|---|
| 1 | fill in : fill out | 7.06 | 0 |
| 2 | [*day]to : through/thru [*day] | 1.18 | 0 |
| 3 | get on (with) : get along (with) | 1.18 | 0 |
| 4 | at the weekend : on the weekend | 1.18 | 0 |
| 5 | [negative] + for years : [negative] + in years | 0 | 0 |
| 6 | in : on [street names] | 0 | 3.53 |
| 7 | to protest against : to protest [+ DO] | 0 | 4.71 |

Table 3: Frequencies (pmw) of British versus American English prepositional occurrence in the Kano sub-corpus.

Table 3 provides an overview for the investigation of preposition usage patterns in the Kano component of NiTE. Although the Kano sub-corpus is approximately only half the size of the Lagos component, the frequencies of occurrence are almost twice as high as those of the Lagos sub-corpus. It is also apparent that the use of British English prepositions is almost exclusive, which is not surprising since Hausa English has always been more standard since the colonial times. The exception to this pattern is found in features 6 and 7.

In more detail, however, we can discard features 2 to 5, because the British English variants per feature occur at most only once and the American English ones occur never, i.e. no American English influence in prepositional choices. The same lack of influence is visible in feature 1, which additionally suggests an exclusive usage of the British variant. This trend is starkly contrasted by features' 6 and 7 distribution, which suggests an exclusive usage of the American English preposition before street names and the direct object after the verb *protest*. As I mentioned above for whether the differences between the features and the sub-corpora are statistically significant, the assumptions of a chi-square test are not met.

For the predominantly Muslim inhabitants of Northern Nigeria, it seems to be equally valid to claim that both native varieties have influenced and continue to influence Northern NiTE. However, unlike in the Southern part of the country, each of the prepositions seems to be in exclusive use. In case of feature 1, only the British English preposition in the phrasal verb is in the sub-corpus (the same is true for features 2 - 4 disregarded above). In contrast, features 6 and 7 show an exclusive use of the American English prepositions.

The similarity between the Lagos and the Kano sub-corpora is that in the phrasal verb, represented by feature 1, the British preposition is used and that feature 6 and 7 represent an American English origin. This may suggest that, for example, in NiTE, streets are conceptualized in the American way, i.e. as a surface on which objects are located, whereas phrasal verbs might be dominantly British. Having stated that, it must be kept in mind that the reported frequencies of occurrence are quite low; too low to draw any firm conclusions. Additionally, an investigation of a reference corpus might illuminate this issue further. At least it might clarify whether this is a data-specific (or genre-specific) finding or holds true beyond Twitter as well.

In summary, it is important to stress that both native varieties influence the two sub-corpora of NiTE in a similar way, such that feature 1 (and to some degree feature 2) use British prepositions and features 6 and 7 use American prepositions or lack the preposition. The question that may arise from this observation is whether there is a general tendency of young Nigerians to use American English in written language more often or exclusively in only certain domains.

### 4.2. Using GloWbE as a Reference for Prepositional Usage in Nigerian English

Although the texts used in GloWbE (Davies 2013) belong to a similar genre as the ones in the Twitter corpus, the age of their authors remains unknown. Likewise, although GloWbE allows us to track difference in frequencies of usage between web-based texts from different countries, it does not allow us to differentiate Northern Nigerian usage patterns from Southern Nigerian usage patterns. GloWbE can, however, serve as a reference corpus when it comes to answering the question of whether the British English prepositions under investigation in this paper are exclusively used or not and of how often they occur. The GloWbE results might further help – at least in part – to decide whether the findings in the Twitter corpus are data-specific or not.

| Feature No. | Variants | Occ. of British prep. | Occ. of American prep. |
|---|---|---|---|
| 1 | *fill in* : *fill out* | 5.60 | 2.39 |
| 2 | [*day]*to* : *through/thru* [*day] | 7.10 | 0.33 |
| 3 | *get on (with)* : *get along (with)* | 3.31 | 4.20 |
| 4 | *at the weekend* : *on the weekend* | 7.62 | 1.22 |
| 5 | [negative] + *for years* : [negative] + *in years* | 0.45 | 0.73 |
| 6 | *in* : *on* [street names] | 0.82 | 2.06 |
| 7 | *to protest against* : *to protest* [+ DO] | 1.92 | 0.12 |

Table 4: Frequencies (pmw) of British versus American English prepositional occurrence in the Nigerian sub-corpus of GloWbE.

Most apparently, the numbers are similar in size to the ones reported earlier for the Twitter corpus, i.e. none exceeds 10 occurrences per million words. Likewise, it is apparent that British and American English prepositions are mixed in the variety of Nigerian English represented by the 42.6 million words component of GloWbE, i.e. none of the two prepositional usages is exclusive.

When we compare the results from GloWbE with those from the Lagos component of the NiTE corpus, we find that features 1 and 2 are similarly distributed. Both features show a clear preference for the British English preposition. The same clear preference can be found for features 5 and 6, although in these cases the American English alternative is preferred. For features 3, 4, and 7, the results in the Lagos sub-corpus of the NiTE corpus are contrary to those in the Nigerian sub-corpus of GloWbE. While feature 3 never occurs in the Lagos component, it shows a tendency towards usage of the American English preposition in the Nigerian component of GloWbE. Regarding feature 4, a strong preference for the British English usage can be seen in Table 4, contradicting a slight preference for the American English usage in Table 2. The same preference is true for feature 7. It must, however, be emphasized that the frequency of occurrence of feature 7 in the Lagos component of the NiTE corpus is extremely high when compared to the frequency of occurrence in the Nigerian component of GloWbE: 3.64 pmw BrE: 18.22 pmw AmE in Lagos versus 1.92 pmw BrE: 0.12 pmw AmE in GloWbE's Nigerian English. It seems, that this extremely high value in Lagos' NiTE is data-specific, i.e. due to the nature of the content shared in Twitter.

In comparison to the variety of English used in Tweets from Nigeria's north, we cannot corroborate the exclusive usage pattern suggested by the results shown in Table 3. The frequencies of occurrence are slightly higher in number in the Nigerian sub-corpus of GloWbE when compared to the Kano component of the NiTE corpus. The preference for the British English preposition is similar for features 1, 2, and 4, and the preference for the American English preposition is similar for feature 6 in both sub-corpora. The findings between both varieties are contrary for features 3 and 7 with a small preference for the British English preposition in Kano's NiTE in case of the former, and with a small preference for the American English preposition in Kano's NiTE in the latter.

Table 5 shows that, except for feature 5, these preferences for British English or American English prepositional usage patterns are significantly different from the expected frequencies of occurrence – according to a chi-squared goodness-of-fit test. In case of features 1, 2, 4, and 7 the observed frequencies of British English prepositions are significantly higher than the expected frequencies, and in case of features 3 and 6 the observed frequencies of American English prepositions are significantly higher than the expected frequencies. The insignificance of the difference between the British and the American variant in feature 5 means that both variants occur as often as mathematically expected.

| Feature No. | Variants | $\chi^2$ | $p_{\text{one-tailed}}$-value |
|---|---|---|---|
| 1 | *fill in : fill out* | 55.04 | <0.001 |
| 2 | [*day]*to : through/thru* [*day] | 263.47 | <0.001 |
| 3 | *get on (with) : get along (with)* | 4.51 | 0.017 |
| 4 | *at the weekend : on the weekend* | 197.69 | <0.001 |
| 5 | [negative] + *for years* : [negative] + *in years* | 2.88 | (0.050) |
| 6 | *in : on* [street names] | 22.84 | <0.001 |
| 7 | *to protest against : to protest* [+ DO] | 68.15 | <0.001 |

Table 5: Chi-squared and probability-of-error values for the difference between British English and American English *prepositional usage* in the Nigerian sub-corpus of GloWbE.

Despite the prevalence of using the British prepositions significantly more often in the Nigerian component of GloWbE, it becomes obvious that American English prepositions are used in Nigerian web-based English and that the American variants *get along (with)* and *on* + [street name] even occur statistically significantly more often.

In general, it seems fair to conclude that both the British and the American variants are used in Nigerian Web-Based English and that they are a minority variant in all three sub-corpora. Particularly, feature 5 shows very small frequencies of occurrence with no more than 1.04 occurrences per million words maximum. It is further fair to conclude that the preference for the usage of a certain preposition is a function of region and genre. As mentioned in section 2.2, the content of tweets is predominantly babble of the sort "I am eating a sandwich now". In other words, most tweets are intended to inform the online community or imagined target audience about what one is up to – be it for purely informative reasons or for inviting other people to join in or to share their opinion. This genre-specificity thus helps to explain the high numbers of occurrence of the verb *protest* in the Twitter data from Lagos (feature 7), as it makes Twitter the perfect means to invite a potentially large number of random people to join the protests or to raise an awareness of the fact that people are protesting something publicly (cf. Schmied & Opeibi 2017). At the same time, it may be the limited amount of 140/280 characters per tweet that gives rise to the number of frequencies of occurrence of *protest* + [direct object], omitting the preposition *against*. In addition to these features that define the Twitter genre, it may be region that causes the comparatively small number of occurrences of *protest* + [direct object] in the traditionally more standard British English north of Nigeria, represented by NiTE.

Having stated that, it must be kept in mind that the frequencies of occurrence for all features in GloWbE are not representing the prepositional usage patterns of the country's youth. They rather represent the usage patterns of the country's businesses' and companies' websites. 18- to 25-year olds usually do not have websites or represent a minority in businesses and companies. I consider these usage patterns in NiTE – of all features in general and of features 5 and 7 in particular – contrasted by those in GloWbE are unlikely to be a function of age, however, allowing for extrapolation from the GloWbE data.

## 4.3. British and American Orthography in Northern and Southern Nigeria

A level of language that is much more salient than prepositions is orthography (cf. section 2.4). Bearing in mind that one must have had at least some education to set up an (English) Twitter account and use it on a regular basis, most young educated Nigerians are well aware that some words have a British English spelling and others an American English one. An example of competing native spelling influences is seen in lemmata ending in British English *–our* versus American English *–or*.

| Lemma | British orthography | American orthography |
|---|---|---|
| fav[o/ou]r | 65.08 | 32.28 |
| hon[o/ou]r | 36.97 | 23.95 |
| col[o/ou]r | 34.89 | 26.55 |
| lab[o/ou]r | 25.51 | 5.73 |
| neighb[o/ou]r | 13.54 | 14.58 |
| behavi[o/ou]r | 12.50 | 20.31 |
| flav[o/ou]r | 9.89 | 2.60 |

Table 6: Frequencies of occurrence (pmw) of the most frequent lemmata with word-final British English *–our* and American English *–or* in the Lagos sub-corpus of NiTE.

The per-million-word frequencies of occurrence of the most frequent lemmata in the Lagos component of NiTE are shown in Table 6. These occurrences are on average multiple times higher than the occurrences of the prepositions outlined in the previous section. A closer look at Lagos sub-corpus of NiTE shows that a general trend of a dominating British English spelling is not true for each individual lemma (cf. Table 6), as expected from the results in the previous section. Particularly the lemma *behavior* and to some degree the lemma *neighbor* show a higher frequency of occurrence in American English orthography than in the British one.

In more general terms, Table 6 is striking because it provides clear evidence against the notion of exclusive use of either an American English variant or a British English one. This clarity could not be shown in Table 2, particularly for feature 2, which indicated an exclusive use of the British preposition *to* in NiTE from Lagos. As such, Table 6 provides the empirical support for a parallel use of the British and American variants in the Lagos component of NiTE that to this point could only be shown for the Nigerian component of GloWbE – although this support is restricted to orthography.

| Lemmata | $\chi^2$ | $p_{\text{one-tailed}}$-value |
|---|---|---|
| favor : favour | 21.12 | <0.001 |
| honor : honour | 5.38 | 0.010 |
| color : colour | 2.17 | (0.070) |
| labor : labour | 24.07 | <0.001 |
| neighbor : neighbor | 0.07 | (0.392) |
| behavior : behavior | 3.57 | 0.029 |
| flavor : flavor | 8.17 | 0.002 |

Table 7: Chi-squared and probability-of-error values for the difference between word-final British English *–our* and American English *–or* in the Lagos sub-corpus of NiTE.

Table 7 shows the chi-squared goodness-of-fit test results for the spelling of the lemmata shown in the previous table. Except for the spelling variants of *color/colour* and *neighbor/neighbour*, the frequency distributions of the two spellings deviate significantly from the expected ones. That is, British *favour, honour, labour,* and *flavour* occur significantly more often than expected, and American *behavior* occurs significantly more often than expected.

| Lemma | British orthography | American orthography |
|---|---|---|
| fav[o/ou]r | 60.03 | 51.79 |
| hon[o/ou]r | 40.02 | 32.96 |
| neighb[o/ou]r | 27.07 | 10.59 |
| lab[o/ou]r | 25.89 | 3.53 |
| flav[o/ou]r | 24.72 | 0 |
| col[o/ou]r | 22.36 | 27.07 |
| behavi[o/ou]r | 4.71 | 16.48 |

Table 8: Frequencies of occurrence (pmw) of the most frequent lemmata with word-final British English *–our* and American English *–or* in the Kano sub-corpus of NiTE.

In case of the traditionally standard British English dominance in Kano, we can observe a similar trend as mentioned above for Southern Nigerian Yoruba English used in Twitter (cf. Table 8). Most of the lemmata are spelled more often in a British English manner than in an American English manner, except for the lemma *color* and the lemma *behavior*.

The traditional status of Hausa English in the North of Nigeria is maintained through the virtual absence of the lemma *labor* and the absence of the lemma *flavor*. This finding stands in interesting opposition to the usage of prepositions shown in section 4, as the use of British orthography is not exclusive in most of the cases.

| Lemmata | $\chi^2$ | $p_{\text{one-tailed}}$-value |
|---|---|---|
| favor : favour | 0.52 | (0.236) |
| honor : honour | 0.58 | (0.223) |
| neighbor : neighbor | 6.13 | 0.007 |
| labor : labour | 14.44 | <0.001 |
| flavor : flavor | | not tested |
| color : colour | 0.38 | (0.269) |
| behavior : behavior | 5.56 | 0.009 |

Table 9: Chi-squared and probability-of-error values for the difference between word-final British English *–our* and American English *–or* in the Kano sub-corpus of NiTE.

The first four features in Table 3 were showing the use of British prepositions exclusively. It is also worth mentioning that the lemmata *favor* and *honor* are much more frequent in their American spelling than in the comparatively innovative South of the country. Likewise, the lemma *color* is used more frequently in its American English orthography. Another interesting finding is that the lemma *behavior* is used more often in the American English spelling in both sub-corpora of NiTE. This may suggest a lexical effect, meaning that American orthography is only dominant in this lexical item.

Startlingly, only two lemmata occur significantly more often in their British orthography than expected (*neighbour* and *labour*). The same is true for *flavour* as it only occurs in its British spelling in NiTE-Kano. The only other significant deviation from its expected frequency is the observed frequency of the lemma *behavior*, which – in addition to the fact that the frequencies for *favor, honor*, and *color* are not significantly different from the expected frequencies – is surprising for the traditional character of the northern Nigerian variety of English.

| Lemmata | $\chi^2$ | $p_{two\text{-}tailed}$-value | $\phi$ |
|---|---|---|---|
| favor : favour | 4.19 | 0.041 | 0.12 |
| honor : honour | 0.36 | (0.551) | 0.04 |
| color : colour | 1.23 | (0.268) | 0.09 |
| lab[o/ou]r | 0.16 | (0.692) | 0.04 |
| neighb[o/ou]r | 3.69 | (0.055) | 0.21 |
| behavi[o/ou]r | 0.94 | (0.333) | 0.11 |
| flav[o/ou]r | | | not tested |

Table 10: Chi-squared, probability of error, and effect size for the difference between the Lagos and Kano sub-corpora of NiTE regarding word-final British English *–our* and American English *–or*.

As outlined in section 3.3, I use a chi-squared test for independence and $\phi$ as effect size, to statistically asses the differences in frequencies of occurrences between British and American orthography shown in Table 6 and in Table 8. The results in Table 10 indicate that the frequencies of occurrences in NiTE-Lagos and NiTE-Kano do not correlate significantly with one another, except for lemma *favor/favour*. As stated by a chi-squared test for independence, this correlation is significant ($\chi^2 = 4.19$; $df = 1$; $p_{two\text{-}tailed} = 0.041$). However, the effect size is small, suggesting that, although the correlation is not random, it is not strong as well ($\phi = 0.12$).

In general, it is apparent that orthography does not vary as a function of region. The only exception to the rule seems to show a significant deviation, because of the variable level combination lemma *favor* and NiTE sub-corpus Kano, which is more often observed than expected (squared residual of 1.94). The contribution of this variable level combination is graphically represented in Figure 1, in which the extents of the rectangles relate to the difference in observed and expected frequencies. The figure visualizes that *favor* is strongly preferred in Kano, but not preferred in Lagos. The opposite kind of preference is found for *favour*.

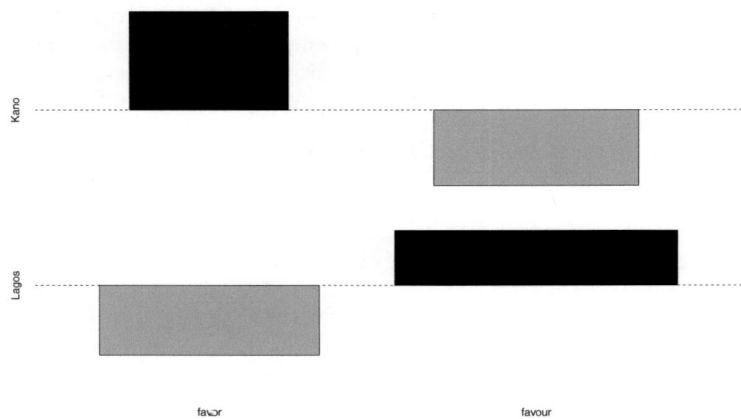

Figure 1: Association plot for research site and the orthographic realization of the lemma *favor/favour*.

Orthography thus provides good support for the increasing influence of American English, as stated by Alo & Mesthrie (2008), because it shows that both variants – the British and the American English one – exist alongside one another. This may reflect an ever-increasing influence of American English through increasing frequencies of occurrence that eventually may surpass the frequencies of British English spelling variants in two to four generations time.

Whether this influence is caused by or "due to American broadcasts (*CNN* and *Voice of America*)" (Alo & Mesthrie 2008: 338) remains highly doubtful. As Foulkes & Docherty (2000), for example, have shown in an L1-English setting, television rather serves as a catalyst instead of introducing new features, so that speakers redeploy the linguistic resources already available to them. Their speech may shift towards the linguistic features of imagined socially attractive speakers (cf. Bell's 1991 Audience Design). At least, they may change their attitudes towards existing features through broadcasts (cf. Stuart-Smith 2007) or become more aware of standard forms (cf. Milroy & Milroy 1985). In case of an L2-English setting as in Nigeria, it seems that the linguistic forms speakers are aware of (spelling/orthography) show higher American English variants than those speakers are less aware of (prepositional usage) – at the very least in *Twitter English*. This could thus mean, that the American English variants have gained value in social attractiveness and that broadcasts like *CNN* have made young and educated Nigerians from Lagos more aware of orthographical features. Naturally, this interpretation only holds true, if the same processes apply for L2-English speakers as those mentioned above for L1-English speakers.

## 5. Conclusion

The investigation of tweets from young Hausa English speakers in Northern Nigeria and from young Yoruba English speakers in Southern Nigerian has shown that, most importantly, the traditional status of Hausa English is still maintained by the young generation of 18- to 25-year olds. Most of the prepositions they use in NiTE-Kano are of British English origin. The young generation of Yoruba English speakers behaves somewhat opposite to the former speakers regarding the investigated prepositions. Not surprisingly, they tend to use the American prepositions more often, which is particularly striking for feature 7. The patterns that both varieties of NiTE show are not an artifact of the Twitter data or their genre-specificity, as they are corroborated by the web-based English in the Nigerian component of GloWbE for the country. Most of the differences found in GloWbE are statistically significant, which does, however, not mean, that the use of a British or an American preposition is exclusive. Both variants are used alongside one another in Nigeria.

On a much more salient level of language – orthography – the findings are a little bit different. In spelling words, the young standard British English favoring Northerners show higher frequencies of occurrences for some American English orthographic realizations than the young, linguistically more liberal, Southerners in Nigeria. This difference is, however, not statistically significant, except for the lemma *favor/favour*.

These findings may suggest that among the upcoming generation, much of the traditional linguistic differences on a sub-national level can be considered to play a continuing role in the future of the country's online discourse. It may be the case that some Hausa speakers change their spell checker from British English to American English on their mobile phones to use American English spelling, but on a structural level, their British English standard is still measurable.

Twitter appears to be a rich and promising source of urban youth speech in African countries such as Nigeria, although the tools to collect data should attempt to collect as much sociolinguistic meta-information about the tweeters as possible. Even if most Nigerians using Twitter will not provide their socio-demographic background, the vast number of collectable tweets will help to differentiate tweeters from one another. Additionally, it may even allow for deletion of so many tweets that keeping the ones with the vital sociolinguistic information is still providing plenty data worth investigation. Such an approach requires, however, a broader scope than the current paper has, by including a longer data collection period, more prepositions and high-frequency prepositions to investigate, and a more sophisticated means of statistical assessment.

# References

Adedeji, K. (2015). RP in Nigeria: Prestige vs. intelligibility. In Opeibi, T., Schmied, J., Omoniyi, T., Adedeji, K. (Eds.) *Essays on language in societal transformation: A Festschrift in honour of SegunAwonusi* (REAL Studies 9). Göttingen: Cuvillier, 29–40.

Albrecht, S. & Schmied, J. (2015). TwitCollect (28 November 2017).

Alo, M.A. & Mesthrie, R. (2008). Nigerian English: Morphology and syntax. In Rajend, M. R. (Ed.) *Varieties of English 4: Africa, South and Southeast Asia*. Berlin: Mouton de Gruyter, 278-339.

Anthony, L. (2014). *AntConc*. (Version 3.4.4) [Computer Software]. Tokyo, Japan: Waseda University. Available from http://www.laurenceanthony.net/.

Bamman, D., Eisenstein, J. & Schnoebelen, T. (2014). Gender identity and lexical variation in social media. *Journal of Sociolinguistics*, 18(2), 135–160.

Bell, A. (1991). Audience Accommodation in the Mass Media. In Giles, H., Coupland, N., Coupland, J. (Eds.) *Contexts of accommodation: Developments in Applied Sociolinguistics*. Cambridge: Cambridge University Press, 69–102.

Bernardini, S., Baroni, M., & Evert, S. (2006). A WaCky introduction. In Baroni, M., Bernardini, S. (Eds.), *WaCky!: Working papers on the web as corpus* (Studi interdisciplinari sutraduzione, lingue e culture). Bologna: Gedit Edizioni, 9–40.

Burghardt, M. (2015). Introduction to tools and methods for the analysis of Twitter data. *10plus1: Living Linguistics* 1, 74–91.

Davies, M. (2013). *Corpus of global web-based English: 1.9 billion words from speakers in 20 countries (GloWbE)*. Available online at https://corpus.byu.edu/glowbe/.

Foulkes, P., & Docherty, G. J. (2000). Another Chapter in the Story of /r/: 'Labiodental' Variants in British English. *Journal of Sociolinguistics*, 4(1), 30–59.

Gries, S.T. (2013). *Statistics for linguistics with R: A practical introduction*, 2$^{nd}$edn. Berlin: De Gruyter Mouton.

Gut, U.B. (2008). Nigerian English: Phonology. In Mesthrie, R. (Ed.) *Varieties of English 4: Africa, South and Southeast Asia*. Berlin: Mouton de Gruyter, 35–54.

Heyd, T., & Mair, C. (2014). From vernacular to digital ethnolinguistic repertoire: The case of Nigerian Pidgin. In Lacoste, V., Jakob, R., Leimgruber, E., Breyer, T. (Eds.) *Indexing authenticity: Perspectives from linguistics and anthropology*. Berlin: De Gruyter Mouton, 242–266.

Hundt, M., & Nesselhauf, N. (Eds.).(2007). *Corpus linguistics and the web*. Amsterdam: Rodopi.

Hutchinson, A. 2017. Top social network demographics 2017 [Infographic]. https://www.socialmediatoday.com/social-networks/top-social-network-demographics-2017-infographic (6 November 2017).

Jowitt, D. (1991). *Nigerian English usage: An introduction*. Lagos: Longman Nigeria.

Jowitt, D. (1995). Nigeria's national language question: Choices and constraints. In Bamgbose, A., Banjo, A., Thomas, A. (Eds.) *New Englishes: A West African perspective*. Ibadan, Nigeria: Mosuro, 34–56.

Kelly, R. (2009). *Twitter Study - August 2009: Twitter study reveals interesting results about usage*. San Antonio, Texas.

Kilgarriff, A. (2007). Googleology is bad science. *Computational Linguistics*, 33(1), 147–151.

Lipsman, A. (2009). What Ashton vs. CNN foretold about the changing demographics of Twitter. http://blog.comscore.com/2009/09/changing_demographics_of_twitter.html (6 November 2017).

Mair, C. (2013). Corpus-approaches to the vernacular web: Post-colonial diasporic forums in West Africa and the Caribbean. *Covenant Journal of Language Studies* 1(1), 17–30.

Mesthrie, R., & Bhatt, R. M. (2008). *World Englishes: The study of new varieties*. Cambridge: Cambridge University Press.

Milroy, J., & Milroy, L. (1985). *Authority in language: Investigating language prescription and standardisation* (Language, education and society). London: Routledge & Kegan Paul.

Murthy, D., Gross, A., &Pensavalle, A. (2016). Urban social media demographics: An exploration of Twitter use in major American cities. *Journal of Computer-Mediated Communication* 21(1), 33–49.

Nguyen, D., Gravel, R., Trieschnigg, D. & Meder, T. (2013). How old do you think I am?: A study of language and age in Twitter. In *Proceedings of the seventh international AAAI conference on weblogs and social media, 8-11 July 2013, Cambridge, Massachusetts, USA*. Palo Alto, CA: AAAI Press, 439–448.

Opeibi, T. (2011). *Discourse strategies in election campaigns in Nigeria*. Saarbrücken: Lampert Academic Publishing.

Osisanwo, A. (2015). A morphological study of the use of pidgin in selected Nigerian electronic media advertisements. In Opeibi, T., Schmied, J., Omoniyi, T., Adedeji, K. (Eds.) *Essays on language in societal transformation: A Festschrift in honour of SegunAwonusi* (REAL Studies 9). Göttingen: Cuvillier, 155–172.

Pomikálek, J. (2014). *jusText*. Brno: Natural Language Processing Centre of Masaryk University.

Schettler, T. (n.y.). *Twython*. Available online at http://www.ling.uni-potsdam.de/~scheffler/twitter/.

Schmied, J. (1995). National standards and the international corpus of English. In Bamgbose, A., Banjo, A., &Thomas, A. (Eds.) *New Englishes: A West African perspective*, 337–348. Ibadan: Mosuro.

Schmied, J. (2012). Social digital discourse: New challenges for corpus- and sociolinguistics. *Topics in Linguistics - Approaches to Text and Discourse Analysis*, 10, 43–56.

Schmied, J. (2015). Internet English in Nigeria: New data - new discourses? In Opeibi, T., Schmied, J., Omoniyi, T., & Adedeji, K. (Eds.) *Essays on language in societal transformation: A Festschrift in honour of SegunAwonusi* (REAL Studies 9). Göttingen: Cuvillier, 189–208.

Schmied, J., Opeibi, T. (Eds.) (2017). *From the virtual sphere to physical space: Exploring language use in Nigerian democracy* (REAL Studies 13). Göttingen: Cuvillier.

Schneider, E. W. (2007). *Postcolonial English: Varieties of English around the world*. Cambridge: Cambridge University Press.

Sousa, A., & Ivanova, A. (2012). Constructing digital rhetorical spaces in Twitter: A case-study of @BarackObama. *Topics in Linguistics - Approaches to Text and Discourse Analysis* 9, 46–55.

Stuart-Smith, J. (2007). The Influence of the Media. In Llamas, C., Mullany, L., Stockwell, P. (Eds.) *The Routledge Companion to Sociolinguistics*. New York/London: Routledge, 140–148.

Stuart-Smith, J., Gwilym, P., Claire T., & Barrie, G. (2013). Television can also be a Factor in Language Change: Evidence from an Urban Dialect. *Language*, 89(3), 501–536.

Taiwo, R. (Ed.) (2010). *Handbook of research on discourse behavior and digital communication: Language structures and social interaction*. Hershey, PA: IGI Global.

Trudgill, P. (1974). *Sociolinguistics: An introduction*. New York: Penguin.

Trudgill, P. (1999). Standard English: What it isn't. In Tony Bex& Richard J. Watts (Eds.) *Standard English: The widening debate*. London: Routledge, 117–128.

Wardaugh, R. (1986). *An Introduction to Sociolinguistics*. Oxford: Basil Blackwell.

# Makerere University English Variety: Is there an Emerging Youth-Urban Language Variety?

*Saudah Namyalo* (Makerere University, Uganda)

## 1. Introduction

The English variety spoken today in Uganda's urban space is characterised by striking linguistic variations. This is particularly true with the varieties of English spoken by the youths in informal circles compared to that which is spoken by the older generation. As a result of these variations, the subjects of 'language decay' and 'language corruption' have hit and continue to be at the axis of debates in Uganda's media, in formal and informal circles. However, apart from casual observations that have been made by linguists and English speakers, no linguistic study has been undertaken to study these varieties. In this paper, I describe the variety of English spoken by Makerere University students' population which feeds into the English variety spoken by the youths in urban contexts. I particularly analyse: (a) the linguistic strategies the speakers of Makerere university English students' variety use to expand its lexicon and b) the functions of Mak-Eng within its community of practice. Using the linguistic strategies observable in Mak-Eng and the functions of this variety, I argue that Mak-Eng represents a new youth-urban language based on English, but also with substantial borrowings from indigenous languages, especially Luganda (see 4.7 and Table 3 below). Although still in its infancy, Mak-Eng is likely to grow into a distinct code like the case of Luyaaye, a youth urban language based on Luganda.

This chapter is part of an on-going larger study in which I am investigating and documenting formal and informal language varieties in Uganda's urban space. The data analysed in this chapter, however, are based on speech data that were collected between June 2013 and September 2014 from Makerere University main campus, which is located in Kampala, the capital city of Uganda. The data were mainly collected through transcription and analysis of various types of speech. These data included recorded students' political rallies and self-recorded casual speeches that were both in audio and video forms. In addition, my students and I conducted sociolinguistic interviews in different colleges that make up Makerere University. Speech data that were collected using sociolinguistic interviews included 50 female and male students aged between 19 and 38 years.

In these interviews, narratives were elicited from participants on a specific set of topics, especially those that interest students. Such topics included sex and sexuality, relationships, life on campus, students' politics in Makerere, inter-hall social politics, among others. In some cases, students were encouraged to choose their own topics for discussion. The speeches were transcribed for analysis.

I use the data elicited to sketch a description of the variety of English spoken by Makerere University students' population. First, I describe the linguistic ecology in which Mak-Eng is spoken, especially highlighting some of the factors that account for the emergence of this variety. I then examine the linguistic strategies the speakers of Mak -Eng variety use to expand its lexicon. These linguistic strategies appear to be a case of 'word-play' and 'conscious language manipulation' depicting a high degree of creativity of its speakers like it is with Luyaaye and possibly other youth urban languages in Africa and beyond. Further discussion of the functions of this variety within its community of practices is made. In an attempt to answer the question of whether there is an emerging youth-urban language, I compare the functions of Mak-Eng and the linguistic strategies observed in this variety to advance a claim that Mak-Eng is an emerging youth-language although it is still in its infant stages.

The chapter is organised as follows. The first section is introductory and highlights the key concerns of the chapter and the employed methodological approach. The second section provides a brief review of the growth and spread of English varieties globally, with the view to placing Mak-Eng within the existing categories. The third section describes the linguistic strategies used by Mak-Eng speakers to expand their lexicon. The fourth section examines the functions of Mak-Eng within its community of practice. The fifth section compares the linguistic strategies and the functions of Makerere University Students' English, henceforth referred to as Mak-Eng, with the general characteristics of youth-urban languages elsewhere in Africa with the view of establishing whether there is an emerging youth language in Uganda based on English.

## 2. English Varieties in Uganda and Beyond

The late twentieth century saw the spread of English across the globe. The global spread of English presented a major component of a 'language revolution' characterised by language hybridization, linguistic variations and innovations (cf. Crystal, 2004, Jantmary and Melor, 2012). Consequently, linguists proposed different models to account for, as well as categorise the different varieties of English spoken in different regions of the world (cf. Kachru, 1982, Schneider, 2007). The main feature that distinguishes these varieties is the range of fluency that often deviates from the so-called 'Standard English' in terms of pronunciation, lexis, expression and grammar (cf. Kubota, 2001). The deviations are quite often a reflection of the different social and cultural environments in which English is spoken as a native and a non-native language. In due course, these deviations have culminated in home-grown forms of English such as Nigerian, Bangladeshi, Indian, Kenyan, Malaysian, Pakistani, Philippino, Singaporean, Sri Lankan, Tanzanian, and Zambian Englishes. Such varieties fall into what Kachru (1994) refers to as the outer circle of the three concentric circles of English. In some countries, such varieties remain informal and continue to co-exist with the varieties considered 'standard' or formal. This is true for Uganda. In Uganda, some of the varieties of English spoken are considered standard and others non-standard, thus informal. Three varieties of English in Uganda are distinguishable and they are typical to the three levels of lectal continuum used by Baskaran (1987) in his description of Malaysian English. Baskaran (1987) identifies three levels of lectal continuum that include: a) acrolect, the official, standard use, b) mesolect – unofficial, informal use c) basilect, broken substandard use. Following this line of classification, the first variety of English in Uganda is equivalent to the acrolect level and is the so-called 'standard variety'. This variety is mainly taught in schools and is grammatically similar to standard British English, even though it is spoken neither with the same pronunciation nor with the prosodic features of a native speaker's standard variety of English. The standard or taught variety is the most prestigious and often preferred in formal communication. The second variety is what may be equated to the mesolect level. This is the informal or unofficial variety mainly spoken in informal settings especially by the youths in urban circles. This variety is what linguists like Kiessling and Mous (2004) and Hollington and Nassentein (2015) have termed as youth language practices or youth languages spoken in the urban contexts. The third variety, basilect, is considered broken English or ungrammatical. Despite the fact that this variety is ungrammatical, it is also widely spoken due to the low levels of education among most Ugandans.

## 2.1. Makerere University Students' English Variety and the Environment in which it is Spoken

Mak-Eng is informally spoken by Makerere University Students. This variety is evident mainly in the students' casual conversations and political rallies. However, unconsciously, this variety spills out into their formal communication in both their lecture discussions and written essays. The use of informal registers in formal communications has been a concern to many Ugandans especially the teachers at different levels of learning. The teachers in particular struggle to eliminate what they describe as 'poor' or even 'strange' English, especially varieties spoken by the students. In Makerere University, an introductory English Communication course was introduced. It is aimed at addressing and teaching university students 'Standard English' which they are supposed to use in formal spoken and written discourses. Despite these efforts, the use of the informal English variety, Mak-Eng, is rapidly growing and influencing the indigenisation of English in Uganda.

Because of its prestigious and influential status, Makerere University serves as the centre for linguistic innovation, which ultimately influences the other varieties spoken in Uganda, especially in urban areas such as Kampala. First, we observe that Makerere University is located in the urban centre and it shares the intricate linguistic ecology that exists in the area. Secondly, the waves of globalisation characterised by technological innovation, increased media interaction, human mobility, as well as the new forces of social, political and economic development, have had significant impact on the urban space's linguistic landscape, ultimately having an effect on the way students speak English during their interaction at Makerere University and beyond. Thus, the urban space in general and Makerere University in particular, is now characterised by new waves of multilingualism, language hybridisation, linguistic differentiation, language change and variations. These waves are progressively affecting the different languages spoken in the urban space. This is especially true for English, which is widely spoken as a second language due to its status as Uganda's official language, and a lingua franca for individuals from different linguistic backgrounds.

In addition to its geographical location, Makerere University campus by itself presents a fertile ground for the emergence and growth of informal language varieties. To begin with, the ethnic diversity of the students' community at Makerere University creates a multilingual society with many languages spoken in a small place. The Academic Registrar's admission records, for example, reveal that the students' body at Makerere University comprises students who come from different ethnic communities (Makerere University students' records, 2012, 2013, 2014, 2015, 2016). By matching names to ethnic identity, the 2016 records indicate that students in that year alone came from close to 33 different ethnic groups. Multilingualism and the emergence of world English varieties in general and youth languages in particular are synonymous, thus not peculiar to Makerere University. In their discussion of World English varieties, Kachru and Smith (2008: 5) observe that "the main push for the adoption and diffusion of English came from the local multilingual populations". Closely related to this Mansour (1993) observes that multilingualism covers two distinct phenomena, i.e. (a) the coexistence and close contact of several languages within a given community where, owing to the nature of community life, a special pattern of language use needs to be adopted; and (b) the co-existence of several ethnolinguistic entities within a community, with each entity occupying a relatively well-defined territory. In agreement with Mansour, the emergence of Makerere university students' English variety is perhaps due to the multilingual nature of Makerere university community which calls for the need to adopt a more neutral 'language' or style of speech that differs from the dominating varieties, in this case English, which is used as an official language, and Luganda, which is the dominant indigenous language in Kampala. In addition to the multilingual nature of Makerere University, students join the university with different distinctive school-lects or codes acquired from different schools where they attended their primary and secondary education. These feed into the Makerere variety to create a youth language practice that can be characterised as Makerere University students' English variety, with characteristics that are similar to youth urban language varieties spoken in Africa.

## 3. Linguistic Strategies Used to Expand Mak-Eng's Lexicon

Mak-Eng speakers make use of a variety of linguistic strategies to expand the lexicon of the Mak-Eng language variety. Characteristic of these methods is the playful nature and high degree of creativity the speakers use to ensure that they create a lexicon that is incomprehensible to the uninitiated. In the sections that follow, I discuss these strategies with ample examples from the data collected.

## 3.1. Semantic Manipulation

In their discussion of the youth's languages in Africa, Kießling & Mous (2004: 23) provide a general observation that "characteristic of youth languages is the far-fetched extension or change in the meaning of words with the function of insult, ridicule, exaggeration or simple enjoyment and play". Semantic manipulation is well attested in Mak-Eng as demonstrated in extracts 3, 4, 5, 6 and 7 below:

- Extract 3: You have been *chopping* lectures *mob times*
- Extract 4: My *body-blood packed*!
- Extract 5: The problem those guys *cook* a lot.
- Extract 6: Did the *white guys* do something?
- Extract 7: Oh! Kololo, a *city dog*?

In the extracts 3-7 above the italicised English lexical items are semantically modified to convey meanings which are only known to the in-group members and thus excludes those that are uninitiated. The extended meanings are as follow:

1. *Chopping lectures* – to miss lectures
2. *Body-blood* – close friend
3. *To pack* – to die
4. *To cook a lot* – to smoke marijuana a lot
5. *City dogs* – city born with no home in rural areas

In an interview with one of the participants, when asked to explain why they change the meaning of the English words, the participant highlighted that they modify the meanings mainly to come up with a vocabulary that is incomprehensible to the outsiders, but also it makes them feel 'cool', as he explains: "when you go downtown, those people speak their *Luyaaye* which some of us do not understand. Therefore, we also change meaning of the words so that those who are not from Makerere get lost when we speak our own English variety" (Musoke Busuulwa, interviewee, 2014).

Besides the semantically-modified words and phrases shown in the extracts above, the data provide other semantically-modified English words including but not limited to the following:

6. *Vegetarian* – a male university student who is still a virgin
7. *Weed* – borrowed from Jamaican English and used to mean drugs
8. *A shuttle* – 'sugar-daddy', an elderly man who sees a young girl
9. *Big brackets* – mainly used to describe girls with big hips
10. *Player* – a university student who sees multiple partners for the sake of getting money from them
11. *Bullet* – a leaked exam

12. *Buffalo* – an expression that sounds grammatically incorrect
13. *Detoother* – a person who sleeps with a woman or man for sake of getting money from him/her

The productivity of this strategy signifies the possibility of this variety of English growing and sieving into the mainstream variety of English. This is because the speakers have a variety of English words to manipulate and there is no mechanism to deter the freedom to manipulate them. Besides, there are possibilities of the speakers of Mak-Eng to continue interacting formally and informally with their peers using this variety beyond the university circles; for instance, public places and work places after graduating from university. The longer the users keep interacting, the broader the spectrum of its influence becomes.

### 3.2. Use of Metaphors

In addition to semantic manipulation as a linguistic strategy, the data reveals that Mak-Eng speakers make use of other semantic processes such as metaphor, metonym, synecdoche, hyperbole, euphemism and dysphemism to expand their lexicon. Lakoff & Johnson (1980) broadly define a metaphor as a comparison that shows how two things that are not alike in most ways are similar in another important way. For example, *to be sent to heaven* is figuratively used by Mak-Eng speakers to mean 'to die'. The association here, at least from a religious point of view, is that you cannot go to heaven without death. Similarly, *to cook a lot* is figuratively used to mean 'To smoke marijuana or other types of drugs in excess'. An act of puffing marijuana resembles the smoke that comes out firewood while cooking. Other metaphors in the data include:

14. *To be binned* – to leave your room when your roommate's girlfriend visits
15. *General happiness* – common burial place
16. *White guys* – policemen (Uganda's traffic officers put on white uniforms)
17. *Investor* – 'sugar-daddy' or an elderly man who sees young girls. In order to sustain the relation he gives her a lot of money.
18. *Shopping bags* – posh cars used by 'sugar daddies' to bring stuff for their girl friends

Other metaphors are summarised in Table 1 below:

| Metaphors | Meaning in Mak-Eng | Figurative use |
|---|---|---|
| *Part-timer* | lecturers who routinely miss lectures | Part-time lecturers by nature of their job teach just a few lectures in a semester. |
| *Chillers or visitors* | unserious students who rarely attend lectures | Visitors by comparison are meant not to be regular. |
| *State General* | Hall chairperson | Assumed to have similar administrative responsibilities as a State General. |
| *Full stop* | someone who is short | A full stop is a brief character used as a punctuation marker. |
| *Boy's quarters* | used to mean girls/women's bums' | Boy's quarters are small rooms behind the main house. The link is that bums are behind. |
| *Parasite* | Someone who depends on others for survival | Similarity in behaviour. |
| *White angle* | Popcorn (popped corn) | White represents purity. |
| *Campus flies* | A student who participates in many of the university activities – he/she is everywhere | It is a common phonemon to find flies almost everywhere. |
| *Airport* | Students' hall of residents | They are always as busy as airports. |
| *Opener* | A man who defiles a minor | Children are expected to be virgins so someone who defiles them 'opens' them the way an opener opens a bottle. |
| *Sleeping pill* | Boring lecture or lecturer | Both may invoke sleep. |
| *To type* | To eat using fingers (without a spoon/fork) | Typing is normally done with bare fingers. |
| *Ice cream* | Oral sex | Both involve using a tongue/mouth. |
| *Political virus* | (opinion leader) or a well known politician whose acts are always imitated by others | Viruses spread quickly like the opinions of outstanding politicians. |

Table 1: Examples of metaphors used by Mak-Eng speakers (Fieldwork, 2014)

## 3.3. Use of Metonymy

Besides using metaphors, Mak-Eng speakers make use of metonymy as a linguistic strategy to expand their lexicon. Lakoff & Johnson (1980: 35) define metonymy as "using one entity to refer to another that is related to it". Similarly, Bonvillain (1993) views metonymy as a type of semantic transfer in which one entity is taken to stand for another based on contextual relationship. Lakoff and Johnson (1980) add that this transfer quite often allows us to refer by association as well as to conceptualize one thing by relating it to something else, i.e. two domains are linked together". In relation to this, Mak-English speakers usually link two domains together as a strategy to expand their lexicon. Metonymies in Mak-Eng are not as many as metaphors. Some of the examples observed in the data include: *Intruder* which means 'unwanted pregnancy' and *Gorilla* which means a fifty thousand Uganda shillings note.

Figure 1: Uganda's fifty thousand note (Photo taken by Namyalo, 2015)

The gorilla in the currency note above is used to represent a fifty thousand Uganda shillings' note. In extract 8 below John tells Mariam that she earned 250,000 Uganda shillings and he expresses this as:

> Extract 8: Mariam, I was lucky to kill five gorillas today. That is good blood.
> Meaning: 'Mariam today I was lucky to be paid 250,000. That is good money'.

This choice also has the potential to expand the lexicon of this variety. This is because the speakers have a pool of entities to refer to and the reasons for their selection of any entities to use in their communication are always there.

### 3.4. Euphemism

Mak-Eng speakers also make use of euphemism as a linguistic strategy to extend their lexicon. The use of euphemism is a common strategy not only in youth language varieties, but also from a number of Uganda's indigenous languages, especially Luganda. Drawing from their experiences, Mak-Eng speakers prefer to use informal terms to avoid using standard lexical items which may not only be associated with the harsh and unpleasant reality of the meaning of the terms, but also may have numerous undesirable associations with the offensive references which may be against the social and cultural practices of speech community. As such, most of the taboo words relating to sexual organs and sexual activities are replaced by words that speakers of Mak-Eng consider 'decent'. Examples of euphemism can be found in Table 2.

| Word | Meaning (sense) attached to it |
|---|---|
| *Faculty* | Man's private organ |
| *Zubula* (source unknown) | Man's private organ |
| *Boxer* | Man's private organ |
| *Whopper* | Man's private organ |
| *Kadaaga* (name of honourable speaker of parliament) | Woman's private organ |
| *Kandahar* | Woman's private organ |
| *To drive* | To have a running stomach |
| *To arrive* | To reach orgasms |
| *Ice cream* | Oral sex |
| *Old Kampala* (name of a place) | Woman's private organ |

Table 2: Euphemism used in Mak-Eng (Fieldwork, 2013-2014)

The use of such words spreads very fast through the media, and especially the social media platforms. There is a possibility of these terms being taken on by other speakers who want to use them for similar global reasons. However, the earlier they become popular, the earlier users will look for a different term to use for the same purpose and the earlier the used word can begin to sound obscene to those who are already familiar with it.

### 3.5. Phonotactic manipulation

Phonological manipulations in Mak-Eng mainly include truncation. Words are truncated and a final vowel from a selection of vowel <i, e, o> is thereafter inserted. At times two of the vowels in a combination <i, e> or <ee> are inserted at the end of the truncated word. In cases where a name of place is truncated a semantically empty, a final consonant /s/ is added. Some of the truncated words are summarised in Table 3 below:

| Truncated word | Full word |
|---|---|
| *Progie* | Program |
| *Nanks* | Nankulabye (name of a place) |
| *Wandes* | Wandegeya (name of a place) |
| *Bweyos* | Bweyogerere (name of a place) |
| *Ginos* | Groundnuts |
| *Probs* | Problems |
| *Sato* | Saturday |
| *Pregee* | pregnant girl |
| *Marko* | Market |
| *Lapi* | Laptop |
| *Curri* | Curriculum |

Table 3: Truncated words in Mak-Eng (Fieldwork, 2013-2014)

The consistence in the manipulation results highlights the extent to which this process can be productive. And based on the principles of least effort, language users are likely to opt for such words instead of their standard counterparts.

## 3.6. Abbreviations

Speakers of Mak-Eng make use of abbreviation as a strategy of creating new vocabularies. For example STM stands for 'Sexually Transmitted Marks'. This is refers to unethical practice among some male students who give free marks to students in exchange for sex. Other examples include:

19. A.T – Airtime: money
20. B.P – Beeping Power: having low credit on your phone
21. UK – United Kikoni: Kikoni is a slum area where students go for cheap stuff
22. 1 GB – (one Giga Bite): used to mean a short person
23. T.P – Transport

In order to test out the universality of some of these abbreviations, a list of the above abbreviations was given to 120 students to provide the equivalent of these abbreviations. Of these, 115 students provided similar equivalents while 3 of them elaborated T.P as toilet paper, and 2 elaborated UK as United Kingdom. These scores indicate that the majority of students are familiar with Mak-Eng terms.

## 3.7. Derivation Using the Agentive Marker -*er*

New Mak-Eng words are constructed using the derivational agentive marker –*er*, as used in Standard English. The agentive marker –*er* is added to common nouns to derive agentive nouns. Although the use of derivational affixes to create nouns is not peculiar to this variety, it is interesting to note that the forms that might be unacceptable in Standard English are the norm in Mak-English. In addition, these new derivates are semantically manipulated to sound not only unique but also incomprehensible to the non-speakers of this variety. Such new coinages include the following examples:

(i) *Bencher* – 'someone who sees a university student'
  *Jackson is Susan's bencher*
  Meaning: 'Jackson is Susan's boy friend'
(ii) *Booker* – 'someone who reads a lot (bookworm)'
  *That sexy is too much of a booker*
  Meaning: 'That university female student reads a lot'
(iii) *Dodger* – 'non-trustworthy person'
  *Do not parse with that chic, she is a dodger*
  Meaning: 'Do not club with that girl she is untrustworthy'
(iv) *Driver* – someone with a running stomach

(v)   *Checker* – 'man who sleeps with different girls and drops them after having sex with them'
(vi)  *Eater* – 'corrupt government officer/worker'
(vii) *Sacker* – 'girl who sleeps with different men for money'
(viii) *Carrier* – 'girl who sees many men'
(ix)  *Rider* – 'boy who uses condom during sex'
(x)   *Cutters* – 'students who dodge classes/lectures'

The new derived words are then used as new lexical items in Mak-Eng. For example, one would say: *The dog bite turned her into a driver* meaning 'HIV has caused her to have a running stomach.' Or *He is a safe rider, he cannot be a war victim* meaning 'he uses condoms during sex; therefore he cannot be HIV positive.'

Since the formation of words under this strategy is based on a common morphological pattern in English, students find it easy to use this to expand their Mak-Eng lexicon. The choice of this strategy may not be to shut out non-members from following the communication, but to paint an obvious picture of the word which should mean: the person who does that action.

### 3.8. Borrowing

The contact between English and other languages spoken by Makerere University students has led to massive borrowings, which include mainly core borrowings and a few cultural borrowings. According to Myers-Scotton (2002)

> Cultural borrowings are words for new objects (e.g. *espresso*) or words for new (non-object) concepts (e.g. *zeitgeist*), and they usually appear abruptly when influential groups use them. Core borrowings, by contrast, are words that more or less duplicate already existing words. Core borrowings usually begin life in the recipient language when bilinguals introduce them as singly occurring code-switching forms in the mixed constituents of their code-switching. (Myers-Scotton 2002: 239)

Cultural borrowings according to Myers-Scotton (1993) enter the lexicon abruptly and are used to fill lexical items that are non-existent in the receptor language while core borrowings meet no real lexical needs and may be redundant in one way or the other. Another view is that non-indigenous words generally start out as innovations and may become entrenched and propagated (cf. Backus, 2005, Gardner-Chloros, 2009). The corpus gathered in this study suggests that most of the borrowings in Mak-Eng are core borrowings which start as innovations aimed at making the youth's communication incomprehensible to the uninitiated. Core borrowings in Mak-Eng occur as lexical items, calques, loan-blends, affixes and transitional discourse markers that duplicate the already-existing ones in English. Table 4 below provides a list of borrowings found in Mak-Eng.

| Loan | Meaning in source language | Meaning in Mak-Eng | Donor Language |
|---|---|---|---|
| Kasanja | A small piece of banana leaf | Re-take (failed examination) | Luganda |
| Federo | Type of governance | A male Ganda student | Luganda |
| Muswiba | Problem | Problem | Arabic via Luganda |
| Pakalast | Here to stay | Forever | Sheng |
| Kalooli | Marabou stork | Ugly person | Luganda |
| Mwana | Child | Friend | Luyaaye |
| Essasi | Bullet | Illegal materials smuggled into an examination with the purpose of copying | Luganda |
| Kaliga | Small sheep/lamb | Type of alcohol | Luganda |
| Kasawo | Small bag | A rich person | Luganda |
| Omupaatiri | A catholic priest | Someone who prays a lot | Luganda |
| Yungwe | Mad person | Mad person | Luyaaye |
| Kanyama | Bouncer | Examination invigilators | Luyaaye |
| Kazende | Parent | Parent | Luyaaye |
| Bong | To greet | To greet | Sheng |
| Jjajja | Grand father | Close friend | Luganda |
| Kasaayi | Purple-like colour | Being poor | Luganda |
| Bade ache | Daughter in law | Beautiful girl | (one of the Indian languages) |
| Mmumbwa | Local herb mingled in clay | Money | Luganda |
| To nose | To sleep | To sleep | Jamaican English |
| Kawologoma | Small lion | Type of alcohol | Luganda |
| Nawolovu | Chameleon | 1 million shillings | Luganda |
| Waaggwaan | What is up? | How are you? | Patois (Jamaican slang) |
| Liklmour | See you | See | Patois |

Table 4: Borrowed lexical items in Mak-English

From Table 4, we observe that speakers of Mak-Eng borrow lexical items mainly from Luganda. The rest of the borrowings are from language varieties spoken by youths within Uganda and beyond. The youth urban languages from which Mak-Eng borrows include Luyaaye, which is a youth language variety spoken mainly in Kampala, but also gradually spreading to other parts of Uganda; *Sheng,* which is a youth-urban vernacular spoken in Nairobi-Kenya and *Patois,* a type of English slang spoken in Jamaica. The increased exchange of the youth's culture through media and music, the increased youth mobility as well as social media like Facebook, Twitter, Viber, Skype and many others perhaps explains the borrowing from Sheng and Jamaican slangs. It is however interesting to note that despite the multilingual nature of Makerere community, Mak-Eng mainly borrows from

Luganda. Luganda is the dominant language spoken in the region and carries the prestige of being the language of the capital city, Kampala, and a language of trade and entertainment.

Striking to note is the semantic modification of the borrowed words in Mak-Eng. Most of the borrowed words are semantically modified perhaps to fulfil the students' desire to make this variety incomprehensible. For example, the word *kasanja-busanja is* derived from a Luganda word, *ekisanja* which means (a) piece of dry banana leaves (b) Days assigned to different wives by a husband in polygamous families (c) recently extended to mean a political term of office. In Mak-Eng, however, it does not take any of these senses but it is used to mean a re-take (a failed examination that you have to re-write when next offered). Again, '*kalooli*' is a Luganda word that refers to a type of a bird called marabou stork. In Mak-Eng *marabou stork* is used to mean 'an ugly person', though in other contexts it is also used to refer to 'lecturers who are committed to their work'. This is so because Marabou storks are ever seen loitering around Makerere Campus. Thus, a lecturer who is always at Makerere is called *Kalooli* as opposed to 'part-timers' (those who are infrequent) even though they are supposed to be full time lecturers.

Besides borrowing lexical items, Mak-Eng also borrows affixes of Uganda's indigenous languages for morphemic hybridisation. Whereas Mak-Eng speakers speak different mother tongues, our data shows that all the affixes are borrowed from Luganda, which is the language of wider communication and a lingua franca in Makerere University. Some of the borrowed suffixes are the diminutive marker *ka-* (12ka-) and plural form *bu-* (13bu-). For example, the *ka-girl with obu-toothpicks* is used figuratively to mean 'a small girl with toothpicks like legs'. The use of the prefix *ka*is not only in Mak-English, it is widely used by speakers of English regardless of age, gender, class among other sociolinguistic variables. It has also gone beyond informal registers and now characterise Uganda's English variety (cf. Isingoma, this volume).

Similarly, Mak-Eng speakers borrow transitional discourse markers like '*kale*'-*okay* from Luganda *and 'peku'-till* from Luyaaye. Unlike core and cultural borrowings transitional discourse markers retain the same meanings (sense) as those in the source language.

## 4. The Functions of Mak-Eng within their Community of Practice

Mak-English's main function is that of identity marking. It plays an important role in marking social group identity and solidarity. Using this code identifies you as a Makerere university student but more so as an educated urban youth from the 'ivory tower[1]'. In of-the-group discussion, Susan Mubiru, a third medical student, highlighted that "speaking Mak-Eng promotes a sense of belonging". The code

---

[1] Ivory tower is term used symbolically to refer to Makerere University as the oldest and most prestigious university in Uganda and the first university in East Africa.

helps us to bridge the differences that exist in Makerere University. For example the ethnic differences, the differences in social status let alone the differences based on the courses that we offer in this university. So it does not matter whether you are an Acholi or Muganda, as long as you use this code you become part of a bigger community. That is why this code is a key campaigning strategy, it is a cloud puller. (Field interviews, 2014).

In addition to marking group identity and solidarity according to the students, Mak-Eng serves as a symbol of modernity, being urban, trendy and anti-traditional. One of the respondents observed that "Standard English portrays you as someone who is traditional and who does not understand new trends and styles of the urban youths" (Field interviews, June 2015-Makerere). Mak-Eng speakers therefore constantly make every effort to strike a balance between locally motivated social and cultural ideologies with those from across the world. For example they copy and mimic Jamaican youth languages vocabulary such as *wagwani* to mean 'how are you', *lirk mour* to mean 'see you later' as well as youth expressions from Europe like *blood* to mean 'my friend', *bring-bring* to mean 'jewellery' among others. In addition to using words from other countries they also adopt dressing codes, walking styles and hair styles from across the world. The integration of ideologies especially from developed countries into the socially and culturally homemade styles of the urban youths has resulted in a new social-cultural hybrid, which in their view portrays them as being 'modern' and 'trend setters'. Thus, Mak-Eng constitutes a means of asserting one's distinctiveness from others, specifically creating a distance from the other people, particularly the older generation.

Mak-Eng also serves as a secret code within the students' community. Whereas Mak-Eng may not be linguistically categorized as purely an anti-language or a secret code, it serves and functions as such. This is so because this code excludes the *out-group* from the *in-group*. This is achieved by using a vocabulary which is only known to the in-group members as exemplified below:

Extract 1: *The professor launched his manifesto but he was chilled off for an investor. He finally dived for a heavily loaded sugar mummy whose wallet is ever happy.*
Translation: 'A boy who is very poor at his studies asked the girl for marriage but the girl decided to go with a rich old man. As an alternative, he also went for an old woman who is very rich and willing to give him money for his survival'.
Extract 2: *The comeback tomorrows disappointed the professor again.*
'The university staff disappointed the a student who has failed several examinations'

In extract 2, *the comeback tomorrows* refers to the staff of Makerere University who never attend to the students and instead keep telling them to come back tomorrow. While *professor* means a student who has failed more than four examinations in one academic year.

The kind of lexicon used in extract 1 and 2 excludes the out-group members thus maintaining secrecy among the students. This is achieved by using semantically modified English words which are unintelligible to the uninitiated. Besides being used as a secret code, Mak-Eng is also commonly used in entertainment and corporate advertisement. In relation to entertainment it is mainly used in stage plays, comedies and music. In describing Ugandan English from which youth languages draw some of their vocabulary, Sabiiti (2014) explains that some Ugandan English terms come from popular songs. For example, Hillary Kiyaga, who raps under the name Dr. Hilderman, links the English phrase "double bed" to a made-up word, *mazongoto*. The catchy hook 'Double Bed Mazongoto' is now used to mean King-size, a big mattress or when describing government corruption especially government officials who swindle huge sums of money. However, Mak-Eng speakers use the term 'double bed – Mazongoto' to mean a big woman with big breasts.

## 5. Is Mak-Eng an Emerging Youth Urban Language Based on English?

Mak-Eng shares a lot of common characteristics with other youth urban languages in Africa. For example, Mak-Eng, like other youth language varieties, is highly stigmatised and is often looked at not only as a threat to the existing standard English variety taught in schools but also a distortion of other of Uganda's indigenous languages (See Namyalo, 2015). In an interview with Buganda Kingdom's chiefs one of respondents commented that "The speakers of youth language varieties are not only uncultured but also agents of doom who are killing our languages as well as the culture associated with these languages" (Field interviews June 2015 - Kampala – Uganda). Despite this stigmatisation Mak-Eng indexes urbanism and modernity, and serves as a youth identity marker especially identifying and expressing a sense of belonging, opposition to traditionalism and an anti-culture stance. Like stigmatisation, this trait is common to many African youth urban languages such as Nouchi from Ivory Coast, Town Bemba from Zambia, Tsotsitaal from South Africa, Camfranglais from Cameroon, Wolof from Senegal, Sheng from Kenya, Yanke in DRC-Congo, Luyaaye from Uganda among others.

In addition to the above, Mak-Eng has emerged out of the multilingual nature of Makerere University. Multilingualism and multiculturism have been key and continue to be so, as far the emergence of informal languages in Africa is concerned. Cohen (2010: 5) emphasises that youth languages "quite often have emerged out of conditions of multilingualism, globalisation and super-diversity and largely as a response to colonialism". Mak-Eng, as already observed, is a response to the continued use of English which is still considered as a language of the colonial masters. In order to break away from colonialism, the youth have created their own variety of English which is seems to be closer to their cultural environment. This argument can be supported by the increasing use of loans from various languages such as Luganda and other youth languages such as Luyaaye, Sheng and Patois.

In addition to these similarities, Hollington & Nassenstein (2015: 2) observe that

> ...similarities between African youth language practices can be observed in the strategies of linguistic manipulations that the speakers employ in order to deliberately create their language, to maintain secrecy and to develop a certain style, which is only known among their particular community of practice.

The range of linguistic strategies used by Mak-Eng speakers is typical of youth urban language varieties. These strategies, as discussed in Section 3, can be classified as phonological or phonotactic manipulations, morphological manipulations and semantic manipulations (See also Namyalo, 2015). Closely related to what Hollington & Nassenstein highlight, Hurst (2015) emphasises that

> urban youth languages have been associated with, *inter alia*, the following similarities: Innovation in the lexicon, including neologisms, (...) metaphor, borrowing, form manipulations, semantic manipulations, circomlocutions (...); [they] are often seen as moving targets with little to distinguish them linguistically from the base languages they rely on other than a shifting lexicon. (Hurst, 2015: 102)

Beside the similarities observed above, Mak-Eng, like other youth language practices, is primarily spoken by youths in urban centres. Although this is true to a large extent, Namyalo (2015) observes that youth languages like Luyaaye in Kampala and Sheng in Nairobi are no longer spoken by the youths only. There is an increasing number of children and young adults who also speak these language varieties which were earlier confined to the youth only. Further, we note that whereas youth languages in Africa are predominantly spoken in urban contexts, they are now spreading to rural areas. This has been due to liberalized airwaves and the constant movements of the youths from the urban areas to the rural parts.

Another common similarity of youth language practices in Africa is that they are always based on a major language predominantly spoken in the community. This is also true for Mak-Eng variety. Mak-Eng is based on English and thus retains the phonological, morphological and syntactic structure of Standard English, however with obvious influence from Ugandan English and the indigenous languages spoken in Uganda, especially Luganda, which is widely spoken as a lingua franca. The primary characteristic of Makerere English students' variety is that it deviates from Ugandan English by its special lexicon that is in a constant process of rapid renovation. This is done by "way of deliberate manipulation of existing lexical items, as an expression of an attitude of jocular and provocative violation of linguistic norms" (Reuster-Jahn and Kießling, 2004: 7). The violation of linguistic norms is observable at different linguistic levels that include phonology, morphology, syntax and semantics among other levels.

Youth language practices in Africa heavily depend on code-switching and code mixing as well as borrowing from different languages (Kießling & Mous, 2004: 3). This method of language formation is also discernable in Mak-Eng. We, however, observe that borrowing and code mixing is not very common in Mak-Eng compared say to Luyaaye, a youth-urban language spoken in Kampala, and Sheng spoken in Nairobi. What seems to be a common factor in all these informal varieties such as Mak-Eng is that they are all typical for conscious language manipulation with the aim of making their language incomprehensible to the uninitiated.

## 6. Conclusion

This chapter has highlighted the strategies used by Mak-Eng speakers to expand their lexicon. They draw from a variety of sources including the indigenous languages of Kenya. These strategies reveal the linguistic creativity of the students as well as the playful nature of youths. The strategies also reflect the speakers' awareness and control of their linguistic repertoires and their abilities to make meaningful choices, especially in terms of the lexicon they need in particular situations and contexts. In addition, the linguistic strategies used by Mak-Eng as well as its functions reveal that the creation of incomprehensive vocabulary is a conscious process geared towards achieving secrecy within their community of practice. These characteristics are similar to other youth urban languages and one may argue that Mak-Eng is a youth language variety mainly spoken by the educated urban youth with the potential to grow and spread beyond Makerere University.

## References

Backus, A. (2005). Codeswitching and language change: one thing leads to another? *International Journal of Bilingualism,* 9, 307–40.
Baskaran, L. (1987). Indigenization of English (Malaysian English – its development & features), in *Proceedings of the Modern Language Association Conference on The Language Situation in Malaysia.* Kuala Lumpur, Malaysia.
Bonvillain, N. (1993). *Language, culture and communication: The meaning of messages.* New Jersey: Prentice Hall.
Crystal, D. (2004). *The language revolution.* Cambridge: Polity Press.
Gardner-Chloros, P. (2009). *Code-switching.* Cambridge: Cambridge University Press.
Hollington, A., & Nassenstein, N. (2015). Youth language practices in Africa as creative manifestations of fluid repertoires and markers of speakers' social identity. In Nassenstein, N., & Hollington, A. (Eds.) *Youth language practices in Africa and beyond.* Berlin: Mouton de Gruyter, 1-22.
Hurst, E. (2015). Overview of the tsotsitaals of South Africa; their different base languages and common core lexical items. In Nassenstein, N., Hollington, A. *Youth language practices in Africa and beyond.* Berlin: Mouton de Gruyter, 169-184.
Kachru, Y., & Smith, L. E. (2008). *Cultures, contexts, and world Englishes.* New York: Routledge.
Kachru, B. B. (1994). Teaching world English without myths. In *Intelec '94, perpustakaan Negara Malaysia,* Kuala Lumpur, Malaysia.
Kachru, B. B. (1982). *Models for non-native Englishes, in the other tongue: English across cultures.* Urbana, Illinois: University of Illinois Press.
Kießling, J. R., & Mous, M. (2004). Urban youth languages in Africa. *Anthropological Linguistics* 46(3), 304–341.
Kubota, R. (2001). Learning linguistic diversity from World Englishes. *Social Studies,* 92(2), 69–72.
Lakoff, G., & Johnson, M. (1980). *Metaphors we live by,* IL: University of Chicago Press.
Makerere University students' records (2012). Academic Registrar's office, Makerere University Kampala Uganda.

Makerere University students' records (2013). Academic Registrar's office, Makerere University Kampala Uganda.

Makerere University students' records of (2014), Academic Registrar's office, Makerere University Kampala Uganda.

Mansour, G. (1993). *Multilingualism and nation building*. Clevedon: Multilingual Matters.

Myers-Scotton, C. (2002). *Contact linguistics: Bilingual encounters and grammatical outcomes*. Oxford: Oxford University Press.

Myers-Scotton, C. (1993). *Duelling languages*. Oxford/Clarendon Press.

Namyalo, S. (2015). Linguistic strategies in Luyaaye: Word play and conscious language manipulation. In Nassenstein, N., & Hollington, A. (Eds.) *Youth language practices in Africa and beyond*. Berlin: Mouton de Gruyter, 313-344.

Reuster-Jahn, U., & Kießling, R. (2006). Lugha ya mitaani in Tanzania – the poetics and sociology of a young urban style of speaking. In Beck, R. M., Diegner, L., Dittemer, C., Geider, T., & Reuster-Jahn, U. (Eds.) *Swahili forum 13* (Special issue), Department of Anthropology and African Studies, Johannes Gutenberg University, Mainz, Germany. 1614–2373.

Sabiiti, B. (2014). *UgLish: Dictionary of Ugandan English*. Kampala: Inside.

Schneider, E. W. (2007). *Postcolonial English. Varieties around the world*. Cambridge: Cambridge University Press.

# Le contact des langues chez les jeunes Algériens
# Lecture d'un corpus sociolinguistique hétérogène

*Souheila Hedid* (Université de Constantine, Algeria)

## 1. Introduction

Depuis que les sociolinguistes ont commencé à s'intéresser à la situation sociolinguistique de l'Algérie, ils ont mis en exergue la complexité apparente de son terrain, et les difficultés qu'il présente pour la conception d'un corpus d'étude. Selon les chercheurs (Cherrad-Benchefra & Derradji, 2004; Taleb Ibrahimi, 1996; Morsly, 1996) la présence de plusieurs codes linguistiques est une caractéristique dominante dans tous les espaces discursifs de ce terrain. De plus, le mélange des codes en présence est souvent constaté. D. Morsly explique d'ailleurs que « *le mode de communication préféré des Algériens est de loin l'alternance, le mélange des langues* » (Morsly, 2004: 112). C'est justement cette pratique qui rend l'étude des comportements linguistiques des locuteurs algériens parfois très difficile à réaliser.

Les corpus sur lesquels se fondent ces recherches sont de nature diverse. L'hétérogénéité des données collectées et analysées permet de mieux cadrer le contexte sociolinguistique local. La variation linguistique est intense et les codes en présence ne bénéficient pas tous de la même situation. Le statut, la fonction, la place de ces langues (tant sur le plan institutionnel que social) attestent de l'existence d'un rapport de force, si certaines sont dominantes, d'autres sont dominées.

English summary
Since the sociolinguists began to take an interest in the socio-linguistic situation of Algeria, they have highlighted the apparent complexity of its terrain, and the difficulties it presents for the design of a body of study. According to the researchers (Cherrad, 2004; Taleb Ibrahimi, 1996; Morsly, 1996) the presence of several linguistic codes is a dominant characteristic in all the discursive spaces of this field. In addition, the mixture of the codes in the presence is often found. Morsly explains that "the preferred mode of communication for Algerians is by far the alternation, the mixing of languages" (Morsly, 2004: 112). It is precisely this practice that makes the study of the linguistic behavior of Algerian speakers sometimes very difficult to achieve.

The corpora on which his research is based are of a different nature. The heterogeneity of the data collected and analyzed makes it possible to better frame the local sociolinguistic context. The linguistic variation is intense and the codes in the presence do not all benefit from the same situation. The status, function, and place of these languages (both institutional and social) attest to the existence of a balance of power, while some are dominant, others are dominated.[1]

---

[1] English translations of the first two paragraphs have been provided above by the editors as an English guide to the chapter.

Le bilinguisme, le plurilinguisme, la situation diglossique conflictuelle, tous ces phénomènes et d'autres sont les grands pôles autour desquels s'organisent les études linguistiques en Algérie.

Dans ce cadre, l'arabe et le français ont souvent été décrits comme les deux codes les plus représentatifs de la situation sociolinguistique locale. Le premier, car langue officielle et nationale, donc soutenu pas l'Etat. Elle constitue pour la majorité des locuteurs une langue maternelle. Un code qui (dans sa version dialectale) bénéficie d'une valorisation épilinguistique de la part de la communauté linguistique en question. Le français, quant à lui, est considéré comme la langue de la modernité, des sciences et de la réussite professionnelle en Algérie. Cette langue est très enracinée dans le paysage sociolinguistique local, elle bénéficie ainsi, d'une place privilégiée de la part des locuteurs.

Mais ce paysage à deux facettes n'est pas réellement fidèle à la réalité. Une autre composante, assez importante que les deux premières, a été longtemps ignorée et passée sous silence. En effet, le tamazight couvre de larges territoires linguistiques ; les berbérophones forment aujourd'hui une communauté linguistique assez large et assez importante. Avec la mondialisation et la montée en puissance de l'anglais, le contexte décrit est devenu plus riche car ce plurilinguisme a donné naissance à plusieurs phénomènes de contact de langues. Les corpus sociolinguistiques élaborés ici attestent de cette richesse et montrent que les pratiques langagières comme les représentations sociolinguistiques sont souvent imprégnées de ce phénomène. Les locuteurs algériens et particulièrement les jeunes sont considérés, aujourd'hui plus que jamais, comme des sujets d'étude très intéressants.

Dans notre travail, il s'agit d'étudier les représentations sociolinguistiques relatives au phénomène du contact de langues, telle qu'elles sont produites par les jeunes Algériens, et ce à travers l'analyse de leurs pratiques langagières. L'étude part du postulat, selon lequel, ces jeunes locuteurs ont des représentations positives du mélange des langues, ce qui les motive à alterner plusieurs codes linguistiques. Une situation déjà étudiée par plusieurs chercheurs (Bedjaoui, 2018; Cherrad-Benchefra & Derradji, 2004; Hedid, 2017; Taleb Ibrahimi, 1996; Morsly, 1996; Tounsi, 1997) qui parlent d'un répertoire verbal très riche et des pratiques langagières parfois difficiles à étudier.

Nous allons considérer que le contact de langues revêt chez ces jeunes une fonction plus symbolique que communicative, leur permettant de créer un univers épilinguistique et socio-discursif propre à eux. Autour de cette réflexion, une kyrielle de questions se pose, nous retenons ces deux interrogations: Comment se conçoit le mélange de langues dans les interactions verbales des jeunes algériens? Quelles représentations ont ces locuteurs de ce phénomène?

L'objectif de cette étude est d'actualiser les schémas descriptifs déjà faits. Le pays a connu de grands changements socioéconomiques, politiques et même culturels. Les politiques linguistiques ont changé ; le Tamazight, par exemple, a fini par être reconnu comme langue officielle. L'anglais devient de plus en plus demandé et même exigé sur le marché de l'emploi ; il devient ainsi évident que les descriptions déjà faites doivent être renouvelées et que les données récemment relevées doivent intégrer les descriptions précédemment faites. Au cœur de ce circuit, les jeunes semblent être extrêmement sensibles à la situation sociolinguistique. Dans leurs pratiques langagières comme dans leurs représentations, les jeunes se montrent très sensibles à la question linguistique de leur pays (Hedid, 2015b). L'usage qu'ils font de ces codes est révélateur d'une envie irrésistible de les approprier, d'agir sur eux, de les structurer et les restructurer. Les différentes configurations étudiées par les chercheurs laissent apparaître des mécanismes, des techniques, des stratégies utilisées par ces locuteurs pour appréhender le contexte plurilingue dans lequel ils vivent (Cherrad, 2004; Hedid, 2015a; Morsly, 1996; Tounsi, 1997).

## 2. Méthodologie et protocole d'enquête

Les interactions verbales fournissent dans le cadre des études sociolinguistiques un corpus patent. Les productions langagières des jeunes sont mieux exploitées, une fois captées dans les circuits des échanges quotidiens. Les corpus oraux sont révélateurs des spécificités des parlers. L'authenticité des données collectées permet aux chercheurs de mieux comprendre le fonctionnement des pratiques en contexte et de capter les facteurs extra langagiers (contexte sociolinguistique) qui influent sur leurs productions langagières.

La démarche expérimentale permet d'atteindre des résultats fiables dans le cas présent. Cette démarche est susceptible de porter des réponses plus certaines dans les cas des études sociolinguistiques. L'approche adoptée est de nature sociolinguistique, elle étudie les productions langagières en contextes. Le facteur « social » est considéré ici comme déclencheur du processus linguistique, découlent de ce facteur : le choix de la langue, son usage, sa maîtrise, l'image qu'elle véhicule dans l'imaginaire collectif. La société est ainsi le générateur par excellence des interactions verbales, interpersonnelles. Il devient ainsi évident que le point de départ de toute réflexion sociolinguistique doit partir de la société, le noyau producteur des interactions verbales et qui confère dans la plupart des cas, les spécificités de ces productions des locuteurs.

### 2.1. Une triangulation méthodologique pour une problématique éclatée

Pour répondre à nos questions, nous nous proposons à une enquête de terrain auprès d'un groupe de jeunes algériens. Nous nous référons à une triangulation méthodologique (Savoie-Zajc, 2009: 285) basée sur un corpus hétérogène, composé principalement d'un questionnaire et d'un corpus oral (enregistrement d'interactions), en plus d'une prise de notes. Le choix de ces outils n'est pas aléatoire, il répond bien à des besoins épistémologiques et scientifiques relatifs à la nature des questions traitées. En effet, les corpus oraux semblent extrêmement bénéfiques quant à la description des pratiques langagières des locuteurs (Baude et al., 2006). L'on sait que l'enregistrement des interactions a permis d'établir des typologies riches en matière de classification des discours (Vion, 1992; Kerbrat-Orecchioni,

1998), il a contribué à l'analyse minutieuse des stratégies discursives. L'on sait notamment que les enquêtes par questionnaire sont généralement conçues pour atteindre les représentations sociolinguistiques. Dans les sciences sociales et précisément dans les sciences du langage, le questionnaire constitue un instrument fiable pour la lecture des contenus latents (Singly, 2005). Les représentations qui se définissent comme des constructions de la réalité sociale et linguistique des individus prennent naissance dans le circuit des interactions sociales. Le questionnaire permet de clarifier les instances organisatrices de ces représentations. L. J Calvet explique que « *tout le monde sait qu'une enquête par questionnaire ne mesure pas la pratique réelle des gens mais l'image qu'ils ont des pratiques* » (Calvet, 1999: 121), il s'agit pour nous de relever, en plus des images mentales, les mécanismes qui les activent. Pour mieux affiner notre analyse et valider notre collecte, nous utilisons une autre technique celle de la prise de notes : « *il s'agit d'une activité continue de consignation par écrit des comportements, activités et lieux observés, des conversations entendues, et des réflexions méthodologiques ou théoriques (voire existentielles) suscitées chez le chercheur par la conduite et le contenu de cette observation* » (Paillé, 2009: 162). La prise de notes permettra de relever les aspects contextuels qui caractérisent la collecte des données, des aspects susceptibles d'apporter plus de détails à notre analyse. Les données qui résultent de la triangulation sont souvent plus fiables car l'hétérogénéité des supports fait que l'analyse devient plus sure, et l'interprétation des résultats se confirme de plus en plus.

## 2.2. Terrain d'enquête, informateurs et premières représentations

Nous réalisons notre enquête à Constantine, ville de 2297.2 km², avec une population de près d'un million d'habitants. Grâce à sa situation géographique et à son potentiel économique, elle occupe une place stratégique sur les plans commercial et socioculturel. C'est une ville universitaire par excellence. Elle dispose de quatre grandes universités, en plus de plusieurs écoles supérieures et centres universitaires qui reçoivent chaque année des étudiants venus de toute l'Algérie et un nombre important d'étudiants étrangers (surtout Africains et Moyen-Orientaux). Comme toutes les villes algériennes, Constantine connaît depuis l'indépendance (1962) une urbanisation galopante. Effectivement, grâce aux conditions de vie et de travail qu'elle offre, cette ville attire de plus en plus les individus et enregistre un exode rural important. Selon les recensements effectués à Constantine, 60% de la population totale occupe la ville (la commune de Constantine, le chef lieu de la wilaya), un espace pourtant limité et ne représente que 08% de la surface de la wilaya. La création d'une nouvelle ville a accentué les phénomènes relatifs à l'urbanisation, tels que la mobilité sociospatiale, la gentrification urbaine, en plus d'une territorialisation spatiale, linguistique et même épilinguistique.

Nos lieux d'enquête sont avant tout des espaces dynamiques, très actifs et propices à l'observation des pratiques langagières des jeunes (Cherrad, 2004; Hedid,

2010). Nous réalisons nos enquêtes dans des espaces diversifiés : à l'université, dans le Centre culturel de la ville, et dans un club sportif. La sélection des lieux d'enquête s'est effectuée après une pré enquête menée auprès d'un groupe de jeunes. À l'aide d'un questionnaire (Annexe), nous avons tenté d'identifier les lieux que ces jeunes fréquentent habituellement et de façon régulière. L'étude de leurs réponses nous a permis de relever plusieurs espaces, les trois retenus sont plus adaptés à une enquête ethnographique: ouverts, dynamiques, riches en interactions et échanges verbaux, en plus d'être des lieux de rencontres quotidiennes des jeunes locuteurs.

Pour cette première investigation, nous avons pu avoir un groupe de 40 informateurs. 10 se sont désistées, expliquant qu'ils ne peuvent rien apporter d'intéressant à l'enquête du fait qu'ils ne maîtrisent aucun code linguistique et qu'ils passent régulièrement d'une langue à une autre pour pouvoir s'exprimer. Le groupe que nous avons interrogé se compose de 30 jeunes étudiants, 21 filles et 09 garçons.

Le rejet de notre enquête est une donnée extrêmement importante du point de vue épilinguistique. Il met en avant des orientations explicatives des représentations sociolinguistiques que ces jeunes développent à propos de leurs propres pratiques. Les discours épilinguistiques formulés ici attestent d'une dévalorisation et d'une sous-estimation de leurs pratiques langagières et de leurs comportements verbaux. La non-maîtrise est considérée ici comme un handicap, une anomalie qui peut paralyser une enquête sociolinguistique. Vue sous cet angle, ces jeunes reconnaissent déjà leur plurilinguisme. La présence, dans le répertoire verbal de ces jeunes, de plusieurs codes linguistiques est incontestable (Ferguson, 1956; Fishman, 1971), et leur mélange est reconnu comme une pratique défectueuse. L'observation minutieuse de leurs discours laisse apparaître un des éléments fondateur de cette dévalorisation. L'alternance des langues est considérée comme un manque de maîtrise du fait que le discours n'est jamais conçu sur une seule langue (Marçais, 1930; Calvet, 1993; Caubet, 2004). L'unilinguisme tant réclamé et enseigné à l'école, un modèle fondé sur « *la langue unique* » est toujours présent dans l'esprit de ces jeunes et soustend la construction de leurs représentations. Cette donnée se définit dans les écoles et les institutions où les jeunes sont obligés parfois d'utiliser l'arabe standard. À l'extérieur, les contraintes institutionnelles ne sont pas dépassées et elles pèsent sur l'imaginaire des jeunes. En effet, si à l'école ils doivent parler en arabe standard, à l'extérieur et dans leurs cités ces jeunes adoptent une attitude de défenseurs et critiquent tout usage qui s'écarte de cette norme.

Ceux qui ont participé à l'enquête ont entre 20 et 26 ans, 28 d'entre eux sont constantinois, deux viennent des villes avoisinantes (Annaba et El Milia). Les corpus relevés (oral et questionnaire) sont riches et montrent une dynamique langagière et une richesse du répertoire verbal des jeunes.

Pour la fiabilité des données, nous avons préféré rester à l'écart et confier le matériel aux jeunes (Labov, 1978). Cette façon de procéder nous a permis d'avoir des interactions plus spontanées et d'étudier des pratiques langagières plus authentiques. En effet, notre présence aurait pu gêner les informateurs et faute d'insécurité linguistique, ils auraient certainement modifié leurs comportements langagiers. Les enregistrements ont été effectués de façon extrêmement discrète, les locuteurs ne savaient pas qu'ils étaient enregistrés, leurs camarades avaient placé les magnétophones dans leurs cartables et dans leurs poches et les discussions étaient très animées.

### 2.3. Ce qu'ils disent dire: les pratiques en question

L'étude de des pratiques langagières des jeunes et leurs répertoires verbaux révèle une certaine homogénéité. En effet, les jeunes répondent à l'unanimité que leur langue maternelle est l'arabe. De plus, ils affirment à 100% que leurs mères sont aussi arabophones. Cependant, deux d'entre eux disent que leurs pères sont bilingues « *de nature* » (selon leurs propos) car ils ont l'arabe et le français comme langues maternelles. Concernant les langues d'enseignement, l'arabe et le français dominent toutes les réponses. Elles sont, la première langue nationale du pays et donc enseignée depuis la première année de scolarisation, la seconde, enseignée depuis la 4$^{ème}$ année primaire, car considérée comme la première langue étrangère du pays (au sens politique du terme). L'anglais vient s'ajouter comme seconde langue étrangère, son enseignement débute dès la seconde année fondamentale et continue jusqu'à la troisième année secondaire.

Pour répondre aux questions portant sur leurs représentations, les données relevées sont parfaitement intéressantes. Les jeunes, unanimes affirment qu'ils alternent les langues. Certains nous expliquent que c'est : « *c'est plus qu'une habitude chez nous les algériens. Notre dialecte est déjà un mélange* ». Pour mieux préciser cette donnée, nous relevons les positions suivantes : 60% disent que l'alternance est une nécessité, contre 40% qui affirment le contraire. Cette répartition confirme la justification donnée, et qui définit le parler algérien comme basé sur l'alternance des langues, les jeunes alternent par habitude et le passage d'une langue n'est pas perçu comme une opération nouvelle, mais un comportement habituel perçu comme acquis. Pour inciter les informateurs à préciser davantage leurs réponses, nous leur posons une question pour savoir si l'arabe, seul, est suffisant à s'exprimer et à transmettre leurs idées. Les jeunes affirment à 100% que l'arabe seul ne répond pas à leurs besoins et que le recours à d'autres langues est une obligation. Paradoxalement, pour répondre à la question qui porte sur la langue qui les aide à mieux s'exprimer, les données relevées sont les suivantes : 65% disent que c'est l'arabe, contre 35% qui affirment que c'est le français. On le voit bien, bien que l'arabe soit une langue privilégiée, le français n'est pas mal placé. Cette position se confirme dans les réponses qui suivent, où les jeunes confirment à 95% que le français est la langue la plus importante « *l'arabe n'est pas une langue à négliger mais son utilisation et sa maîtrise ne permettent pas l'obtention d'un travail ou d'accéder à une ascension sociale* ».

## 3. Le corpus oral: entre diversité linguistique et langue déstructurée

L'étude se base sur deux corpus. Le premier est oral, il se compose de 40h d'enregistrement, il a été effectué dans plusieurs espaces (déjà cités). Plusieurs techniques de collecte ont été utilisées ; les magnétophones employés n'ont pas été tous capables d'enregistrer les interactions notamment dans le club sportif et à l'université, à cause du bruit. Notre présence sur les lieux était quasi obligatoire, nous avons observé le déroulement des interactions et nous avons noté minutieusement tous les éléments qui ont influencé le contexte discursif. Grâce à cette triangulation méthodologique, nous avons pu relever un corpus assez important. Au niveau des pratiques langagières, l'enregistrement a permis d'affirmer deux constatations. Les interactions enregistrées affichent une diversité linguistique frappante : où sont utilisées plusieurs langues. Pour illustrer cela, nous présentons l'extrait suivant[2] :

> Loc1: salem, how are you, wach rak, ça va? (Trad.Comment ça va?)
> Loc2 : salut, ça va, ounti wach raki ça va ? (Trad. Salut, ça va, et toi comment vas-tu ?)
> Loc1: dert les TD taa go out (Trad. T'as fait les TD de « go out » (un appellatif pour désigner un enseignant qui fait sortir les étudiants si jamais ils ne font pas leurs travaux)
> Loc2 : j'ai pas fait, dirili copier coller (Trad. Je n'ai pas fait, peux tu me faire un copier coller de ton travail)
> Loc1 : never, maniche bonicha (Trad. Jamais, je ne suis pas ta bonne)

Entre les deux locuteurs se déroule une très longue interaction. Les sujets traités sont différents (examens, devoirs, vacances...). L'extrait choisi montre une diversité linguistique remarquable, où sont employées trois langues : le français, l'anglais et l'arabe algérien. La cohabitation des trois codes dans le même extrait, et au cœur de la même intervention montre que l'alternance des langues se situe à tous les niveaux (Myers-Scotton, 1993; Caubet, 1993). Les deux locuteurs affichent les mêmes choix linguistiques dans les autres interventions. Le mélange des langues constitue plus qu'un choix, une stratégie de communication que les jeunes emploient pour garantir leur intégration au "*réseau jeunes*" (Milroy, 1980) et pour certifier l'intercompréhension entre eux. Cette négociation des rôles (Vion, 1992) s'effectue par la langue et qui va permettre au locuteur de bien se positionner dans une interaction verbale. Le choix linguistique se pose lui aussi comme problématique, l'on s'interroge sur la correspondance entre la langue et la séquence dans laquelle elle est employée. Il semble clair que les jeunes alternent ces langues à des fins ludiques et que les séquences concernées sont en réalité des actes directeurs (Moeschler, 1985: 88), qui dirigent toute l'intervention. Sur le plan pragmatique cette attitude permet d'accorder à la langue choisie une place plus importante que les autres.

---

[2] Pour une meilleure lecture de cette interaction, nous préférons employer une transcription orthographique

## 4. Des créations lexicales: humour ou revendication?

Cette diversité linguistique montre que les jeunes jouent avec les langues. C'est le français qui subit le plus de métamorphose et de modifications. Le corpus oral révèle un grand nombre de créations ludiques ; le français est complètement ou partiellement déstructuré. Nous présentons dans ce qui suit, l'ensemble de ces créations relevées dans le corpus enregistré que les jeunes emploient souvent pour exprimer leurs idées. Ces données sont répertoriées selon des sections :

### 4.1. Les nouveaux signifiés

4.1.1. Une polysémie simple: on réalise un nouveau signifié sur la base d'un signifiant existant. Comme par exemple : *Mehchacha* qui désigne en l'argot « un lieu mal fréquenté, où les fumeurs de hachich se rencontrent ». Ici, les jeunes l'utilisent pour parler de l'université, ce terme évoque la présence de certains étudiants qui consomment des drogues et des boissons alcoolisés au sein de cet établissement.

4.1.2. *L'emprunt: ici, plusieurs types sont attestés:*

1. L'emprunt intégral: tout le terme est emprunté (forme et sens). Comme dans: *self-service*
2. L'emprunt partiel: où la forme prend les règles de la langue d'accueil. Comme dans: vesta (veste), batta (boite)…
3. La déviation sémantique: qui consiste à dévier la signification d'un énoncé. Comme dans *LMD (Licence-Master-Doctorat) dévier vers : Laissez-Moi Dormir*

4.1.3. *L'interférence*

Selon William. F. Mackey, l'interférence est « *l'utilisation d'éléments appartenant à une langue tandis que l'on en parle ou que l'on en écrit une autre* » (Mackey, 1976: 397). Nous avons l'exemple suivant : *Batatalogue* : qualificatif utilisé pour désigner les agriculteurs qui cultivent les patates (par interférence avec l'arabe le mot débute par un « b » et non par un « p ». Avec la montée excessive du prix de ces légumes, ces cultivateurs sont devenus trop demandés. Les jeunes ajoutent « logue » à la fin pour rapprocher le terme des noms des sciences en latins, comme : dermatologue, psychologue, …

D'autres créations très intéressantes sont attestées dans le corpus :
  i. *Chintoc*: pour désigner la mauvaise qualité de certains produits chinois vendus en Algérie. « Toc » fait référence au fait que ces produits sont souvent trafiqués et leur fiabilité est douteuse. Cette création s'inscrit dans la perspective d'un discours ludique que les jeunes produisent pour évoquer leur réalité et la forte présence des chinois en Algérie.
  ii. *Portablove*: pour parler des individus trop attachés à leurs téléphones, ou ceux qui ne cessent de les utiliser.

*iii. Disque fluide*: pour les femmes dont les menstruations sont irrégulières et souvent hémorragiques (langage d'informatique modifié, disque dure, fluide pour évoquer un liquide)

*iv. Annouch*: garçon poli et bien élevé, considéré comme efféminé, car il adopte des comportements trop corrects et qui ne s'adaptent pas avec le caractère masculin.

Une lecture plus attentive de ces données laisse apparaître quelques conceptions du mélange des langues chez ces locuteurs.

### 4.2. La déstructuration de la langue française et l'influence de l'anglais

Les exemples 1, 2, 3 attestent du besoin de ces jeunes d'agir sur la langue. Les procédés varient, les exemples 1 et 3 se basent sur une combinaison des préfixes et des suffixes sans toucher pour autant le sens et à la force illocutoire de chaque élément. Cette déstructuration du français permet apparemment une appropriation et une maîtrise de cette langue.

### 4.3. L'influence du domaine des TIC:

Le domaine de l'informatique leur offre la possibilité d'enrichir leurs créations. La fonction principale ici est bien ludique. Faire rire leurs interlocuteurs est le premier objectif de ces jeunes, en comparant une personne à un appareil ou à une machine et à utiliser les propriétés de ces objets pour qualifier les êtres humains.

Le mélange des langues, confirmé par l'enquête menée, montre qu'il n'y a rien d'aléatoire. Si les langues sont sollicitées c'est parce qu'elles permettent de répondre à des besoins bien particuliers. Les jeunes ne se servent pas d'une langue correcte, le plus important pour eux est de transmettre un message et de se faire comprendre par la communauté jeune.

## 5. Que conclure?

Le questionnaire utilisé dans cette étude situe la question de l'alternance dans une perspective pragmatique. Le fait est que l'objectif n'est pas de constater si cette pratique existe, ce qui est évident, mais de voir les mécanismes qui sous-tendent son émergence chez les locuteurs et les représentations qu'elle génère chez eux. De ce point de vue, la tranche d'âge de personnes jeunes est intéressante, leurs pratiques langagières et leurs représentations sociolinguistiques sont un terrain d'enquête fertile.

Les données présentées ci-dessus résultent d'une enquête de terrain, la triangulation méthodologique nous a permis de capter les deux dimensions : linguistique et épilinguistique. Les pratiques langagières exposent une dynamique et une hétérogénéité remarquable ; plusieurs langues sont sollicitées. L'arabe constitue la langue dominante, le français est la langue souvent attestée, et l'anglais celle qui s'impose le mieux dans le contexte de la mondialisation.

Bien que beaucoup d'entre eux refusent de l'admettre, l'alternance des langues bénéficie d'une place importante dans les représentations des jeunes. La lecture des réponses laisse apparaître qu'ils nient parfois la nécessite de cette pratique, car ils ne maîtrisent pas les langues étrangères, notamment le français. Toutefois, ils affirment que l'arabe ne suffit pas à transmettre les idées et que le recours à d'autres langues est une obligation, ils ajoutent que le français est une langue importante, que son utilisation ouvre bien des perspectives. Ces données se contredisent en apparence, mais leur mise en synergie permet de détecter une profonde cohérence. Ce qui motive ces locuteurs à utiliser l'alternance codique c'est certainement ces représentations, l'idée qu'ils se font de leur dialecte, qu'ils conçoivent comme un mélange. L'alternance n'est pas considérée comme une pratique, mais comme la logique qui sous-tend le parler de ces jeunes ; tel est leur point de vue.

## Références bibliographiques

Baude, O., Blanche-Benveniste, C., Calas, M., Cappeau, P., Cordereix, P. Goury, L., Jacobson, M., de Lamberterie, I., Marchello-Nizia, C., & Mondada, L. (2006). *Corpus oraux, guide des bonnes pratiques*. CNRS Editions, Presses Universitaires Orléans. Accessed on 16 Aug. 2017 at https://hal.archives-ouvertes.fr/hal-00357706/.
Bedjaoui, N. (2018). Les étudiants algériens face au français. *Taikomoji kalbotyra*, 11, 3-23.
Calvet, L.-J. (1993). *L'Europe et ses langues.* Paris: Plon
Calvet, L.-J. (1999). De l'analogique au digital. À propos de sociologie du langage et/ou sociolinguistique et/ou linguistique. *Langage et Société*, 89, 125-137.
Caubet, D. (1993). *L'arabe marocain*. Paris/Louvain: Peeters.
Caubet, D. (2004). La "darja", langue de culture en France. *Hommes & Migrations*, *1252*(1), 34-44.
Cherrad-Benchefra, Y. & Derradji, Y. (2004). La politique linguistique en Algérie. *Revue d'aménagement linguistique*, 107, 145–170.
Ferguson, C. A. (1956). Diglossia. *Word* 15, 325-340.
Fishman, J. A. (1971). The sociology of language: An interdisciplinary social science approach to language in society. In Fishman, J. A. (Ed.) *Advances in the sociology of language*. The Hague: Mouton, 217-404.
Hedid, S. (2010). Le corpus urbain: un puzzle à reconstruire. *Corpus entre donnée sociale et objet d'étude, Actes du colloque*, Alger: Université d'Alger, 127-137.
Hedid, S. (2015a) Le français dans le plurilinguisme urbain algérien : les jeunes en parlent. In Abecassis, M. & Ledegen, G (Eds.). *De la genèse de la langue à Internet. Variations dans les formes, les modalités et les langues en contact*. Oxford: Peter Lang, 181-200.
Hedid, S. (2015b). Les parlers urbains vus par les nomades. Des discours autours des villes et des langues. *Lengas. Revue de sociolinguistique*, 78. Accessed on 16 Aug. 2017 at https://journals.openedition.org/lengas/956.
Hedid, S. (2017). La formation des nouveaux enseignants de FLE à l'évaluation de l'écrit. Discours sur une pratique enseignante. *La formation initiale des enseignants de français langue étrangère, Dialogues et Cultures* 61, 102-110.
Kerbrat-Orecchioni, C. (1998). La notion d'interaction en linguistique: Origines, apports, bilan. *Langue française*, 51-67.
Labov, W. (1978). Where does the linguistic variable stop. *Working papers in sociolinguistics*, 44. Austin: Southwest Educational Development Laboratory.
Mackey, W. F. (1976). *Bilinguisme et contact des langues*. Éditions Klincksieck. Paris
Marçais, W. (1930). "La diglossie arabe". *L'Enseignement Public* 14, 401-9.
Milroy, L. (1980). *Language and social networks,* Londres. Blackwell.

Moeschler, J. (1985). *Argumentation et conversation. Elements pour une analyse pragmatique du discours*. Berne : Peter Lang

Morsly, D. (1996). *Génération M6, Le français dans le parler des jeunes algérois*. In *Plurilinguismes* N°12, 111–121.

Morsly, D. (2004). Revisiter la langue. *Le siècle des féminismes*. Paris : Les éditions de l'atelier, 319-332.

Myers-Scotton, C. (1993). Elite closure as a powerful language strategy: The African case. *International journal of the sociology of language, 103*(1), 149-164.

Paillé P. (2009). Notes (prise de). In Mucchielli A (Ed.). *Dictionnaire des méthodes qualitatives en sciences humaines et sociales*. 3rd ed. Paris : Armand Colin.

Savoie-Zajc, L. (2009). *Technique de validation par triangulation*. In, Dictionnaire des méthodes qualitatives en sciences humaines. 3ème édition. (Sous dir A. Mucchieilli), 285–286.

Taleb Ibrahimi, K. (1996). *Remarques sur la parler des jeunes algériens de Bab El Oued*. In *Plurilinguismes,* 12, 95–109.

Tounsi, L. (1997). Aspects des parlers jeunes en Algérie. In *Langue française*, 114, 104–113.

Vion, R. (1992). *La communication verbale: analyse des interactions*. Hachette.

# Annexe

Dans le but d'étudier le mélange des langues chez les jeunes Algériens, nous procédons une enquête par questionnaire. Nous cherchons à comprendre précisément comment ces jeunes conçoivent ce phénomène. Notre travail consiste à étudier les pratiques langagières et les représentations sociolinguistiques de ces locuteurs. Ainsi, nous vous adressons ce questionnaire auquel nous vous prions de répondre. Nous vous garantissons que le plus strict anonymat sera respecté.

1. Sexe :      F ☐     H ☐
2. Âge
3. Lieu de naissance
4. Langue maternelle
5. Langue maternelle de la mère
6. Langue maternelle du père
7. Langues d'enseignement
8. Parlez-vous une seconde langue ? Laquelle ?
9. Dans quels contextes avez-vous appris cette langue ?
10. Dans quelles situations de communication utilisez-vous souvent cette langue ? Pourquoi ?
11. Utilisez-vous plusieurs langues pour communiquer habituellement ? Pourquoi ?
12. Pensez vous que le recours à plusieurs langues est une nécessité ?
13. Est-ce que vous pensez que votre langue maternelle ne suffit pas à transmettre tous vos messages et toutes vos idées ?
14. Quelle est la langue qui vous permet de mieux vous exprimer ? Pourquoi ?
15. Y a-t-il une la langue que vous considériez comme plus importante que les autres ? Pourquoi ?

# Le nouchi: une menace ou un tremplin pour la promotion des langues ivoiriennes?

*Jean-Claude* Dodo (Université Félix Houphouët-Boigny, Cocody-Abidjan)
*Yves Marcel* Youant (Université Félix Houphouët-Boigny, Cocody-Abidjan)

## 1. Introduction

Apparu en 1970, le nouchi était à l'origine l'argot des délinquants et des jeunes non scolarisés. Cependant, depuis près d'une décennie, cet argot a commencé à se généraliser au point de devenir un discours urbain. Les jeunes ivoiriens, dans leur majorité, parlent de plus en plus le nouchi parfois au détriment de leur langue maternelle. Cette situation peut nous amener à savoir si le nouchi constitue une menace réelle pour les langues ivoiriennes. D'une part, on pourrait penser qu'en empruntant massivement des mots des langues ivoiriennes, le nouchi met en péril ce dernier. D'autre part, l'hétérogénéité de nouchi marquée en substance en empruntant des langues locales peut être un atout pour la continuité de ces langues.

English summary
Appearing around 1970, Nouchi was originally considered the slang of delinquents and out-of-school youth. However, for nearly a decade, this slang has begun to become generalized to the point of becoming an urban youth langage. Ivorian youth in their majority speak this language more and more, sometimes at the expense of their mother language or first language. This situation has led us to the question whether Nouchi constitutes a real threat to the Ivorian languages or not. On the one hand, one might think that by borrowing and mixing words massively, Nouchi jeopardizes the indigenous languages. On the other hand, the heterogeneity of Nouchi marked in substance by borrowing from Ivorian local languages can be an asset for the continuity of these languages.[1]

Selon Gnagra Nazaire, un des tous premiers locuteurs nouchi, à l'origine, le terme « nouchi » signifie « voleur ». Par ailleurs, ce dernier avance que le nouchi est né en 1970. Durant plusieurs années, le nouchi a été voué aux gémonies. Cet argot était exclusivement réservé aux délinquants et aux jeunes déscolarisés. Après quelques décennies écoulées, le regard sur le nouchi n'est plus le même. Cet argot a évolué. Il s'est généralisé. Le nouchi est usité maintenant par toutes les franges de la population. Il est devenu un parler urbain. En outre, il s'incruste, de plus en plus, dans les endroits de prédilection du français standard comme l'administration, l'école et autres (Aboa, 2011 ; Ploog, 2000 ; Kube, 2004).

Sa structure est ancrée sur le français tandis que ces lexèmes sont issus de langues occidentales et africaines. Ce parler émergent emprunte beaucoup de mots

---

[1] English translation is here provided for the first paragraph above as an English guide to the chapter.

aux langues ivoiriennes. Il s'invite dans pratiquement toutes les conversations. De ce fait, le nouchi constitue-t-il une menace pour les langues ivoiriennes?

Avant de répondre à cette interrogation, une brève présentation du cadre théorique s'impose. Les corrélations langue, temps, espace trouvent leur fondement dans la sociolinguistique urbaine. Il est important que les études sur les parlers de jeune prennent nécessairement en compte les marqueurs de langue et discursifs dans leur context espatio-temporel (Bulot et Veschambre, 2006). La jeunesse urbaine africaine construit sa propre identité (Kießling et Mous, 2010; Dodo et Allou, 2016). L'une des matérialités prépondérantes de cette identité demeure sans nul doute le langage. Pour la Côte d'Ivoire, le nouchi est un exemple remarquable. Les locuteurs du nouchi font preuve d'une déconcertante créativité et d'un dynamisme vertigineux (Kouadio, 1990; Dodo, 2015). L'analyse de notre corpus (en diachronie) permettra de montrer l'hétérogénéité de ce parler.

Pour cette étude, le corpus est essentiellement composé de chansons et textes. Ces compositions vocales et textes sont entièrement ou partiellement produits en nouchi.

## 2. Le nouchi, un parler hétérogène

Le nouchi est un parler hybride. La base du nouchi est le français avec cependant, un nombre important d'emprunts aux langues locales et étrangères (africaines et occidentales). Les langues locales enrichissant le nouchi sont : le dioula, le bété, le baoulé et autres. Le lingala, le pidgin nigérian, le pidgin ghanéen, des langues camerounaises, le camf-anglais sont les langues africaines pourvoyeuses de mots au nouchi. Enfin l'anglais et l'espagnol constituent essentiellement la source d'emprunt du nouchi pour les langues occidentales. Dans cet article, nous nous appesantirons sur les emprunts aux langues locales.

**2.1.** Les emprunts aux langues locales

Plusieurs mots sont empruntés aux langues locales par le nouchi. Le choix de ces langues n'est pas fortuit. En effet, le dioula, le baoulé et le bété sont des langues qui possèdent le plus grand nombre de locuteurs. Pour cette étude, nous avons recensé une liste non exhaustive de mots.

2.1.1. *Le dioula (malinké)*

C'est le plus gros pourvoyeur de mots au nouchi pour les langues ivoiriennes. Cela s'explique par deux raisons. La première est que nombre de locuteurs nouchi sont dioulas. Et la seconde, vient du fait que le dioula constitue une langue véhiculaire. Par conséquent, plusieurs parlent et ou comprennent plus ou moins cette langue. C'est la langue qui possède le grand nombre de locuteurs dans le groupe Mandé. Quelques mots nouchi issus du dioula :

Ata kabori [atakabori]: prostituée, volexécuté à la tire
Babougô [babugɔ] > [gbagbugu] / gbagbougou: frapper, bombarder
Bara [bara]: travail
Bakrôni [bakrɔni]: cabri
Bobara [bobara]: fesse
Bori [kurir]: courir
Bôrô [bɔrɔ]: sac
Djandjou [dʒãdʒu]: prostituée
Djandjouya [dʒãdʒuja]: prostitution
Djêguê/djêkê [dʒɛgɛ] / [dʒɛkɛ]: laver, se laver, êtrepropre
Dji [dʒi]: eau, (se dji) se laver mystiquement
Djinanmori [dʒinãmori]: prestidigitateur, magicien, magie
Fohite [fojite] > [yafoji] Yafohi: iln'y a rien
Fraya [fraya]: fuir
Froto [froto]: piment
Gnagami [ɲagami]: mélanger, déranger
Kabadji [kabadʒi]: eau de maïs, bière
Kouman [kumã]: dire
Kounglo [kũŋglo]: tête
Malo [malo]: riz
Mlouti [mluti]: fâché
Mousso [muso]: femme
Naloman [nalomã]: stupide
Nassidji [nasidʒi]: décoction mystique
Sôgô [sɔgɔ]: couteau, couper
Soutra [sutra]: aider
Soutrali[sutrali]: aide
Tassouman [tasumã]: feu
Tchonou[tʃonu] > [tʃũ] tchoun: dénoncer
Toubabou [tubabu]: Européen, Blanc
Trômi-trômi [trɔmitrɔmi]: se tordre
Wélé [wele]: appeler
Wolosso [woloso]: prostituée
Yougouyaga [jugujaga]: sécouer

## 2.1.2. *Le bété*

C'est le second pourvoyeur de mots au nouchi au plan local. Certains locuteurs natifs comme Boni Dagrou (RAS), Kéké Kassiry et John Pololo ont intégré plusieurs mots bétés au nouchi. C'est la langue qui a le plus de locuteurs dans le groupe Kru.

Quelques mots nouchi issus du bété
Abi: frère
Awouli [awuli]: mon ami

Gnétè [ɲetɛ]: seins
Gnézédré [ɲezedʀe]: pitié
Gnoukouli [ɲukuli]: oreille
Gnrin [ɲʀĩ] ou Gninrin [ɲĩʀĩ]: vagin
Gninnin [ɲĩʀĩ] > [ɲĩnĩ] odeur: saoul, ivre
Guédji [gedʒi]: drogue
Lalé [lale]: appeler, téléphone
Poagnon [poaɲɔ̃]: orphelin
Soukou [suku]: école
Woody [wudi]: garçon
You [ju]: enfant en bété, policier en nouchi

### 2.1.3. *Le baoulé (Kwa)*

Le baoulé est une langue de groupe Kwa. A l'instar du dioula et du bété, c'est la langue qui possède le plus grand nombre de locuteurs dans le groupe Kwa.

Ahoko [aoko]: instrument de musique baoulé, masturbation en nouchi
Blêblê [blɛblɛ]: doucement
Blô [blɔ]: faire le malin
Blôfouê [blɔfuɛ]: blanc
Djêtê [dʒɛtɛ]: argent
Likefi [likefi]: rien
Nanwlê [nãwlɛ]: vérité
Souklou [suklu]: école

### 2.1.4. *Les autres langues locales*

Le wobé, le guéré, le sénoufo et le touraontune influence moins prépondérante sur le nouchique le dioula, le bété et le baoulé. Toutefois, ils donnent quelques mots au nouchi.

Cobo [kobo]: vieux en wobé devient père en nouchi
Bahi [baji]: habit en guéré mais malchance en nouchi
Gbêlê [gbɛlɛ]: boisson (sénoufo)
Pongué-pongué [pɔgepɔge]: rien (toura)
Maplo [maplɔ] ou plo [plɔ] (Wobé): faire l'amour

Tous les mots empruntés énumérés ci-dessus ont une forte récurrence en nouchi. Ces mots sont dans différents énoncés.

## 2.2. Les onomatopées et idéophones

Les onomatopées et les idéophones sont également utilisés dans le nouchi. Ce sont des mots en partie empruntés aux langues locales ou tout simplement crées par les locuteurs. Selon Hagège C. (2009: 307), un idéophone est : « une peinture sonore d'une idée, pour symboliser un état, une impression sensorielle, une manière d'être ou de se mouvoir, une action qui n'est pas nécessairement elle-même reproductrice d'un bruit ». Cependant, l'idéophone est très souvent confondu à l'onomatopée qui est l'imitation d'un bruit naturel.

### 2.2.1. *Les onomatopées*

Les mots onomatopéiques sont de nature diverse. Il y a des verbes, des adjectifs et des adverbes.

Bao [bao]: pistolet (imitation du bruit d'un pistolet mis à feu)
Bêhê [bɛɛ]: homosexuel (imitation du cri du mouton)
Boudoum [budum]: tam-tam (imitation du son du tambour)
Djomolo [dʒomolo]: téléphone bas de gamme (imitation de la sonnerie d'un telephone bas de gamme)
Dj(ou)roudj(a)ra: éventrer, blesser grièvement (imitation du bruit de l'éventration)
Douhi [duji]: explosion (imitation du bruit d'une explosion)
Doum [dum]: déflagration (imitation du bruit d'une forte explosion)
Gbô [gbɔ]: salutations (imitation du son du croisement de deux poings)
Gbrin-gbrin [gbʀin]: somme d'argentin signifiante, petite monnaie
Kiakiakia oukiokiokio: rire aux éclats (imitation du rire sans retenue)
Kpakpa [kpakpa]: chaussure (imitation du son des talons d'une chaussure)
Kpayaille [kpajaj]: rencontre, choc (imitation du son d'un choc violent)
Kprass [kpʀas]: canif (imitation du son du canif quand on le déplie)
Krikata [kʀikata]: dj au sens péjoratif (imitation du son des galops du cheval)
M(ou)roum(ou)rou : long couteau, machette (imitation du son de l'entaille faite par ces objets)
Tchra [tʃʀa]: déchirer, blesser (imitation du son d'une entaille)
Teunneunneun, tinninnin [tɛ̃nɛ̃nɛ̃]: téléphoner (imitation de la sonnerie d'un portable)
Roukasskass: Roulade de batterie de musique
Wouhoo [wuoo]: joie (imitation de bruit exultation de la foule après un but)
Zaga-zaga [zagazaga]: mitraillette (imitation du son des tirs à répétitions d'une mitraillette)

Excepté les items dj(ou)roudj(a)ra, m(ou)roum(ou)rou qui sont issus du dioula, tous les autres items sont des creations des locuteurs nouchieux-memes.

### 2.2.2. *Les idéophones*

Ces mots idéophoniques sont composés de verbe, adverbe, nom et adjectif.

Agbolo, digba, doungba: personne musclée
Blagada [blagada]: sans force, veule, avachi
Flêkê-flêkê [flɛkɛflɛkɛ]: personne très mince, sans force
Fouin [fuɛ̃]: petit
Gbougbou [gbugbu]: braquer, faire un hold-up
Gbra [gbʀa]: descendre, enlever, destituer

Graou [gʀau]: voleur
Kaba-kaba [kabakaba]: vite
Krakra [kʀakʀa]: courageux, téméraire
Mouinoumouin-mouin: timide, nonchalant
Mougou-mougou [mugumugu]: somme d'argent insignifiante, petite monnaie
Fian-fian qui devientpian-pian [piãpiã] en nouchi: vantard, fanfaron
Pôtchô [pɔtʃɔ]: bon, excellent
Prin-prin [pʀẽpʀẽ]: Plaisantin, bouffon, plaisanterie, bouffonnerie
Nguê [ngɛ]: petit, enfant
Souê [suɛ]: silencieusement, calmement
Sri [sʀi]: attraper
Tchoko-tchoko [tʃokotʃoko]: quoi qu'il advienne, coûte que coûte.
Tchoun [tʃũ]: dénoncer
Tuss [tys]: petit
Zou [zu]: bien habillé, tiré à quatre épingle
Zouinouzouin-zouin [zuẽ zuẽ]: timide, nonchalant

Les idéophones **flêkê-flêkê, mougou-mougou** et **tchoko-tchoko** sont issus du dioula. Tandis que **fianfian, mouin-mouin, zouin-zouin** et **souê** sont des idéophones qui proviennent du baoulé. Les autres idéophones sont des créations originales ou d'origine inconnue.

Dans ce corpus, nous constatons qu'il y a peu d'onomatopées et d'idéophones empruntés aux langues ivoiriennes.

## 3. Le nouchi : un allié pour les langues ivoiriennes

Nous constatons au vu de ce qui précède que cette variété du français (le nouchi) s'appuie fortement sur les langues ivoiriennes. Ce qui en ce sens peut constituer un moyen de promotion de cesdites langues. Le nouchi n'est donc pas une menace pour les langues ivoiriennes mais plutôt un allié, un partenaire stratégique pour la promotion de ces langues.

En outre, le nouchi dans un environnement plurilingue tel que celui de la Côte d'Ivoire, le nouchi assume la fonction de langue véhiculaire tout comme le français, par ailleurs, langue officielle.

Le nouchi constitue donc un trait d'union entre les langues ivoiriennes dans la mesure où elle l'intersection de celles-ci.

## 4. Conclusion

En définitive, il ressort que le nouchi ne peut constituer une menace pour les langues ivoiriennes. Il est plutôt un tremplin pour la promotion de ces langues. Ce sociolecte constitue un trait d'union du fait de son hétérogénéité marquée en substance par un emprunt massif aux langues ivoiriennes.

# Références bibliographiques

Aboa, A. L. (2011). Le nouchi a-t-il un avenir? *Dans Sud langues*, 16, Dakar, 44-54.
Bulot, T. et Veschambre, V. (2006). *Mots, traces et marques. Dimensions spatiale et linguistique de la mémoire urbaine*. Paris: L'Harmattan.
Dodo, J-C. et Allou, S. (2016). Les parlers urbains africains: Regard sur la construction d'une nouvelle identité endogène. Communication présentée au Colloque International Pluridisciplinaires du LAASSE. *Regards croisés des Sciences sociales et humaines sur les dynamiques actuelles des sociétés africaines.* Université Félix Houphouët-Boigny, WASCAL, Campus Bingerville, 16-17 mars 2016.
Dodo, J-C. (2015). Le nouchi : étude linguistique et sociolinguistique d'un parler urbain dynamique. Thèse unique de Doctorat, Université Félix Houphouët-Boigny, Cocody-Abidjan.
Hagège C. (2009). *Dictionnaire amoureux des langues*. Plon/Odile Jacob.
Kießling, R. et Mous, M. (2010). Vous nous avez donné le français, mais nous sommes pas obligés de l'utiliser comme vous le voulez. In *Youth Languages in Africa*, 362–37.
Kouadio, N. J. (1992). Le nouchi abidjanais, naissance d'un argot ou mode linguistique passagère ? *CIRL* 32. ILA. Université d'Abidjan.
Kube, S. (2004). Le rôle des locuteursdans les actions sur la diversitélinguistique – voixd'élèvesd'Abidjan.*ColloqueDéveloppement durable.Leçonset perspectives*. 1-4 juin 2004. Ouagadougou, http://www.francophonie-durable.org/documents/colloque-ouaga-a1-kube.pdf.
Ploog, K. (2000). La Norme dans l'observation des normes abidjanaises: étude d'un continuum linguistique. *Lengas*, 23(48), 103–128.

# The Urban Film Narrative as a Space of Linguistic Hybridity in Africa

*Shikuku Emmanuel Tsikhungu* (Jomo Kenyatta University, Nairobi)

## 1. Introduction

The African urban cinema is one of the cultural productions through which a multiplicity of languages comes into dialogue. It is thus important to address urban cinematic narratives between African cities as sites where a multiplicity of languages jostles for space. The different languages used in telling the urban story must be weighed against the discourse of linguistic syncretism because "each language reflects a unique worldview and culture complex, mirroring the manner in which speech community has resolved its problems in dealing with the world, and has formulated its thinking, its system of philosophy and understanding of the world around it" (Wurm, 1991: 13).

The African urban film provides an expressive site for the coexistence of a multiplicity of languages, hence creating a linguistically hybrid zone. The urban youth seize this opportunity to further expand linguistic horizons at the social level within the cities. In this article, I choose to interrogate the way languages are imagined and hybridized in the films for the reason that languages organize cultures, thereby giving the right of inclusion or exclusion, and it is in the linguistic field that perhaps cultural confluences are designed and defined.

## 2. Hybridizing Urban Youth Languages in Films

The two films explored in this chapter are Tosh Gitonga's *Nairobi Half Life* (2012) and Claus Wischmann's and Martin Baer's *Kinshasa Symphony* (2010). The hybridization of youth language in the films follows three strategies, which are: code-mixing, creolization and linguistic assignment of characters. Code-mixing, which is characterized by the use of words of different languages in the same sentence, is present in the two films; it is also characterized by the use of sentences of different languages in a speech phrase. One of the major processes creolization involves is the creation of new words by contracting or bringing together stems of words from different languages. Assigning different languages to characters depends on various factors. For example, geo-spacing or tempo-spacing character identity is a strategy popularized by filmmakers like Sembene Ousmane (see Shohat & Stam, 1997).

These strategies of hybridizing language act as agents of discrete communication revealed through either conformity or deviation from mainstream local and official languages. While the strategies are used to get close to the urban dwellers as a special brand of users and consumers of the languages, hence achieving verisimilitude, they are also meant to shut out unwanted attention. Moreover, such hybridized languages act as forms of social communication that break down official barriers within the cityscape. This is particularly true of Lingala as used in the documentary *Kishsasa symphony*. The languages also act as character identity markers revealing the fragmented history of their users.

## 2.1. Hybridity in Kinshasa Symphony (2010)

*Kinshasa Symphony is* a documentary set in the informal settlements on the periphery of Kinshasa city of the Democratic Republic of Congo. The documentary film gets its strongest appeal from the exterior wide angle shots that sweep through the streets of Kinshasa to reveal a space fraught with lack and want and yet so vibrant and colourful. The story itself narrates the quest of a band of ambitious Congolese musicians who try what they did not know and end up knowing by singing and playing Beethoven's Symphony Nine. Orchestra Symphonique Kimbanguiste is a musical outfit under the directorship of Armand, a strict leader who always speaks fluent French, marking the language as that of serious business in the film. In one of the documentary interviews in the film, Armand reveals that he is actually not just the band leader but also a spiritual leader of the Kimbanguiste sect; a sect formed and named after a famous spiritual leader Kimbangu.

Apart from the cinematography, the success of the documentary as an Afropolitan story comes from the use of hybridized forms of languages of Kinshasa – Lingala, Swahili, French and sometimes a mixture of all. French is the language of official communication, particularly when instructing anyone who may not understand the different varieties of Lingala or Swahili. For example, and as noted earlier, Armand the conductor addresses his members in French.

Swahili, which is predominantly spoken in various Eastern and South Eastern parts of Congo and brought to the centre of the city by migrants to the capital, acts as a centre language amidst the competing languages of Lingala and French. As much as it is not widely used in the film in its pure sense as it is in East Africa, it forms communicative linguistic fragments in between Lingala and French.

Lingala circulates as the language of social communication, or what Bokamba (2009) refers to as "language of wider communication" (LWC). It is also the dominant language used for daily communications in Kinshasa metropolis. Bokamba further notes that Lingala serves several functions in Kinshasa, key of them being to unite migrants who come from other parts of the country as well as to create Congolese music.

It must also be noted that Lingala has variations, as Nassenstein (2015) posits.[1] These variants are creolized by several sections of the society to serve their own needs. For example there is the Yankee variety, which is mainly used by street children, and the Langila, which is an elite creolization that serves the linguistic interest of artists of Congo. The latter is popularized by the Soukous and Rumba singers (Nassenstein, 2015). However, these creolizations are really isolated and

---

[1] In this article, Nico Nassenstein details the two Lingala varieties, i.e. Yankee and Langila. However there is another variety called Kindoubil. For a discussion on this variety of Lingala creolization, see Wilson (2012).

serve interests of various communities of practice. Lingala in its standard form forms the spine of the hybridization since French and Swahili rotate around it. It Africanizes the film *Kinshasa Symphony,* as can be seen in the excerpt below:

> *Eza qui est cache. Eza qui a zala qui on dirait moin ba Rhythm moko yaba Rhythm Africaines eza Beethoven*
>
> ("And that is what is hidden. We can say or conclude that there is African rhythm in Beethoven.")

It can be noted from the above that most Lingala words (*Eza, zala, moko,* etc.) co-exist side by side and are interrelated and intertwined with French words (*qui est cache, rhythm Africaines,* etc.) to create meaning. It should also not be lost that the use of 'Ba' as a Bantu human noun plural prefix to signal belonging is Bantu in nature (Bokamba, 2009: 67). So when Tresor talks of *ba Rhythm Africaine* to mean African rhythms, he is simply borrowing from the Bantu prefix to make sense to the Bantu language speakers, while using French words to sound official. Through code mixing, he is making the message accessible to those listening to him.

## 2.2. Linguistic "Disorientation" in *Kinshasa Symphony*

In *Kinshasa*, and as noted earlier, the language spoken in the offices is French. Thus it is marked clearly as the official language to the extent that when the interviewer is interviewing the members of the orchestra Kimbanguiste, they all speak in French. However, all these change in the streets and in the market places as well as homes where the hybridized language that meets at the interstice of Lingala, Swahili and French takes over. Since the language is free flowing, the filmmakers even position the camera in such a way as to sway the audience into feeling the disorientation that the language causes to non-speakers by picking the fragmented scraps of the motor vehicle being repaired as the members of the group pass on the road as well as the derelicts that would have been the Institute of Teaching Media Studies. For example, when the young chorist Tresor Wamba of the Orchestra Kimbanguiste is exchanging banter with his fellow Kinshasa youth in his neighbourhood while distributing posters announcing the night of the orchestra, he uses the hybridized Lingala thus:

> *Nazala Tresor, la tressurya familliena Ngai. Na zalakuimba Tenor naya Orchestra Kimbanguiste. Oho lo navingthuit, ce qui mwa ye te. La eza belle on va joule ba Handel, Ba Verdi ba Beethoven*
>
> ("I am Tresor, the treasure of my family... I sing tenor in the Orchestra Kimbanguiste. On the 28th all of you should come... We sing many sing very beautiful of the likes of Handel, Verdi, Beethoven...")

The excerpt above mixes languages and virtually disorients one. It is neither French nor Swahili nor Congolese language per se but a mixture of the three. However, one does not need be fluent in the three languages to understand the excerpt. Urban youth languages, as Karanja (2010) posits, are understood by their speakers by the context rather than based on the meaning of the words. One who understands French would simply understand that the name Tresor is a play on *trésor* which means treasure as Tresor thinks of himself.

### 2.3. Localizing and Hybridizing the Urban Vernacular in *Nairobi Half Life*

The most conspicuous example of linguistic hybridity exhibited in the urban film narratives explored in this chapter is to be found in Tosh Gitonga's *Nairobi Half Life*. The film recounts the story of a young man who abandons the tribulations of the rural Kenya to try his luck in the city, only to encounter greater tribulations that are well expressed in the fragmentation of his life, and in his language. He joins groups of boys whose background he does not know, but in whose company he resigns himself in order to make a living. In this film, the filmmakers employ Sheng, a hybrid language between English and other local Kenyan languages, but mainly Swahili to fuse and represent the Nairobi Narrative. Sheng is characterized by phrasal switching, reversal of letters as well as of words in phrases and formation of new words. Language is used to mark geo spatial territories whereby Kenyan indigenous languages like Gikuyu, Luo, Meru and Kamba are for the rural dwellers. What is in-between these rural and the urban core is marked by Sheng while the urban centre is marked by English. But Sheng, the in-between language, whose hybridity is extolled by Karanja (2010) as fluid and almost elusive, can be seen from the excerpt from *Nairobi Half Life* below:

> MWAS: *Inaweza Kuaje?* ("Can you find a way out for me?")
> JOSE: *Ukopoa, ukopoa, ukopoa. Ubayaniukoocha.* ("You are a good actor. Problem is you are in the rural area")
> MWAS: *Naezakam Nairobi* ("But I can come to Nairobi")
> JOSE: *Halafu?* ("And then?")
> MWAS: Can you help me?
> JOSE: *Kuna vile, eeh, kuna vile. Lakini Ukikam Nai lazima utafute agent.* ("There is a way but you must look for an agent once you are in Nairobi".)
> MWAS: *Aaah, Agent, Naeza get aje agent?* ("Oh, an agent, but how can I get an agent?")
> JOSE: *mi hukuaga agent* ("I am usually an agent")
> *Haki*!? ("Really?")
> JOSE; *Eeeh*! ("Yeah")
> MWAS: Can you help me?
> JOSE: *Kukuokole hukuaga chapchap. Ikohapa. Bora tuunipe 5k* ("Helping you is easy. I know how. Just give me 5K")

A speaker of English, Swahili, Kikuyu and Luo would be able to understand that all these languages have been amalgamated in this language in various forms.[2] Such forms include contraction, e.g. *Naeza* instead of *Naweza*, code-mixing, e.g. *Naeza get* (where *naweza* is Swahili and "get" is English), *Ukikam* (*Uki* is Swahili

---

[2] English is the official Language in Kenya but Swahili is the national language, while Luo, Meru, Gikuyu and Luhya are some of the local languages spoken by the corresponding ethnic communities.

stem, while 'come' is English), and new formations, e.g *Ocha* to mean 'rural' where *Ocha* is from a Luo language stem among others. Sheng, in this context, is not only unifying the other linguistic zones but also mapping out its own territory that only its users and consumers can understand.

In *Nairobi Half Life*, it can also be noted that there are occassionally some words from local Kenyan languages in the film, which in these contexts act like Sheng. Some examples of various uses of local languages which may easily pass as Sheng words are as follows:

1. *Ngai* – exclamation in Kikuyus language to mean "God!"
2. *Kalife, kaworks*: "Some life, some work" – the prefix 'Ka' coming before a noun is a Gikuyu diminutive prefix to explain something that can help in a holding position.
3. *Morio* – "friend" in Gikuyu
4. *Murume* – "male human" in the film context although in Meru it transcends masculinity.
5. *Nairobi Vitu Huendangahivo* – "That's how it happens in Nairobi." The suffix '-nga' is Luhya used to suggest present continuous tense. Adding it at the end of a Swahili word makes the Swahili word sound more Luhya than Swahili.
6. *Ocha* – rural home. 'O-' is the prefix that signifies luofication of a word. Prefixing the 'O-' on a name gives it a Luo register.

The use of these borrowings and affixations from local languages and languages at the interstice seems to emanate from the difficult situations that the users find themselves in. Youth characters have been positioned as entrapped by economic hardship, living precariously and on the margins of the soft core of the cities. On one hand, the mixing of languages is a manifestation of the characters' search for a way out of their own worlds that seem to not have a bright future. It is a vain search for responsibility, respect, prestige and economic freedom in a world that shuts them out through capitalistic tendencies of cultural and material production. On the other hand it is a manifestation of their search for identity in multiple and competing ethnic linguistic variants in the city. The youth seem to be using words from local communities that they have no ethnic affiliation to perhaps so as not to be seen to belong to one or the other through language. This in a way may be a linguistic camouflage strategy in a city and country that experiences political tensions arising from negative ethnicity.

The above assertion may be further qualified when one interrogates the names that characters are given in the film. The main character, whose full name is *Mwangi*, is simply contracted to *Mwas*, and his partner in crime is *Oti*, which one can speculate is a contracted form of *Otieno*. The head of the rival criminal gang is *Dingo*, a name that sounds local but cannot be placed in any ethnic community. The criminal merchant's name is *Waya*, perhaps a covert corruption from the English word *wire*. This use of contracted and covert local names seems to unconsciously give the urban youth a safety net in a city that fails to positively harness its ethnic diversity.

## 3. Local Languages as Hybrid Markers in Urban Film Narratives

Film, being an instrument of artistic representation, cannot be presumed to be linguistically innocent. It must be tasked to bear responsibility to what it carries through language as a means of representations. As an instrument of artistic representation, it draws synergy from the social phenomena, which in turn feeds it in a reflexive manner. Thus, film reflects upon the reality in which it was created.

In urban narrative and discourse especially within Africa, the urban dweller is a dislocate figure. The urban dweller in Nairobi, and Kinshasa, is a migrant who is ambivalently at home away from home. Karanja's eponymous paper describes this state as "'homeless' at home" (2010). With close to over ten million other city dwellers in Kinshasa and approximately five million dwellers in Nairobi and all coming from different parts of the respective countries, such a dweller finds him or herself at once at home and at the same time dislocated. While his or her language is that of "home" (rural), where he/she migrated yet he/she must seek to fit in the metropolis by interacting with other migrants. This therefore results in a language that is, just like the speaker, dislocated, but is trying to fit into the multiplicity of other languages. This then gives birth to a language that is comprehensible in the city but not necessarily away from it. This hybrid language feeds from the local languages as has been noted above.

Such a situation calls for an understanding of these phenomena from a hybrid perspective: a perspective popularized by Homi Bhabha in his various writings on the postcolonial situation. It is perhaps the African city that has experienced the greatest effects of the postcolony in the sense that Achille Mbembe uses the term (Mbembe, 2001). The perspective of hybridity evokes notions of consciousness and agency as well as seeing urban dwellers as subjects that exist at the linguistic interstice and aware of their own reality. Furthermore it calls for reading identity, especially linguistic identity, as hybrid, since it challenges the dominant/colonial/official language through merging it with the other peripheral and local languages (Bhabha, 1994). The perspective warns of complacent optimism about the relationship between the dominant Europhones and the multiplicity of third world African languages which should be tempered with a dose of historical reality. Bhabha offers this dose of reality when he notes:

> So no culture is full unto itself, no culture is plainly plenitudinous, not only because there are other cultures which contradict its authority, but also because its own symbol-forming activity, its own interpellation in the process of representation, language, signification and meaning-making always underscores the claim to an originary, holistic, organic identity. (Rutherford & Bhabha, 1990: 210).

## 4. Conclusion

Dislocated figures (as most urban dwellers are) exhibit linguistic fragmentation that reflects their self-fragmentation in order to fit in fractured spatio-temporal situations, so that the language they speak has traces of both the host culture and the parent culture. Their language is rarely essential, pure and free of the two influences of their lives since the city is a confluence of many fragmentations. The characters in Gitonga's *Nairobi Half Life* and Wischmann and Baer's *Kinshasa Symphony* have to keep shifting between local languages to Nairobi English and back to Swahili in order to fit into their role as Nairobi dwellers. The infusion of the local languages in the resultant mix is conspicuous. However, shifting from one language to the other affords them acceptance in both spaces and thus truncates any idea of essentializing language and identity. Since urban dwellers are already dislocated subjects, one expects traces of the different languages that embody these dislocations in their speeches; thus, films about such characters would remain alive to this fact of dislocation. The films are alive to the environment (cultural, political and social and even economical) and therefore use linguistic syncretism to tell the stories at the interstice of cultures.

## References

Bhabha, H. K. (1994). *The Location of Culture*. London and New York: Routledge.
Bokamba, E. (2009). The Spread of Lingala as a Lingua Franca in the Congo Basin. In McLaughlin, F. (Ed.) *The Languages of Urban Africa*. London and New York: Continuum, 50–70.
Karanja, L. (2010). "Homeless" at home: Linguistic, cultural and identity hybridity and third space positioning of Kenyan urban youth. *Education Canadienne et Internationale, 39*(2), 1–11.
Mazrui, A. A. (2003). Maintaining linguodiversity; Africa in the twenty first century. In Tonkin, H., & Timothy, R. (Eds.) *Language in the twenty first century*. Amsterdam/Philadelphia: John Benjamins Publishing Company, 97–113.
Mbembe, A. (2001). *On the postcolony*. Berkeley: University of California Press.
Nassenstein, N. (2015). The Emergence of Langila in Kinshasa (DRC). In Nassenstein, N., & Hollington, A. (Eds.) *Youth language practices in Africa and beyond*. Berlin: Mouton de Gruyter, 81–98.
Preusse, H. (Producer) & Baer, M., Wischmann (2010) Kinshasa Symphony [Motion picture]. Germany: Salzgeber & Co. Medien GmbH.
Rutherford, J., Bhabha, H. K. (1990). The Third Space. Interview with Homi Bhabha. In: Rutherford, J. (Ed.) *Identity: Community, Culture, Difference*. London: Lawrence & Wishart, 207-221.
Shohat. E., & Stam, R. (1997). *Unthinking Eurocentrism*. London: Routledge.
Tykwer, T. (Producer) & Gitonga, D. T. (Director) (2012). Nairobi Half Life [Motion picture]. Kenya: Indigo.
Wilson, C. (2012). *The Congolese Yankee: Language and identity among youth in Kisangani*. Leiden: University of Leiden.
Wurm, S. A. (2001). *Atlas of World languages in danger of disappearing*. Paris: UNESCO Publishing.

# Performing Urban-Rural and Modern-Traditional Identities through Popular Zambian Music

*Felix Banda* (University of Western Cape, South Africa)

## 1. Introduction

Zambian musicians construct multiple identities and localities (urban and rural, and traditional and modern) through exploiting lexico-grammatical features and rhyming across urban and rural forms of Zambian languages (Bemba and Nyanja) and English. In this chapter, I use the notion of *multivocality* (Bakhtin, 1981) to show how the resulting linguistic capital becomes the tool through which the musicians recontextualise the rural and the urban, and the traditional and the modern to produce new cultural *selves* and to remake the world around them. I show how they use the resulting linguistic capital as semiotic material in the co-articulation of the rural and the urban, and traditional and modern ways, as the contemporary lifestyle. I contend that the resulting translanguaged forms, comprising English and urban and rural Zambian languages are transformative of the 'original' languages, the musicians, music fans and society at large. I conclude that the resulting linguistic and cultural dispensations are reflective of the transcultural and transmodal communicative practices constituting the glocalized world in which they live – a world in which the rural-urban and traditional-modern lifeworlds are morphed into one.

## 2. Language and Music in Zambia

Multivocality, multilocality and hybridity can be seen as constituting the frames of discourse practice in popular Zambian music. Zambia is a landlocked country found in South-Central Africa. It is said to have more than 72 ethnic groups who speak more or less related 72 tongues (Marten and Kula, 2008) as the languages belong to the Benue-Congo family, a branch of the Niger-Congo family, which in turn is a subdivision of the Niger-Kordofanian (Miti, 2006). Specifically, all the languages belong to the Bantu language family. Bemba is clustered as M42 and Nyanja as N31 in the Guthrie (1967/1971) classification. The government had zoned the country into seven linguistic areas in which seven languages are used for local administration. The languages are Bemba, Nyanja, Tonga, Lozi, Luvale, Lunda and Kaonde. Bemba is mainly spoken in the Northern area, while Nyanja is spoken in the Eastern side, and in Mozambique and Malawi where it is called Chewa.

Bemba is the most widely spoken language in Zambia, followed by Nyanja. Both languages are used as lingua francas. Both languages have urban versions with urban Bemba mainly spoken in the cities on Copperbelt mines, while urban Nyanja is mainly spoken in Lusaka, the capital city of Zambia. However, since there is a lot of mobility of Zambians across the rural-urban divide and from one linguistic zone to another region, one finds languages spread outside their official zones.

In evaluating how musicians stylize multiple musical affiliations, ethnolinguistic, cultural identities as well as multiple locality through their music, I specifically draw on lyrical and visual performances in the popular video *Kapilipili* by JK (featuring Salma) (2010/2014). JK is the stage name of Jordan Katembula, while Salma is the stage name of female Hip Hop artist Salma Dodia.

## 2.1. Zambian Music

There has been very little in terms of published research on Zambian music in recent times, and there is little or no literature on popular music and performance of identities and localities in contemporary Zambia. Most of the literature is from the 1980s and before, and focused on the spiritual and cultural aspects of traditional music and instrumentation. For instance, Mapoma (1988), Mensah (1970, 1971) and Davidson (1970) focused on ethnomusicology. The healing properties of traditional music have also been of interest. Mapoma (1988) investigated the role of music in healing among the Bemba speakers of Northern Zambia.

Traditional Zambian music and dance styles are known for their energetic expression and versatility in performance. Traditional music has been used for social commentary, in rites of passage, birth, funerals, and for entertainment purposes from time immemorial. It is also the case that traditional music and dance styles are not static as they change with the times, or what they are being performed for. Mtonga (2006) describes the masquerade dance called *Gule Wamkulu* ('Big Dance') of the Chewa found in Zambia, Malawi, Mozambique and Zimbabwe as an enterprise, whose performance and symbolisms change with occasion and time. *Gule Wamkulu* is not only versatile in execution, but also innovative in the manner in which the dancer through the symbolisms depicted by the mask, dress and other accessories portrays past and present history, as well as the social, economic and political structures and discourses. Kunkeyani (2014), in her evaluation of HIV and AIDS campaign in Malawi, has argued that through suggestive dance moves, gestures, lyrics and masks, *Gule Wamkulu* has been used to parody aspects of tradition and modern lifestyles, colonialism, Christianity, and as form of social commentary. Innovation with times and situations has continued with the *Gule Wamkulu*, as in contemporary times special masks, lyrics and dance styles have been 're-originated' and new ones formed for use, for example, in HIV and AIDS and malaria prevention programmes (Kunkeyani, 2014). The same can be said of other traditional music and dances, including Kalindula traditional music on which the sounds in the video to be analysed are partly based.

The negative portrayal of women in popular Zambian music has found focus in Longwe and Clarke's (1998) study. They approach the topic from a feminist perspective and are critical of the patriarchal social structure for engendering gender-biased lyrics. Banda and Mambwe (2013) suggest that it is not only in popular music that gender biases are found; they list a number of both traditional and modern Zambian music in the 1950s and before, as portraying women to be subservient to men, and meant for the home and as cultural keepers. Banda and Mambwe

(2013) also focus on the positive role that Zambian music is playing as a vehicle for social messages and societal cohesion, as well as in the fight against HIV and AIDS.

In trying to capture the dynamism of Zambian music and dance, especially the transformation and repurposing of semiotic material, Banda and Mambwe use re-semiotisation (Iedema, 2003) and semiotic remediation (Prior & Hengst, 2010) to demonstrate the circulation of semiotic resources in HIV/AIDS messages in Zambian music lyrics and videos. They also show the semiotic appropriation of lived socio-cultural experiences and beliefs, as the producers and singers exercise their creative and authorial stamp on specific compositions. Banda and Mambwe's (2013) study falls short of exploring the re-stylisation and blending of different kinds of music genres into popular Zambian music for multiple affiliations and identity performance.

## 2.2. Multivocality in Zambian Music

The interest of this article is in the influence of the traditional music style called Kalindula on what is increasingly associated with popular Zambian music. Katulwende (2015) traces the origins of Kalindula music to Samfya District in Luapula Province in the northern part of Zambia. Although the music was traditionally used in dirges, Kalindula has evolved different styles so that it is used to define moments related to weddings, love, illness, and marriage among others. As a traditional music, Kalindula is known for its powerful vocal performance (it used to be sung without any instruments), intricate vocal harmonies and complex lyrical content designed to depict multifarious imagery and symbolisms. Modern Kalindula music has incorporated guitars, drums and other electronic instruments. It is also often merged with local and globalised music genres such as Reggae, Caribbean Dance Hall and American R&B, and the West African High Life music genres. The High Life music originated from Ghana but was popularised by Fela Kuti, a Nigerian, is known for jazzy horns and guitar licks, whose general melodic and rhythmic structures are framed in the traditional African harmonies. The interest of this paper is in both the blending of music genres and the use of multiple languages by musicians to produce heteroglossia to express multiple identities, multivocality and multilocality.

When accounting for multiple voices in the lyrics, sound and visual performance of songs, Bakhtin's notion of multivocality is useful. Higgins (2009a: 6) defines multivocality as "a set of interlinked concepts ... on voice as well as the multiple perspectives, or speaking positions, articulated through language." She relates the term to "the different voices" or *polyphony* that single utterances can yield due to their syncretic nature" (p. 7). The creative blending of language leads to the resulting form to be *bivalent* (Woolard, 1999), that is, to belong to two (or more) languages simultaneously leading to double-voiced usage, and hence having multiple meanings all at once. In this article, I suggest that the use of multiple languages is also a strategy to achieve multiple affiliations to different ethnolinguistic groups, regions and even nationalities.

Therefore, ultimately my interest is in how musicians draw on diverse cultural materialities (linguistic and musical) from their multiple universes for use as semiotic material in their music. The notion of multivocality is useful to explain how the multilingual and multicultural contexts provide the semiotic material on which musicians draw, enabling them to transcend social and ethnolinguistic groups and regional and national boundaries.

## 3. Local Production of Globalisation

Overt internationalisation of Zambian music is evident in the official promotion video for the song *Kapilipili,* literally, '[small] hot chili.' It starts with a display of opulence often seen in American Hip Hop/Rap music videos. Note that the diminutive prefix *ka-* is used in Zambian languages generally to denote something small. However, in urban Nyanja and Bemba the meaning extends to things or people who are deemed to be 'nice,' 'beautiful' or 'desirable.' In the song, the 'diminutive' hot chili is a reference to a beautiful and desirable young woman. The materialisation of the 'hot chili' as Salma, the featured female singer, functions to actualise social discourse around 'hot' women and it also also gives visual substance to the theme of the song. The use of hot 'hunks' and hot 'babes' is a staple of Hip Hop/Rap music video genre (see Alim, Ibrahim & Pennycook, 2009).

It can be argued that the video has all the trappings of American pop culture – SUV, flaunted jewelry, body-guards and a beautiful woman. However, the Hip Hop/Rap music genre has been remodeled and reframed around a (Zambian) locality, which is clearly not 'American' as it is layered around hybrid vocal performances combining Zambian languages (Nyanja and Bemba) and cultural materialities through references to well known lyrics from a popular Kalindula traditional song, and to Bemba sayings. In the analysis, I refer to the rural or standard language as Bemba or Nyanja, while the urban versions are referred to as urban Bemba or urban Nyanja. Standard Zambian languages are based on the rural forms.

| Original | Translation[1] |
|---|---|
| We kapilipili kandi/ kulibe wamene anganipatse cikondi/ ceumani pasa | My (little) hot pepper [sung in Bemba]/ there"s no one who can give me the love you/ give me" [sung in Nyanja/urban Nyanja] |
| Angel wanga/ kulibe wamene anganipatse cikondi/ ceumani pasa | My angel/ there"s no one who can give me the love/ you give me [sung in English-Nyanja/Nyanja/Urban Nyanja] |
| Verse 1: Ba PK balimba: 'We bushiku bulalepa ngataukwete aka**k**wisala**ko**, akakwisala**ko** oh oh…" | P.K. (Chishala) once said in his song: „The night is long when you don"t have a little something to hold on to, to touch" [sung by JK in Bemba] |

---

[1] Translation adapted by author from Kitwe Online

| | |
|---|---|
| Notulo tulashupa ngatapali akakwikata**ko**/ ukwalawila**ko** oh, oh | Even sleep is hard to come by when you have nothing to touch/play with [sung in Bemba /urban Bemba?] |
| Eico ndetotela iwe mwandi walipan**gwa** | That is why I am grateful, you (my dear) are quite a creation [sung in Bemba] |
| Eico ndetotela, ala mwandi nalipa**lwa** | That is why I am grateful, I am indeed blessed [sung in Bemba] |
| (JK Raps/Free styles in Nyanja) So, kukusiya mwandi/ Baby iyo/ ndi bigi NO!! | So leaving you, Baby is no/ a big NO!!" [sung in Nyanja/ English-Bemba/ Nyanja-English] |
| Nikalibe kupeza cikondi monga ici/ **so** | I've never come across love like this [sung in Nyanja/English] |
| Siumacinja olo ivute cash **flow** | You never change even when I have problems with my cash flow [Urban Nyanja-English] |
| Ndiye pamene undikondela**ko**/ Baby eh, eh!! | That's when you love me even more!! [sung in Nyanja/English] |
| **Repeat Chorus; Verse 2** Niwe doctor wandi, uwaishiba umuti wakumpe**la**, nganalwa**la** | You are my doctor, who knows the right medicine to give me when I am sick [sung by Salma in Urban Bemba-English] |
| Niwe nurse wandi, uwaishiba epo ekata, ngapalekali**pa** | You are my nurse who knows where to touch when it hurts [sung in Urban Bemba-English] |
| Concoction umpela, ngabwaca ulucelo mbuka nensansa, ninshi nintemwa | The concoction you give me – when I wake up in the morning I'm joyful, I am happy [sung in Urban Bemba-English] |
| So, kukusiya mwandi Daddy iyo/ ni big NO!! | So leaving you Daddy no/it's a big NO!! [sung by Salma in Urban Bemba-English/urban Nyanja-English] |
| Nikalibe kupezapo cikondi monga ici **so** | I've never, ever, come across love like this [Urban Nyanja] |
| Siumazanda olo ivute cash **flow** | You are never out of favour even when we are broke [Urban Nyanja] |
| Ndiye pamene undikondela**ko** Baby, eeh | That's when you love me even more, Baby, eeh [Urban Nyanja] |
| **Repeat Chorus 2X; Verse 3** Bring it back JK!! [Interlude sung with only Kalindula drum beat interspaced with Reggae / Ragga / Dance Hall synthesizer] We bushiku ulalepa ngataukwete akakwisala**ko**, akakwisala**ko** ooh Notulo tulashupa ngatapali akakwikata**ko**, ukwalawila**ko** ooh | |

## 4. Multilingual Lyrics, Multiple Sociocultural and Locality Affiliations

In the lyrics, we see the clever use of poetic devices (consider the rhymes in the bold forms in the lyrics above), in which rhyming is across linguistic boundaries, and which Zambians and those familiar with local languages and culture will appreciate.

The most visible aspect of the song is the blending and use of different languages. My argument is that this is to claim multiple affiliations both locally and internationally. Using English connects the song to the international language and the world; while rural Bemba and rural Nyanja connect the music to both rural and urban areas as well as the traditional and the modern world. Using Bemba and Nyanja not only connects the music to the two most widely spoken languages in Zambia, but also opens the markets in Malawi, Mozambique and Zimbabwe where Nyanja is spoken, and parts of the Congo Democratic Republic where Bemba is spoken. In addition to localities and identities associated with linguistic choices, the use of multiple languages is used for communicative, aesthetic and stylistic effect. For instance, the English choices 'doctor' and 'nurse' are more specific than the Nyanja and Bemba *ng'anga*, which only refers to a traditional African medicine person, while the word 'nurse' would be difficult to translate as one would require a descriptive phrase or sentence. In addition, the Bemba or Nyanja 'Doctor' *Ng'anga* would have negative associations if used in the context of the song. The resulting meaning would also contradict the message of love being generated in the song. This is because *Ng'anga*, traditional medicine man, is socially used to refer to someone who is perceived to be 'ugly' or a scheming person who is up to no good. Doctors enjoy higher socioeconomic status than traditional doctors. In addition, if the Bemba or Nyanja equivalents were used, it would also disrupt the aesthetic and lyrical flow. The phrase 'cash flow' would be difficult to capture in Bemba and Nyanja without bringing in ambiguity. It also enables the musician to create rhymes across languages as 'flow' pronounced [flo] in Zambia rhymes with –*ko*, 'no,' and 'so.'

Bantu languages use verbal extensions to transform verb roots into passive constructions. The morph –w- in Bemba is the passive marker as in *walipangwa* [u-ali-pang-w-a] and *nalipalwa* [n-ali-pal-w-a]. The first phrase can be described as: *u*- 'second person singular', -*ali*- 'future tense', -*pang*- 'verb root' for 'make', -*w*- 'passive marker' and –*a* 'end of word vowel.' The same analysis applies to the second phrase but with *n*- standing for 'first person singular.' Note that the first *u*- changes to *w*- because Bemba, like other Bantu languages, does not often allow successive vowels of different qualities so that *u*- and *a* gives *wa*-. The use of the passive extension enables the construction of the object NP as subject, as the subject NP is absent. This elevates the girl (*Kapilipili*) to the centre of the action and the focus of the sentence. The use of verbal extension also allows for musical rhyming of the words: *wakumpela, nganalwala, ngapalekalipa, nensansa,* and *nintemwa*. In essence, the use of different languages allows the musicians the creative freedom to construct novel lyrics for their music. They are not encumbered by the dictates of standard language, so that they can draw on standard and informal languages depending on the aesthetics and lyrical flow that the musician wants to inculcate in the song.

## 5. Dialogicality and Heteroglossia as Discourse Practice

Bolter and Grusin (2000) and Prior and Hengst (2010) have drawn attention to how developments in media technology and editing tools enable producers to easily reclaim prior semiotic material and reuse it in new applications and modalities for different meanings. The presence of Salma as a featured artist and the linguistic choices are not random but carefully crafted for consumer appeal.

The lyrical content is also arranged in such a way that it allows the singers to 'speak' to each other. The first part of the 'dialogue' is sung by JK. The first line starts with Bemba *We kapilipili kandi* 'My pretty hot angel' and the rest which forms a chorus is in Nyanja *kulibe wamene angani pasa cikondi ceumanipasa* 'No one loves me the way you do'. The standard (rural) Nyanja *Camene umanipatsa* has been contracted to *Ceumanipasa* a form used in urban Nyanja, enabling the musician to affiliate to both rural and urban locations. The voiceless sibilant affricate [ts] is reduced to voiceless sibilant fricative [s] as in urban Nyanja. He repeats the verse but this time in Nyanja-English and he reformulates *We kapilipili kandi* 'My pretty hot angel' as '*Angel wanga*' 'My angel' and slightly reformulates the chorus by fusing *cameneumani* into *ceumani* 'that you give me'. These subtle changes have an impact on meaning making and are also done to enhance the musical and aesthetic effect, as well as to spice up the emotional load on the kind, that is, the 'quantity' and 'quality' of love the two have for each other. Then from *Ba PK balimba…* 'PK once sung…' to *ala mwandi nalipalwa* 'I'm really blessed' is done in Bemba. Reminding the viewer about what PK said and the use of traditional sayings are designed to trigger in the Zambian viewer/listener direct involvement and connection with the content. This affiliation to PK and the traditional is immediately disrupted by an interlude of free style rap in Nyanja by JK ('*So, kukusiya..undikondeleko, Baby eh, eh…*'). This perhaps is done to also involve the modern and the young, who are into free style rap music, but at the same time affiliate with the rural through using Nyanja.

The stanza beginning *Niwe doctor wandi…ninshinintemwa* 'You're my doctor… I'm ecstatic' is a response in the dialogue by Salma, who we now identify as the *Kapipili*. It is interesting that there appears to be a subtle intertextual reference or dialogism (Bakhtin, 1981) to Gregory Isaac's Reggae hit song *Night Nurse*. Unlike in Gregory Isaac's Reggae song in which he calls his lover 'My night nurse,' Salma does not replicate the line but recontextualizes the idea behind the love song and resemiotizes it in Bemba (not English). Moreover, instead of replication and making reference to 'nurse,' Salma describes her lover as both 'Doctor' and 'Nurse.' The use of the word 'concoction' is interesting in that in urban Bemba and Nyanja, it has negative associations as in English, such as 'preposterous or implausible story.' However, in the song the negative associations are defamiliarized, so that the word refers to Salma's appreciation of JK's love.

Just like JK free styled in rap after his dialogue, Salma also free styles in rap in Nyanja starting *So, kukusiya mwandi…undikondelako Baby, eh eh…* What we find is that polyphony (many voices) and multiple localities are not only expressed with language choices; JK and Salma are able to strategically make their music transcend ethno-linguistic, cultural and national boundaries by rhyming across ethnolinguistic and national boundaries. In her description of Brazilian Rap music, Roth-Gordon (2008: 67) comes up with what she calls "conversational sampling" in which singers not only quote and recycle "memorable phrases" from popular songs and familiar themes, they also "creatively draw on global youth culture to align themselves with the power and prestige they associate with the US First World modernity." However, rather than aligning to a particular group, locality or even genre, the song that has been analysed shows a simultaneous disconnection with the various affiliations. For instance, as illustrated above, the affiliation to PK and traditional Kalindula music is immediately revoked by affiliation to 'free style' Rap which relates to America. Note also the seamless shift in music genres as the instrumentation moves from what I shall call Kalindula Rap/R&B to 'Free style' and back. In the process, memorable phrases from other sources are made distinct, and popular songs and familiar themes are made unrecognisable and unfamiliar through semiotic blending, substitution and replacement of lyrical content and soundbites as social semiotic material.

Therefore, the heteroglossic nature of the lyrics and the multifarious nature of the instrumentation and musical framing suggest that the musicians in this case do not claim strong affiliation to a particular ethnolinguistic group, region and nationality, music genre or cultural attachment. However, since this is a deliberate strategy, this dissociation is also the materialisation of who they are and what their music is, and hence constitute a claim to these same affiliations. The creativity that goes into the interfacing of the local / global, traditional / modern lyrical and musical / instrumentation content, regional / national / international, Kalindula / Rap / Hip hop / R&B / Reggae and Dance Hall music genre, is what makes JK and his music unique. The argument here is not that JK, the musician, claims to be everything and affiliates to everything; rather he uses these affiliations, soundbites and musical content as semiotic choices in the construction of a particular sound which constitutes his own brand identity. In this connection, it can be said that JK and Salma, for example, have a particular sound people are able to identify them with even though they might be using the same genre or genre blends. However, when musicians 'feature' others, they are enhancing their own brand identities through infusing those of the 'featured.' This leads to integration of diversity and collaboration and celebration of shared cultural and linguistic knowledge and references, and further integrates the local/global and traditional/modern interfaces and associated cultural materialities and affiliations.

The local and international appeal of the song is captured in the following YouTube comments. The local Zambian flavour in the production of an international popular song is not lost on the commentators, and so too is the link to traditional Kalindula music.

1. "Love it from Sweden too!!"
2. "This Song is Playin Everywhere, And Every City In Zambia :D"
3. "DMMN !! THIS DUDE IS SICK .. I HEARD HIM ON R KELLY TRACK N I WAS LIKE I GOTTA CHECK HIM OUT FOR REAL !! RESPECT FROM SUDAN .."

4. "This guy killed this song,,,very nice song (luv from Nigeria)"
5. "hey yu what i like a genuine zambiuanebeatsbyu know how 2 impress people yuguyz keep up gud luck on yo work god blessblessyuguyz from katimanamibia"
6. "gr8t song peace from Denmark ;)"
7. "this song n video r superb n meet world standards. if JK was trying to be western he wdnt have sang in Nyanja n Bemba n he definitely wdnt have referred to a Zambian kalindula legend, PK in his lyrics. Mind u Salma is coloured Indian but wasnt fluent in the local languages n she had to learn nyanja and bemba to do this song so 2 me that's Zambian enough! if u dont have anything good to say keep it to yo damn self!!"
8. "Lyrics in zambodian and English please"

It is also interesting that the commentators also notice that JK is not trying to imitate Western style Hip Hop/Rap music. The use of more than one language in the lyrics is also highlighted as one of the typical Zambian language practices.

## 6. Conclusion

The complex simultaneous use of diverse linguistic resources or heteroglossia (Bakhtin, 1981) is critical in unravelling the creative genius in popular Zambian music, which enables musicians to traverse regional, national, linguistic and ethnic boundaries to market their music. The linguistic repertoire and semiotic resources at their disposal give 'voice' to their creativity as well as to the performance of multiple identities and to produce multilocalities. The language use in the song is analogous to urban (youth) language in Zambia and elsewhere in Africa. Urban or youth language, as Hurst (2017) notes, is not just spoken by people in urban areas or by the youth only, it is also used by the older generation and people in rural areas. I have argued that urban Nyanja and urban Bemba affilaite the musicians with urbanity and modernity, while English and references to Hip Hop / Rap music, Marvin Gaye and reggae music orient towards transnational affiliations. Standard / rural Bemba and Nyanja and references to PK and Bemba saying appeal to rural and traditional worlds. Since the linguistic practices and sociocultural worlds depicted in the songs describe the life-worlds of the musicians, the affiliations should not be conceived as binary, as they constitute who they are.

In terms of the semiotic material in the video and the lyrical style and instrumentation in the song, there are affiliations with Hip Hop / Rap music. In the influential books *Global linguistic flows* (Alim, Ibrahim & Pennycook, 2009) and *Global Englishes* (Pennycook, 2007), the authors emphasise the localised nature of Hip Hop music world-wide. Whereas American Hip Hop music is sung in African American English vernacular, scholarship has shown that Hip Hop / Rap music in Africa draws on its multilingual heritage (Ojoawo, 2016; Gbogi, 2016; Higgins, 2009a, b; Omoniyi, 2009; Oloruntoba-Oju, 2018; Williams, 2017). Thus, the creative lyrical production of multilingualism and multiculturalism are at the centre of Hip Hop music in Africa. For example, in Nigeria, Hip Hop draws from pidgin English, 'standard' English, Yoruba, Igbo and other languages (Gbogi, 2016; Ojoawo, 2016; Babalola and Taiwo, 2008; Omoniyi, 2009; Oloruntoba-Oju, 2018), while in Kenya and Tanzania, Swahili, Sheng, Dholuo, and Kikuyu are some of the languages used in the music (Higgins, 2009a, b). Hip Hop music strives on keeping it real. This means retaining local culture and content in the music (Pennycook, 2007, 2009). As also shown in the analysis of Kapilipili, there is emphasis on the local production in terms of linguistic and lyrical innovations, as well as in the content and the message being projected. There might be references to African American Vernacular English tropes and even to African American rappers and their music, but the creative genius of the music is in the local experiences of socioeconomic, cultural, and political conditions. It is in this context that the song under study should be appreciated.

In terms of language use in Zambian music, it can be argued that there is increasing recognition by musicians that languages are just one of the many mobile social semiotics available in everyday life. Musicians have come to realise that although using the 'standard'/rural form may be desirable, this does not guarantee commercial success. This limits the number of consumers; the majority of consumers are likely to be urban and modern young adults or adults. There is also a risk that using the 'standard'/rural form would associate the song with a particular ethnic group and hence a particular market. Moreover, since the majority of musicians are young and urban based and raised, singing in a monoglot / monolingual voice would create a self-identity of a mono-ethnic self which they are not. The use of multiple languages or bits and pieces from different languages enables them to express who they are as urbanites. The music becomes an avenue of expression and a platform in which to showcase the appropriated music genres and multiple identities. Through lyrics, instrumentation and soundbites as remediated semiotic material, musicians are able to express multiple affiliations, voices and agency cross ethnic and linguistic, regional and national boundaries. In turn, they are able to bridge traditional/ 'rural' and modern/urban worlds and different music genres, and thus ensuring that there is wide market for their music.

The complexity of music genres and instrumentation and the simultaneous use of diverse linguistic resources, or heteroglossia (Bakhtin, 1981) are critical in unraveling the creative genius in popular Zambian music, which enables musicians to traverse regional, national, linguistic and even ethnic boundaries to market their music. No doubt the development in media technology makes it easy to manipulate the sound coming from musical instruments, while the linguistic repertoire at the musicians' disposal gives 'voice' to their creativity as well as to the performance of multiple identities. Since different language forms are associated with different social groups, localities and regions/centres, I want to conclude that multivocality enables musicians to belong to several localities, social groups and regions and to cross national boundaries at the same time. The notion of multivocality can, therefore, be extended to different sound bites and visual performances associated with particular social groups and identities, localities and regions.

## References

Alim, S., Ibrahim A., & Pennycook, A. (Eds.) (2009). *Global linguistic flows: Hip hop cultures, youth identities and the politics of language*. London: Routledge.

Babalola, E. T., & Taiwo, R. O. (2009). Code-switching in contemporary Nigerian hip-hop music.*Itupale Online Journal of African Studies*, 1, 1–26.
Bakhtin, M. M. (1981). *The dialogic imagination*. Austin: University of Texas Press.
Banda F., & Mambwe K. (2013). Fighting HIV/AIDS through popular Zambian music, *Muziki. Journal of Music Research in Africa*, 10, 1-12, DOI: 10.1080/18125980.2013.852738.
Bolter, J., & Grusin, R. (2000). *Remediation: Understanding new media*. Cambridge: MIT Press.
Davidson, M. (1970). Some music for the Lala Kankobele. *African Music*, 4(4), 103–113.
Higgins, C. (2009). *English as a local language: Postcolonial identities and multilingual practices*. Toronto: Multilingual Matters.
Gbogi, M. T. (2016). Language, identity, and urban youth subculture: Nigerian hip hop music as an exemplar. *Pragmatics*, 26(2), 171–195.
Higgins, C. (2009a). *English as a local language*. Clevedon: Multilingual Matters.
Higgins, C. (2009b). From 'da bomb' to bomba: Globla hip hop nation language in Tanzania. In Alim, S., Ibrahim, A., &Pennycook, A. (eds.) *Global linguistic flows: Hip Hop cultures, youth Identities, and the politics of language*. London: Routledge, 95–112.
Hurst, E. (2017). African (urban) youth languages.Online Publication Date: Mar 2017 DOI: 10.1093/acrefore/9780199384655.013.15 Accessed 20 September 2017.
Iedema, R. (2003): Multimodality, resemiotisation: Extending the analysis of discourse as multi-semiotic practice. *VisualCommunication*, 2(1), 29–57.
JK feat. Salma Uploaded on Apr 13, 2010/ Feb 22, 2014. Kapilipili. (Official Video). Directed and Produced by Vatice of Inzy: MziikiTube. Available www.youtube.com/watch?v=LvwErCptOwM.
Katulwende, M. (2015). Zambia's kalindula music: Of death, drums and poetry. http://theculturetrip.com/africa/zambia/articles/zambia-s-kalindula-music-of-death-drums-and-poetry/. Accessed 1 March 2015.
Kunkeyani, T. E. (2014). Modes and resemiotisation of HIV/AIDS messages in the Eastern Region of Malawi. Unpublished PhD, University of the Western Cape.
Longwe, S. H., & Clarke, R. (1998). *Women know your place: The patriarchal message in Zambian popular song. A research report from the women in music project*. Lusaka: Zambia Association for Research and Development.
Mapoma, M. I. (1988). Glimpse at the use of music in traditional medicine among the Bantu: A case of healing among the Bemba speaking people of Zambia. *Muntu: Revue scientifiqueetculturelle de CICIBA*., 8, 117–123.
Marten, L., & Kula. N. C. (2008). One Zambia, one nation, many languages.In Simpson, A. (Ed.) *Language and national identity in Africa*. Oxford: Oxford University Press, 291–313.
Mensah, A. A. (1971). *Music and dance in Zambia*. Lusaka: Zambia Information Services.
Mensah, A. A. (1970). The music of Zumaile village, Zambia. *African Music*, 4(4): 96–102.
Miti, L. (2006). *Comparative Bantu phonology and morphology: A study of sound systems and structures of the indigenous languages of Southern Africa*. Cape Town: CASAS.
Mtonga, M. (2006). Gulewamkulu as a multi-state enterprise. *Museum International*, 58(1-2), 229–230.
Ojoawo, A. O. (2016). A discourse analysis of sexual themes in Nigerian hip-hop music.*Journal of the* Department of English, ObafemiAwolowo University, Ile-Ife, 12(2), 104–140.
Oloruntoba-Oju, T. (2018). Contestant hybridities: African Urban Youth language in Nigerian music and social media. In Hurst, E. & Erastus, F. (Eds.) *African Youth Languages: New media, performing arts and sociolinguistic development*. London: Palgrave.
Omoniyi, T. (2009). "So I choose to do amNaija style": Hip hop, language, and postcolonialidentities. In Alim, H. S., Ibrahim, A., & Pennycook, A. (Eds.), *Global linguistic flows: Hiphop cultures, youth identities, and the politics of language*. New York: Routledge, 113–135.
Pennycook, A. (2007). *Global Englishes and transcultural flows*. London: Routledge.
Prior, P. A., & Hengst, J. A. (2010). Introduction: Exploring semiotic remediation. In Prior, P. A. & Hengst, J. A. (Eds.) *Exploring semiotic remediation as discourse practice*. New York: Palgrave, 1–23.

Roth-Gordon, J. (2008). Conversational sampling, race trafficking, and invoking the ghetto in Brazilian hip hop. In Samy, H. A., Ibrahim, A. & Pennycook, A. (Eds.) *Global linguistic flows: Hip hop cultures, youth identities, and the politics of language*. New York: Routledge, 63–77.

Williams, Q. (2017). *Remix Multilingualism*. London: Bloomsbury.

Woolard, K. (1999). Simultaneity and bivalency as strategies in bilingualism. *Journal of Linguistic Anthropology* 8.1: 3-29.